COMPLETE GUIDE TO
FLORIDA GARDENING

Stan DeFreitas

TAYLOR TRADE PUBLISHING

Lanham • New York • Oxford

Published by Taylor Trade Publishing
An imprint of The Rowman & Littlefield Publishing Group, Inc.
4501 Forbes Boulevard, Suite 200
Lanham, Maryland 20706

Distributed by National Book Network

Library of Congress Cataloging-in-Publication Data

DeFreitas, Stan.
  Complete guide to Florida gardening.

  Rev. ed. of: Stan DeFreitas' complete guide to
Florida gardening.
  Includes index.
    1. Gardening—Florida. I. DeFreitas, Stan.
Stan DeFreitas' complete guide to Florida gardening.
II. Title.
SB453.2.F6D43 1987   635'.09759   87-5038
ISBN 0-87833-572-2

Revised Edition edited by Kim Lively

Designed by Bonnie Baumann

Printed in the United States of America

In memory of my father and mother,
Frank DeFreitas and Edith Lillian Miller,
and with special affection for my family,
Peggi, Marie, and James

ACKNOWLEDGEMENTS

The author wishes to thank his wife, Peggi, who lovingly and dilligently organized and typed the material for this book, and Colleen Tracy for her original work in houseplants.

Special thanks also go to those horticulture professionals whose guidance, knowledge, and reviews made the book possible—Dr. Charles Peacock, Ph.D. turf specialist, University of Florida, County Extension Service; Dr. Gary Simone, Ph.D. pathologist, University of Florida, County Extension Service; Jim Stevens, vegetable specialist, University of Florida; Lee Schmool, landscape architect and landscape design instructor, Pinellas Vocational-Technical Institute; Ray Smith, landscape designer and co-owner/operator of Smith's Nursery and Garden Supply Center; Dave Smith, co-owner/operator of Smith's Nursery and Garden Supply Center; Mike Karr, annuals specialist; Jack Sweet, a national certified judge for the American Orchid Society with 31 years experience in growing orchids; Jim Boone, turf specialist; Jim Nau, Ball Seed Co.; Opal Schallmo, urban horticulturist, Pinellas County Extension Service; Mitchell and Michelle Crose; Mildred (president of Suncoast Botanical Gardens) and Ken Palmer, co-owners/operators of G. K. Palmer Nursery, which specializes in flowering and fruit trees; Bob Smith, turf specialist; and LaRue Robinson, horticulture agent, Pinellas County Extension Service.

This second edition of the *Complete Guide to Florida Gardening* contains a wealth of new color photographs. A good number of them were taken by the author. A very hearty thanks must go to Denny Mc-Keown, gardening expert and author of the *Complete Guide to Midwest Gardening,* who generously contributed many of his own photographs for use in this volume. McKeown's handiwork with a camera adds much to the second edition's visual appeal and usefulness to the gardener. Other photos were provided by Jim Nau, the Florida Citrus Commission, James Bennett, John and Bonita Lucas, Gregory Van Stavern, William Moriarty, Steve Carlisle, and Polly Jones. The author deeply appreciates their time and skill. Thanks also go to Greenskeepers of Largo, Florida, for their contributions to several of the houseplant photographs.

P R E F A C E

Seems as if I've loved plants forever. I started growing them at the age of six. In my early years, I worked with neighbors, helping them care for their plants. In high school, I worked for a local nursery, which sparked an even greater interest in horticulture. After attending junior college, I completed a two-year horticultural program, during which time I was also a landscape foreman.

Much of my experience and knowledge was gained during my tenure as an urban horticulturist for the Pinellas County Extension Service. In seven years there, I attended numerous short courses, meetings, and seminars; these classroom sessions and meetings with fellow professionals gave me invaluable information about all manner of plant materials. At the same time, I gleaned hands-on practical experience while tackling the many plant problems brought to me by thousands of local residents and nursery personnel.

For the past nine years, radio has played a further role in my reaching and communicating with fellow gardeners throughout the state. Primarily for easy identification with my listening audience, I adopted the name "Mr. Green Thumb," and the label has stuck.

Local newspapers have also given me a vehicle by which to keep in touch with horticultural enthusiasts. Writing tri-weekly columns for the *Clearwater Sun,* and weekly for the *Tampa Bay Tribune,* keeps me abreast of the prevailing interests of Florida gardeners today.

As the years have passed, I have found myself taking a greater interest in educating aspiring green thumbers and fellow horticulturists. Through my 10 years as a teacher, I feel I have learned even *more* about this profession. Hopefully, this time spent in the classroom has been as rewarding for my students as it has been for me.

For the past four years, television has been an important part of my gardening-related activities. I've discovered that presenting weekly shows on the local PBS and CBS affiliates is both challenging and extremely fulfilling. These programs allow me to reach an even greater number of Floridians—those who garden and those who may need a little inspiration to get started.

Through newspapers, television, radio, and the *Complete Guide to Florida Gardening,* I enjoy being able to encourage the sort of enthusiasm for nature that gets everyone involved in creating and maintaining their own outdoor paradise. And what better place is there to do so than Florida?

Stan DeFreitas
"Mr. Green Thumb"
Clearwater, Florida
1987

CONTENTS

INTRODUCTION

When most people think of Florida, they think of orange trees, bright sandy beaches, and tropical foliage—correct perceptions, every one. But Florida is outstanding for another important reason: It's a gardener's paradise!

Florida is blessed with a marvelous climate that enables us to spend as much time outside our homes as inside. Here, we can design and build walls of thick foliage for beauty and privacy, lay a grassy carpet for relaxation, and furnish our outdoor living area with seasonal color for an ever-changing environment. Executed and cared for properly, such a garden is both aesthetically pleasing and personally satisfying.

You don't have to be wealthy to have a beautiful landscape in Florida. A small amount of money yields bountiful returns. Whether you are building a new home or improving an existing one, you can surround your home with a lush living environment; all you need to get started is some gardening knowledge and a little imagination. Keeping in mind your preferences, needs, and lifestyle, you can create a home landscape that will give you years of pleasure. As a bonus—like compound interest on an investment—your property value will increase, literally, before your eyes.

If you recently moved to Florida, you may find that the types of flowers, shrubs, trees, fruits, vegetables, and lawns that grow here are unfamiliar to you, even if you're a veteran gardener. The difference in growing seasons (between Florida and other parts of the United States) can be *months* apart. The soil here—which has a sandy base—is certainly different from the loamy, clay, and rocky soils found in many other areas of the country.

Planting a lawn requires a different perspective here, too. Many of my newly transplanted radio listeners (particularly those from the Northeast) mistake St. Augustine for northern crabgrass, and *remove* the desirable lawn from their landscapes. To these listeners, I reply, "When in Florida, do as the Floridians do." St. Augustine happens to be an excellent lawn grass for our state, when used in the right location, and when watered and fertilized properly. This book is designed to help you learn all about the lawn grasses, other plant materials, and climatic conditions in our area so you can grow a beautiful landscape, Florida-style.

If you live in northern Florida, you will need to plan for cooler winters and later spring-planting dates; in southern Florida and in the Keys, you will be dealing with tropical conditions and almost year-round growth. In central Florida, of course, the climate is temperate but has elements of both extremes, heat and cold. Invariably, these factors will affect your plant selections, planting dates, and care practices.

The chapters in this book are organized to give you a basic, working knowledge of where to plant and how to care for Florida's most viable and popular plants. From the section on how to plan your landscape in Chapter

1, through the chapters on trees, shrubs, fruits and nuts, flowers, vegetables, ground covers and vines, lawns, and houseplants, I've endeavored to provide the most complete information possible. In the chapters on plants, I've reviewed the basic requirements for planting and care, and then touched on each plant's physical characteristics, growth habits, and, where applicable, any peculiarities that may be of interest.

The final chapter is devoted to the most common insects and diseases found in Florida landscapes. While this is certainly not the most scenic section of the book, it *is* important. A good number of pests and plagues are simply a fact of life in our state; as a gardener, if you don't know how to identify and battle these problems, all the time and money you've invested in your beautiful landscape will eventually be for naught!

The charts, maps, and photos used throughout the text not only reinforce certain parts of the discussion, but also offer additional tips for successful gardening. The color photos, in particular, should help you judge the look and appeal of various plant varieties. Depending on selection and usage, colorful plant specimens can "make or break" the overall look of a garden. Thus, I hope the photos and other graphic elements will help make your landscape decisions simpler and more satisfying.

There are important aspects of the text that merit mention here. First, I *cannot* overemphasize the importance of following label directions with respect to chemicals and other materials. No amount of fun in the garden is worth risking your safety and that of your family and pets. To keep things safe and enjoyable, always read the directions on any lawn-and-garden product before you use it.

Secondly, let your nurseryman be your partner in making the right choices of plant materials, fertilizers, and other products for your outdoor environment. His knowledge and expertise may prove invaluable to you as a gardener.

And I hope this book will be a partner of sorts, too, in all of your gardening endeavors. My aim is to give you an "armchair companion" that you can consult anytime—for advice on designing a new flower bed, for information about a particular plant, or for help with a pesky problem.

I think that gardening is one of the most enjoyable pursuits in the world. It's healthy, productive, gratifying, and allows you to form a close bond with the outdoor environment. What could be more natural?

COMPLETE GUIDE TO FLORIDA GARDENING

CHAPTER ONE

Planning Your Garden

Never planned a garden before? Does the prospect of having to landscape your yard bring on an anxiety attack? Don't be disturbed. It's much easier than you imagine. Still, if the idea terrifies you into immobility, you may need help from a professional landscape company. Depending on the amount of work to be done, the cost can range from a very reasonable sum to a major expense.

Professional landscape companies will guarantee their work. Any weak or dying plants will be replaced free of charge, provided you have given them the required amount of care and feeding. You might even want to weigh the comparative cost of doing all the work yourself, and possibly having to replace some plants later, against the initial cost of turning over the job to a landscaper.

You can let a professional design your garden or landscape, advising you on trees, shrubs, and plants. Then you can proceed on your own from that point buying, locating, and installing your own materials. Again, this will depend on your own capabilities and desires, as well as the amount you plan to spend. A good, reputable landscape company certainly can help those who feel creatively inadequate in planning the layout of a garden.

For the ambitious do-it-yourself gardener or landscaper, however, this book can help you get the results you want.

GETTING STARTED

Your first concern should be your family's outdoor needs. How do you plan to use your garden? The front of most homes usually is the public area, to be designed merely as a setting for the house and to enhance its appearance from the street. The back yard and sides of the property usually are the living and entertaining areas, play areas or service areas, and functional areas for storage or a vegetable garden.

To decide the proper use and size of each area, you should draw a scale outline of your property. School graph paper is ideal. Scale down your drawing to ¼ inch to every foot, making the overall outline from fence-line to fence-line. Fill in all driveways, walkways, fences, and other hardscape items, as well as the outline of the house itself. Any existing trees that you wish to retain should be

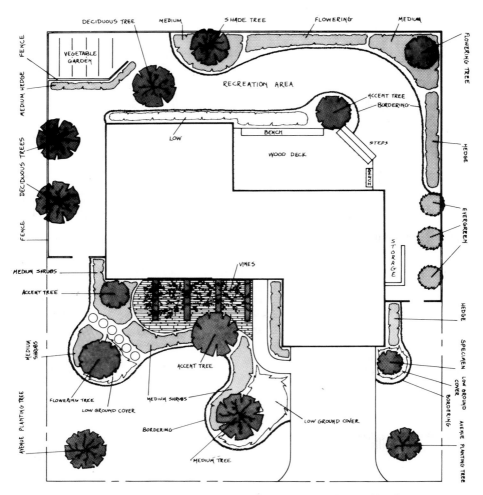

It's helpful to draw a sketch of your landscape plan, indicating plant and hardscape areas.

marked, together with "hot spots" where shade is needed. You may want to check your deed map to determine the exact dimensions of your property. The architect's drawing of your home also is useful to show the placement of doors and windows and the orientation of the house on your lot. You may also have to check a contour map to determine any rises or hills in your yard. Some properties will drop a foot or two over the length of the yard, a factor that will affect your landscaping plan.

Once your scale drawing is complete, you can make decisions on where to put flower beds, trees, shrubs, rock gardens, etc. If you intend to put in a pool, choose a large, open area away from any existing trees. Remember that digging a swimming pool requires working space for men and equipment. Be sure to leave at least 20 feet along the back fence to allow the pool construction crew access

Before you introduce any new plants, be sure to remove any undesirable materials and prepare the soil. Whenever possible, healthy existing trees should be retained and developed into the new plan.

A deck or patio is ideal for Florida landscapes, and provides a smooth transition from indoor to outdoor living areas.

to your yard. Once the pool is installed, you then can determine the placement of shrubs or trees along the fence.

While everyone envisions a landscaped yard or garden in its final form, remember that it often takes several years for such dreams to take real shape. Because of the expense and because of the growing time needed for plants, many homeowners approach landscaping as a "five-year plan." This is especially true if a pool is in those plans. Whether you are able to begin everything you want to do right away or have to spread your budget over a period of time, you should stick to your original landscape plan. In this way, no matter how long it takes to complete, you wind up with a garden or yard that is aesthetically appealing and creatively satisfying.

In Florida, patio landscaping serves as an extension of the living room. Patio landscaping makes small houses seem larger and provides a smooth transition from indoor to outdoor living and recreation areas. Similarly, the placement of trees, shrubs, and flower beds in the front yard should serve to lead visitors to the front door of the house.

CREATE AN INVITING ENTRANCE

Landscape architects plan their plantings at the front of a home to frame the house in the most appealing manner, and, at the same time, point the way to the front door. If your front yard is a jungle of foliage, visitors can wind up at the side or back door by mistake. A well-designed front landscape will have a

The proper placement of trees, shrubs, and other landscape materials enhances and defines a home's front entry.

This circular driveway is accented by an island of lush foliage, including ground covers and small trees.

A brick wall marked by colorful plantings creates a pleasing visual flow in this landscape.

welcoming appearance, a natural flow that guides people to your front door.

For the front of your property, try for visual balance, not symmetry. Noah's Ark had two of everything, but this is not advisable for landscaping. Avoid having two of the same type of plant on opposite sides of a walkway. Vary your plant selection and give a balanced, but not identical, appearance to arrangements. If you have, for example, a large oak tree on one side of the property, you may balance it with two or three smaller trees on the other side.

Always choose plants that will grow in proportion to your house. An 80-foot eucalyptus tree will look out of place next to a typical one-story Florida home. The size and ultimate shape of shrubs and trees is very important, and something you should check out at a nursery before you make a purchase. Many people buy a small Norfolk Island pine or an Italian cypress and plant it close to the house, unaware that it inevitably will grow into the overhang of the roof.

By checking the full-grown size of a tree or shrub, you can avoid planting anything that will become a problem in a few years. The secret lies in maintaining visual balance — creating a pleasing flow of lines and patterns across the landscape and maintaining the right look on your property without any awkward visual distractions.

PLANT SELECTION

Many of us do not know what specific types of plants to buy. Here again, your nurseryman can advise you, not just on size, but on overall appearance and texture, too.

To determine the best plants for your landscape, take a stroll through your favorite nursery. This garden center's railroad-tie planter box gives visitors an idea of how some plant materials can be interspersed for maximum effect.

Trees are the largest living things in the landscape; they are also going to be your largest investment. Since trees are the slowest growing of any plant group, you may wish to spend a little more and buy a more mature tree rather than get a smaller one that will take years to give you the look you want.

In selecting your trees, ask yourself what their purpose will be. To add privacy? To provide shade? To balance the overall look of your property?

Too, take a walk through your nursery and examine the various plants and shrubs. Feel the leaves. Consider whether a shiny plant, such as a philodendron, would be right, or perhaps something light and feathery, such as a fern. Will the plant fit into your plans? Does the plant spread, or does it grow roundheaded and

Don't waste your time and money by purchasing unhealthy plants; inspect each prospect thoroughly. Yellowish leaves such as these denote an iron deficiency.

When selecting plants, keep in mind that some varieties require more care than others. Roses *are* beautiful, but they must be given a good deal of attention.

upright? Should the plant be placed in a corner for best effect, or could it be a specimen by itself, surrounded by lawn? Try to visualize the plant in the location you have in mind before buying anything that might not enhance your overall landscaping ideas.

Selecting an unhealthy plant for purchase is the quickest way to throw money down the drain. When shopping for plants at the nursery, pay special attention to the condition of the leaves. Make sure each leaf is healthy — a rich, dark green rather than a yellowish green (chlorotic) hue that denotes a deficiency or disease. Even plants with naturally variegated leaves should be firm, healthy looking, and free of brown spots that could indicate a fungus infection. Above all, a plant must be free of insects and any sign of insect damage.

Too, check on any *potential* root problems and insect or fungus susceptibility. What are the nutritional requirements? Is the plant prone to nematode infection? Does it require a special pH? How much light and water will it need for optimum growth?

Take a pad and pencil with you to record the information you get from your nurseryman. Your notes will be helpful when you return home and begin putting in your plants. Above all, take heed of the advice you get from your nursery. Most of these stores have qualified personnel familiar with the stock and the growing requirements of each type of plant. They should be eager to help, because a satisfied customer is a repeat customer. Get to know your nurseryman, just as you get to know your doctor or dentist. He can be invaluable when it comes to resolving your particular gardening problems or selecting the right trees, shrubs, and flowers for your yard.

HARDSCAPE SELECTION

Plants aren't the only items you'll be selecting if you're planning to incorporate any new hardscape items, such as walkways, patios, and fences.

One of the greatest joys is to be able to walk comfortably through a yard or garden without tripping over protruding branches or uneven ground. Patios and walkways not only add beauty, but also ease access to your yard and garden.

Concrete often is used for this purpose. It is readily available and very frequently favored by Florida contractors. Gravel and wood chips also can be used for a decorative walkway or patio and formed into any desired shape by using strips of wood along the outer edges. Gravel can be pressed into wet concrete to form a more interesting surface. Bricks, too, are popular and can be laid into many interesting patterns, such as the basket weave (two bricks one way, two bricks at right angles to the first two).

These various types of materials can give you attractive and practical access to your greenery, enabling you to enjoy it to the fullest. If you are laying a pathway or patio yourself rather than hiring a contractor, be sure to place 4 inches of sand on the ground first. This provides a solid base, especially for bricks, and prevents shifting and buckling.

Fences are essential for privacy and containment of pets, but they need not be unattractive. A variety of fencing materials can blend with the image you wish to create in your landscaping.

The chain-link fence is one of the most popular, although when used alone it does little for privacy or noise reduction. However, a chain-link fence is ideal as a solid support for vines. A fast-growing vine of your choice soon will provide an attractive, solid barrier.

Wrought-iron fences lend a touch of elegance to any garden, but again afford little privacy. Still, a wrought-iron fence surrounding a patio area inside your property line can give a picturesque touch to your overall landscaping, sectioning off an outside area for dining or relaxing.

Brick is a popular hardscape material, and can be used in a variety of ways.

Concrete and gravel combine for a sturdy, attractive, and accessible walkway.

A fence can be more than a functional structure; it can also be a "display area" for greenery, such as this Virginia creeper and Boston ivy.

The most practical fences, however, are made of wood. The old-fashioned picket fence adds a traditional rustic touch and can be utiiized as a solid support for climbing roses. Solid wooden fences can be installed in several different ways and — whether left natural or painted — blend with any garden. For durability, use pressure-treated posts, which are well worth the extra cost. For a Western touch to your Florida home, a split-rail fence is unusual and very attractive.

The longest-lasting and most secure fence is one of masonry or brick. These fences are common in Florida landscapes. If cost is a consideration, keep in mind that brick fences, in particular, are expensive.

A fence company can advise you on installation as well as show you a variety of styles from which to choose. You may want to compare the costs of different types of fencing. Any fence is a major expense and is not an item you'll want to replace frequently.

INSTALLATION OF HARDSCAPE AND PLANT MATERIALS

After you have determined the overall layout of your garden and selected your plants and hardscape elements, you're ready to get started on the installation of your project. Whether you are handling the job yourself or have turned it over to a professional, make sure that each element is installed in the proper order.

The first items to be installed are the hardscape elements, if any. Walkways, patios, fences and, especially, pools, must be introduced first, or you run the risk of damaging newly planted trees, shrubs, and flowers during construction.

Now you're ready to start planting the greenery. The trees should be planted first; they are the largest and slowest growing elements in your landscape. They provide the landmarks on your property and create the general character of the landscaping. Something else you should consider: In some areas, you may have

Whether your landscape plan is extremely formal, relaxed and informal or somewhere in between, the installation process is the same. Hardscape materials should always be introduced first, to prevent damaging new plants during construction.

Trees—the largest and slowest growing components in your landscape—should be planted first. They establish the overall ambiance and character of your garden.

to check with city hall for a permit to *remove* any existing trees that you may not want in your new landscape.

Major shrubs are the next item you should plant. Like trees, most shrubs are slow-growing and may take several years to achieve the size and height needed to complete the impression you wish to create.

The next step will be marking out and preparing your flower beds (and vegetable garden, if you choose). If you plan these as raised beds, wooden or masonry edging will have to be installed. Whether you do this work yourself or

After the shrubs are planted, flower beds and planter boxes should be marked out and prepared.

If you'd like to try your hand at vegetable gardening, mark and prepare this area as you define your flower beds and planter boxes.

Marigolds are perfect for Florida flower beds.

have a contractor build them for you, a certain amount of room will be needed for equipment and elbow room. (If doing any construction, no matter how minimal, makes you nervous at this stage, build your raised beds earlier, along with all the other hardscape work.)

The next step is to install your lawn, which fills the space between flower beds, trees, shrubs, and the edges of your property. Putting in the turf at this stage ensures that it will not be destroyed by workmen or equipment needed for building walkways, the swimming pool, flower-bed edgings or any other items.

These five steps are your major installations, after which the main layout for your landscape will be complete. All that is left to do is install any vines, ornamental shrubs, and annuals and perennials you choose.

Vines should be placed so that they help screen heat and excessive light from the windows of your home. Planted along a chain-link fence, they ultimately provide privacy as well as block any unsightly views beyond your property

While some shrubs and variegated plants provide a certain amount of color, nothing is better than the colors offered by perennials and annuals, such as these perky sunflowers.

Perennials such as gazanias are highly recommended for the color they contribute to the garden.

Ageratum is another floriferous favorite in our state.

Annual pansies exhibit a wealth of color and interesting shapes and textures.

lines. Along with vines, you can plant ground cover to conceal problem turf areas, such as beneath shade trees.

Ornamental shrubs, either in the ground or in decorative tubs, can be placed as accents wherever you feel they are needed. A row of various-sized clay pots filled with small ornamental shrubs can enhance a patio or walkway.

Finally, you can fill the flower beds with the annuals and perennials of your choice. While perennial shrubs, such as azaleas, and certain variegated plants, such as crotons, provide some eye-catching color in the landscape, nothing can beat annuals and perennials when it comes to splashy, visual effects.

For a changing palette of color in the garden, annuals are your best bet, not only for variety of hues, but also for interesting flower forms. Petunias, marigolds, zinnias, asters, nasturtiums, and calendulas all do well in Florida. Perennials also contribute their share of color, including gerbera or gazania daisies, carnations, and everybody's favorite: roses. Except for the finicky roses, perennials require less care than annuals; still, the rewards of planting annuals are well worth the effort. A detailed list of suitable annuals and perennials will be found in later chapters.

Mixing flowers of various colors in the same bed can be exciting, but you should be careful that the final result is visually appealing, not flashy or gaudy. Some gardeners like mingling various kinds of flowers in the same bed. This creates an interesting display, but it is a matter of taste.

I generally feel that a ratio of 40 percent tropical plants, such as hibiscus, copper plants, and bird-of-paradise, should be mixed with 60 percent evergreens, such as podocarpus, ligustrums, and viburnum. This should give you a good "hedge" against losing all your plantings in the severe cold we occasionally experience (remember the 1983 freeze), as well as providing a nice mixture of colors.

ADDED BENEFITS

An extra incentive for planning your landscaping is the potential energy savings provided by judiciously planted trees, shrubs, and vines. A large oak tree can reduce the temperature inside your home from 10 to 20 degrees. It has been estimated that a large growing tree can equal 10 room air conditioners in cooling

With a little planning, trees and shrubs can act as energy saving features around a home.

efficiency. Similarly, vines growing against sunny walls cut direct as well as indirect, reflective heat. A lawn also provides cooling, because it is always transpiring water. Concrete, on the other hand, retains and radiates heat.

Well-planned landscaping can benefit your home in the winter as well as the summer. Deciduous trees, such as the golden rain tree, produce shade during the hot months and let sunlight and warmth through in the winter. Large evergreens planted on the north side can block some of the chilly, north winds from your home.

EVALUATING THE SOIL

The most important element in your garden is the soil — the good earth. Without it there would be no life in any form. Nothing is more important to the continued success of your garden than good soil. As in most other states, the soils of Florida vary from north to south. Northern Florida soils are mostly clay. The central soils consist mostly of sand. And in the south, the soil is muck-type. All these soils need attention to transform them into the most suitable consistency and composition for maximum growth of plants.

Most Florida soils are low in essential elements, such as nitrogen, phosphorus, potassium, iron, zinc, manganese, and magnesium. On the other hand, there are plenty of nematodes, bacteria, fungi, and weed seeds in area soils. As every gardener will discover, it takes more than merely turning over the dirt and planting seeds to achieve a truly rewarding display of flowers. Any undesirable elements in the soil have to be removed, and any shortages of essential minerals must be supplemented, much as we take vitamins to provide our bodies with the building blocks to replace tissue and keep us healthy.

Before you begin your landscape installation, you must give attention to your soil. A good, balanced soil mixture is essential for growth and good blooms, as well as for resistance to disease. To determine the quality of your soil, you first must learn its pH balance, which refers to the acidity (sourness) or alkalinity

The quality of garden soil has a direct effect on a landscape's success or failure.

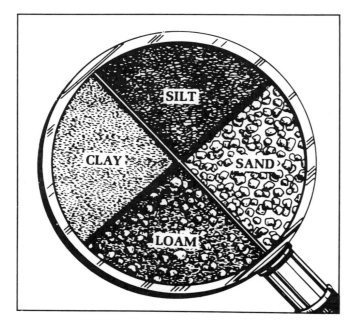

Gardeners should be aware of the various soil types. Sand is the coarsest soil, is well aerated, but drains rapidly. Loam contains equal amounts of clay, silt, and sand, plus some organic material. Loam is ideal for garden soil. Silt is important in loam soil for texture and nutrients, but is not adequate as a garden material by itself; it needs enrichment. Clay contains the smallest particles of any soil; it has high nutrient and water retention, and helps bond sandy soil.

(sweetness). A measurement of 0.0 on the pH scale indicates the highest acidity, while 14.0 is the most alkaline. The halfway mark, 7.0, is neutral.

Soil pH is important because it influences several soil factors that affect plant growth, such as (1) soil bacteria, (2) nutrient leaching, (3) toxic elements, (4) nutrient availability, and (5) soil structure. Bacteria that changes and releases nitrogen from organic matter, as well as the action of certain fertilizer materials, are particularly affected by the pH level of the soil.

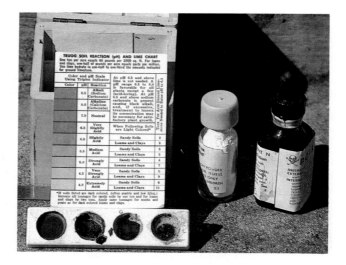

A soil analysis kit, which measures the soil's pH, can help you determine how to enrich your landscape base for maximum plant growth.

MR. GREEN THUMB RULE

Many gardeners tend to overlook the importance of knowing the pH of their soil. But most of the soil in Florida is poor and needs some enrichment. You must check the pH level in your garden and take whatever steps are necessary to adjust it.

The pH level in your garden soil must be tested chemically. You can do this yourself with an inexpensive soil-analysis kit obtainable from a garden shop or feed store.

With a small trowel or soil auger, dig a core sample of your landscape from 2 to 6 inches deep. These are the main depths where plants feed from their root systems. Following the instructions in your pH kit, use this plug of soil to test the pH.

If you don't want to do it yourself, you can send your soil sample to the University of Florida for analysis. For a small fee, you receive not only the pH factor, but also a listing of all minerals and other elements in the soil.

BALANCING THE PH

After you have learned the pH of your soil, you will have to either increase or decrease the pH to achieve the proper or neutral balance that is most desirable for optimum plant growth. Bear in mind that most soil in Florida consists of silicon sand, which is devoid of nutrients. Pure sand has less than 1 percent organic matter, compared with the ideal soil composition of 25 percent organic matter, 25 percent air, 25 percent water, and 25 percent minerals.

To increase the pH, or "sweeten" the soil, use ground limestone or dolomite. Do not use hydrated lime, which will "burn" the plant roots. The greater the amount of organic matter or clay in the soil, the more limestone or dolomite will be required to change the pH. To raise the pH one unit, add 4 pounds of limestone or dolomite per 100 square feet or 40 pounds per 1,000 square feet.

If a high pH reading is created by applying too much lime or dolomite, you can restore an acceptable balance by adding a combination of acid-forming chemicals and compost that enrich the soil.

To decrease the pH chemically, use superfine dusting or wettable sulfur in the following amounts: not more than 1½ ounces of sulfur per 10 square feet, 1 pound for 100 square feet or 10 pounds per 1,000 square feet. Note that it takes one-third of the amount of superfine or wettable sulfur to decrease the pH one unit as it does ground limestone or dolomite to raise the soil pH by one unit.

Applications of sulfur should not be made more than every eight weeks. In the ground, sulfur oxidizes, mixes with water, and forms a diluted sulfuric acid, which can burn the roots of plants. Be careful. Too little sulfur is better than too much.

Since it is difficult to counterbalance excessive alkalinity with chemical additives (such as sulfur) only, compost and other organic soil-builders should be added for structural enrichment of Florida soil. Using a tiller or shovel, add 25 pounds of peat moss and 25 pounds of cow manure for every 100 square feet of growing area.

ESSENTIAL SOIL ELEMENTS

The results you achieve with your plants are directly related to the degree of fertility in the soil, which is influenced by the amount of nutrients available. For instance, approximately 1/7 of protein is nitrogen, which is the element most used by all plants. Important for both the growth and greening of plants, nitrogen is an essential ingredient in most fertilizers. But since it dissolves very easily in water, nitrogen is leached out of the soil more easily than other elements. Nitrogen exists in the protoplasm and chlorophyll of all plants. It is an integral element essential for life and growth. Too much nitrogen applied during fertilization, however, can cause overly fast growth, as well as excessive growth. This will make plants more susceptible to disease and insects and less capable of withstanding strong winds, extremes in temperature, and physical injury.

Other elements necessary to maintain a balanced rate of growth are potassium, phosphorus, and iron. Potassium, or potash, strengthens plants, stems, and leaves, and the holding quality of flowers. Potassium is the main element that helps plants survive a long period of drought. Phosphorus helps in germination and development of seeds, provides rapid development of roots, and is necessary for good flower color. Iron, meanwhile, is vital to the growth and life metabolism of plants. Iron deficiency in the soil will cause new growth to lack the green of a healthy plant. Iron-poor plants often will exhibit green veins in the leaves, while the remainder of the leaf turns yellow, a condition that can be remedied by spraying with chelated iron. Most good fertilizers contain some iron in the formula.

Several minor elements play important roles in plant metabolism. Calcium helps strengthen cell walls and assists in root hair development. Root hairs are essential to plant growth because most nutrients are absorbed into the plant through them. Magnesium is used in the cells of chlorophyll (green coloring) that assist in photosynthesis, the process by which carbohydrates are manufactured by plants. Magnesium also aids in the distribution of phosphate within plants.

A chelated-iron spray will help cure iron deficiency, a yellowing condition found on these azaleas.

Manganese is essential in carrying iron throughout a plant, as well as helping the roots assimilate fertilizer, water, air, and gases. Boron helps prevent the breakdown of structural tissues in the leaves and stems. Small quantities of copper and zinc also are needed by plants to strengthen the growth of young seedlings and ensure proper growth in mature plants. And sulfur is used in the formation of protein and aromatic oils in leaves and stems.

ORGANIC MATTER

All organic matter is derived from living material and contains the most essential building block of life: carbon. So a compost pile is a must in every garden. Not only does a compost pile provide you with a disposal site for grass clippings, leaves, and small twigs, but also, in time, it becomes a never-ending source of the best possible soil conditioner for your garden.

If you do not have a compost pile, you can start one right away. Any yard refuse may be used, such as grass clippings, leaves, and small twigs, as well as any food scraps from the kitchen, including coffee grounds and tea leaves. Start with a 6-inch layer on the ground, followed by a layer of chemical fertilizer or dehydrated cow manure; add another layer of organic refuse, continuing to alternate the layers until you build a large pile. Make a small hollow at the top of the pile to catch and hold moisture, which aids in the breakdown of the organic materials. Once a month, you should turn the pile with a shovel to keep the mixture well-aerated.

To keep your compost pile from spreading, stake a fine wire mesh around it in a circle. This will allow oxygen and carbon dioxide to enter the compost pile and aid in the breakdown. During the process, heat and gas are generated, both of which affect the deterioration of the organic matter, turning it into the soft, crumbly humus that is the finest additive you can find for mixing with your soil.

FERTILIZERS

Although organic matter is important for plants, chemical fertilizers are needed, too. These constitute a fast pick-me-up for plants, just as we get a daily boost from coffee, which contains caffeine, a strong stimulant. Caffeine, however, does nothing for our growth, while fertilizers do possess positive food value for plants through the process of photosynthesis. That word is derived from the ancient Greek: "photo" meaning light and "synthesis" meaning putting together. This natural function within the body chemistry of a plant enables it to absorb and utilize chemical fertilizers, much as the human metabolism relies on minerals and vitamins for much of its function.

Since Florida's soils are generally poor and deficient in texture and nutrients, you should be familiar with the properties of the common fertilizers available for enriching Florida soil. Whether you choose granular fertilizers, liquids, or organic or inorganic materials, the basic properties are very much the same and those properties are spelled out on the product labels.

By law, all product labels must provide information by which you can judge the value of the material to be applied as well as standards of safe handling.

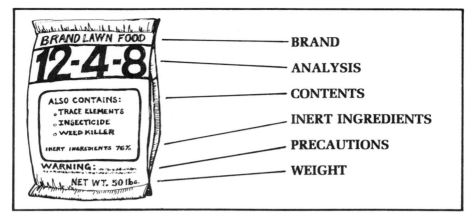

Fertilizer labels should always display the above data.

Fertilizer labels should give the following information:
1. Florida's registration code.
2. The brand name used by the manufacturer to identify the product.
3. The net weight, which tells the exact weight of the material in the bag.
4. The manufacturer's name.
5. The analysis, which lists the percentages of nitrogen, phosphorus, and potassium. This also should include secondary elements, if present, and the percentage of chlorine, which can be toxic to plants when present in high concentrations.

Chemical fertilizers give flowers and other plants a much-needed boost, encouraging their vigor and overall health.

6. Also important is the term "derived from," which gives the actual source of the ingredients.
7. A listing of inert ingredients, which are the fillers and carriers, or the inactive part of the fertilizer.
8. Details of any pesticide, contained on a yellow label with lettering in contrasting colors.

Florida laws concerning fertilizers have undergone many changes since they were first enacted in 1889. There is no magic combination of numbers to denote the best fertilizer. 6-6-6 often has been used. It is the lowest possible analysis that still can be termed a fertilizer under Florida law. By using a more concentrated product, (a fertilizer with higher numbers in the analysis, such as 14-12-20,) you will have fewer salt burn problems. You will save energy, time, and effort by applying fertilizer, and, in general, you will get more for your dollar.

Fertilizers are sold in several forms: liquid, granular, pellets, capsules, and spikes. Each has its own special value and particular application. Label directions will help you determine which will be most successful with your plants. Plants can use fertilizer only in liquid form, however. Even granular products must be dissolved in water before the tiny root hairs can absorb the needed nutrients for growth.

Many people become confused over the relative merits of organic versus inorganic aids for plants. Organic aids are longer-lasting, but elements such as cow manure are more valuable as soil builders than as true fertilizers. Chemicals may not last as long, but they are less expensive than store-bought organics and have a higher concentration of absorbable nutrients. Plants can use both chemical and organic fertilizers. Both should be included on your planned "diet" for your plants, as well as the all-important organic soil builders.

MR. GREEN THUMB RULE

Working organic matter into the soil before planting is the best basis for good, healthy growth. But you still must apply fertilizer. Continued, strong growth will not result from only one application. Small, frequently applied amounts are advised, just as humans thrive better on three small meals a day rather than on just one large meal. Be sure to read label instructions on all fertilizers and consult your nurseryman for a steady nutritional program for your plants.

ALTERING THE GRADE

It may be necessary to change the grade of your landscape to improve soil drainage around trees. Raising the grade is difficult and potentially dangerous to trees if some precautions are not taken. To ensure that roots receive adequate

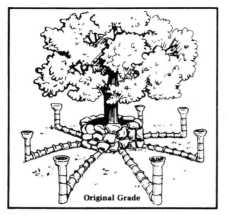

A view of the original grade, with horizontal and vertical pipes and retaining wall in place.

A cross-section view of the new grade, after the placement of soil, gravel, and sandy loam.

drainage, it is best to install a drain system, as shown, with 4-inch agricultural clay tile or perforated plastic pipe, sloping away from the base of the tree to a storm sewer or drainage ditch.

Vertical pipes should be placed to the height you expect to raise the grade, then construct a retaining wall around the trunk, from 3 to 6 feet from the tree. These steps help ensure proper aeration and give the trunk natural exposure.

When filling the grade with new soil, cover pipe openings to keep out soil; then begin filling with coarse gravel, then medium, then fine gravel, then top off with sandy loam.

Once the grade has been raised to the height of the vertical pipes, remove the coverings and fill with coarse gravel. Never fill to the base of the tree. Trees need to rest at natural root level. Then cover the pipe openings with wire mesh to keep out critters. Tiles help to drain off excess water and keep roots from drowning.

Lowering the grade is easier. Most likely, you will need to remove some of the larger, surface roots. Remember to trim some of the top growth to compensate for the loss of feeder roots. This step is similar to the one used when transplanting a tree (as covered in Chapter 2).

WATERING YOUR GARDEN

Eighty to ninety percent of any plant is water. Water is vital to every form of life on Earth. Outdoor plants too often are killed by underwatering, just as indoor plants die from drowning, or overwatering. If a plant starts to turn gray, this is a sign of root stress, a danger signal that water is needed. In some cases, the leaves will cup and curl. What is termed the "critical wilt point" means the point at which the plant has become dehydrated and will die.

Many enthusiastic gardeners complete a landscaping project, water it well for two weeks, then calmly forget it. When plants start wilting and dying, the nurseryman often is blamed when, in reality, the guilty party is the homeowner.

Next to soil itself, water is the most important factor in creating a healthy landscape.

Plants—just like every other form of life on Earth—require adequate water.

Give your garden or landscape daily care and feeding; the results will be worth it.

A garden or landscape is like a new addition to the family, requiring daily attention to flourish. For healthy growth, you must check the moisture level in your soil every week.

In many areas of Florida, especially the coastal regions, salt is a problem that must be faced. A well can be a good source of water for your yard, but it is important to check its salinity. As a general rule, more than one thousand parts of salt per one million parts of water will kill sensitive plants, such as azaleas; they may even succumb to as little as 700 parts per million. If you live in a beach community, you can reduce the effects of salt in your water and air by spraying plants regularly with fresh water and washing down any areas affected by flood or high-water conditions.

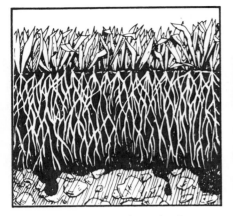 

DO: Water deeply in order to develop deep, sturdy roots. Grass watered less often but more deeply will have greater durability to withstand extremes of cold and heat. The grass above ground is only part of the total plant. Without a deep root system, the grass above ground cannot prosper.

DON'T: Watering lightly, even if it's more often, will not give the kind of saturation and penetration you want. Shallow roots promote weak growth above ground. Extreme temperatures and/or drought can destroy your lawn. Don't let the healthy green color at the surface fool you; the plant's only as durable as the roots that support it.

Many people become confused about watering their plants, shrubs, and trees. "When?" and "How much?" are common questions, and there are no hard-and-fast rules. Plants use water at different rates according to the temperature, rate of growth, time of year, and type of soil.

For most plants, an inch of water a week will suffice, with 2 inches during the summer months. Florida usually gets 50 to 60 inches of rain each year, but this is not necessarily sufficient to keep the ground properly moist, day in and day out. You can test the soil by hand, by pushing your fingers below the surface. If the soil is dry below 2 inches, you need to water. Remember that deep watering, especially for lawns, promotes a strong root system that spreads deep into the soil, enabling the plant to withstand heat and dry spells. Light watering tends to cause the root system to stay near the surface, where it is subject to damage during hot, dry days.

WATERING SYSTEMS

There are so many ways to water a garden effectively, that it will be a matter of personal choice as to how you go about this necessary duty. Many Florida gardeners still use the old-fashioned watering can. It does the job as long as you have the time and the energy. Its chief drawback is the inability to reach spots that may be too high or too densely surrounded by foliage. For convenient flower beds, however, the watering can is ideal, providing a gentle, effective rain that supplies the needed moisture without washing out the root system, especially around small plants.

A hose is possibly the most popular means of watering, both for efficiency

There are many sprinklers and spraying systems from which to choose; which one you select depends on your particular landscape as well as your own preferences.

and savings in time. Hoses come in several sizes, with the ½-inch and ⅝-inch most commonly used. Price ranges are determined by the quality of the hose. Very cheap plastic hoses may seem economical at first, but they tend to fold over and impede the water flow; also, their lifespans are limited. You should invest in a top-quality, reinforced rubber hose that will not buckle. It will outlast any other type.

The type of nozzle for your hose will depend on your personal preference. The adjustable type is the most popular. You can vary the flow of water from a wide spray down to a needle-sharp stream for reaching over shrubs and small trees. The higher priced brass adjustable nozzle is best. With proper care, it should last a lifetime, while plastic nozzles will deteriorate and leak after a period of time. The breaker-bar type of nozzle also is recommended for watering flowers. It turns the flow into a wide, gentle spray that does not damage delicate plant foliage.

Some gardeners prefer automatic watering systems, and several are available. A water bubbler literally bubbles the water out gently like a spring. These also can be attached to wands for broader distribution. Soaker hoses are perforated, porous rubber or plastic hoses that distribute the water in thin, gentle streams. Mechanical sprinklers come in various types, from the stationary version that creates a large, circular spray to the oscillating sprinkler that can be adjusted to distribute a pattern, either square or rectangular. These are particularly useful in preventing water from dropping onto undesired areas, such as pathways. For very large lawns or garden areas, the traveling sprinkler is recommended. These require laying out the hose in the desired configuration where you wish to water. The sprinkler creeps along the hose as it rotates and distributes the water.

For the ultimate in convenience, of course, there is the built-in sprinkler system, which eliminates the need for watering cans and hoses. You can put in a sprinkler system yourself or have one installed. While it is best to have this done before planting your lawn, it can be done in existing gardens without major disruption of your landscaping. Check with a reputable company or discuss installation techniques with personnel at hardware stores that sell the pipe and sprinkler heads. Such a system can be operated manually or by an automatic timer. The automatic system ensures that your garden and yard will be watered regularly. This type is advisable if you are away from home frequently for more than a few days at a time. Remember, if your soil dries out, you cannot expect your garden to flourish. Without water, your lawn, your trees, and your flowers will die.

Another efficient system is drip irrigation, which refers to the slow application of water to soil through mechanical devices called emitters that are located along selected points from the main water supply. Most emitters are placed above ground, but some can be buried at shallow depths for protection. Drip irrigation introduces moisture to the soil through capillary action and is an excellent means of maintaining a proper moisture level. Because it uses less energy, drip irrigation requires less water and is considered 10 to 25 percent more efficient than sprinkler systems. The savings in water alone makes this method very attractive.

Other advantages of drip irrigation:
1. Crops grow faster, yield more, and are of higher quality.
2. It conserves water while providing adequate moisture to root zones at all times.
3. The area between rows remains dry, thereby reducing weed growth.
4. There is no runoff on hillsides or rolling ground.
5. With water of poor quality (a high saline content), there is less damage to crops because the water is applied only to the root area.

Despite its basic advantages, one problem in Florida affects drip irrigation systems. Iron, sulfur, and calcium in irrigation water can react with certain bacteria to produce an ocher sludge or slime that clogs the emitters. If you experience this problem, you should flush out your system occasionally with a solution containing chlorine bleach. Too, while drip irrigation is very efficient for watering trees, shrubs, and flower and vegetable gardens, tests have revealed that overhead sprinkler systems are more efficient for watering lawns.

Drip irrigation kits can be purchased at nurseries or garden supply stores, where you also can get information on installation and maintenance.

Select the most efficient system for your particular needs, bearing in mind that water should be cherished and conserved. Using water efficiently will help you to avoid wasting time and money. Water during the early morning for best results. Watering at midday is not harmful to plants, but it is less efficient due to evaporation in the hot sun. Watering at night, however, is not advised. It tends to promote fungus problems.

TEMPERATURES AND SEASONAL CHANGES

Florida is touted as the land of eternal sunshine and warmth, but every part of the state is subjected to low temperatures on occasion. Even the Keys experience a freeze every 10 to 12 years. Though Florida is largely a subtropical region, heat-loving plants that do well in the southern end of the state are

Even in Florida, cold weather can damage plants, like this ixora.

Freezing temperatures can have a devastating effect on the landscape.

susceptible to injury in the colder, inland areas and in the northern parts. Be warned, therefore, especially if you are a newcomer to Florida!

Winter demands that you take extra care of sensitive outdoor plants, covering them to protect against cold nights. The only part of the state that does not drop into the 20s is the Keys; the rest of the state, especially areas around Tallahassee and Pensacola, can be cold enough to damage some of your plants. It is possible to hop into shorts and sun yourself on Christmas Day; still, Florida winters can be chilly enough to inflict serious damage to some gardens. Before placing tropical plants outside, check the lowest expected temperature for your area. The color-coded map (page 28) also will help you be aware of the general frequency of damaging freezes in your area.

As in most states, spring is a great season in Florida. Cool breezes mixed with warm, sunny days bring out the best in any garden. Azaleas burst forth with color in most areas, while in the northern and central areas, you will see occasional dogwoods in bloom.

Summer in Florida is warm to hot, with extremely high humidity. Daylilies appear, and the annuals, such as zinnias and marigolds, start giving their rich rewards of beauty.

But, for all the blessings of spring and summer, fall is truly the most outstanding season in Florida, particularly favorable to petunias, both in the ground and in the popular hanging baskets that brighten patios. Fall is the time for planting — among other things — cabbage, broccoli, and cauliflower, all cool-season vegetables.

FREEZE FREQUENCIES

The figures on this map indicate the number of times the temperature has dropped below 32 degrees in the past 20 years. The color bars also suggest the general pattern of growing seasons in the state: the coolest in the north, and the warmest and longest season in the south.

300	300
200	200
100	100
75	75
50	50
25	25
10	10

Although not a prevalent sight, dogwoods may be seen blooming in the spring in the northern and central portions of Florida.

Marigolds are a common summer sight in annual beds.

PROTECTING PLANTS FROM HEAT AND COLD

The best insurance against possible plant loss in winter is to select the majority of your plants from cold-hardy species. But just as too much cold can permanently damage your garden, so can too much heat. Even hardy plants can suffer from prolonged exposure to the sun, especially if the temperatures are high, as they often are in Florida in summer. The wind and heat also can dry out foliage, as well as direct sunlight. No one has ever said that keeping a landscape or garden in top shape is easy. You must pay attention to every element that affects growth and appearance. Caring for your greenery, therefore, includes choosing the right annual for the right season as well as taking protective measures for perennials, shrubs, and trees.

A vegetable garden, for instance, can last an extended season if leafy vegetables are planted in the shade, just as young azaleas are a natural for shady spots in the yard.

When a cold spell is anticipated, you must take steps to protect your plants. Burlap, a thermal sheet or a blanket are all good for protection against the frost.

Apply fertilizers containing potassium (K) to protect against heat and cold damage.

Avoid exposing sensitive plants to reflected heat.

Water during a heat wave and before an expected hard freeze.

Mulch with compost, bark or leaves to increase moisture retention and to protect against extreme temperatures.

Shelter cold-sensitive plants from winter winds.

You also can cover the ground itself to preserve the radiant heat stored in the soil. Large cardboard boxes are ideal for this purpose. Plastic (polyethylene film) also is excellent, but be warned: You cannot allow the plastic to touch the foliage, or the plant will be damaged. The plastic must be suspended over a framework of wood or wire. In this way, it creates a small greenhouse that holds in the heat and wards off the cold air.

For some special plants, you can use a low-wattage light bulb placed under a box or protective covering of plastic to raise the temperature a few degrees. Many beautiful theme parks in Florida use heaters on cold nights, but this system is too expensive and hazardous for the home gardener.

Water immersion is another way to save a garden from freezing. One-third inch of water must be applied until the ground temperature rises above freezing. Again, you must be fully familiar with your watering system to employ this means. Also, there are hazards with water immersion: Ice may form on branches or leaves and cause a plant to break. In reality, water immersion should be regarded as a desperate effort to save threatened plants during a freeze. It also increases the danger of rot and mold in the soil.

If your garden does suffer cold damage, do not trim off damaged branches until March or April, when all danger of frost has passed. Some gardeners get out their pruning shears the day after a freeze, but trimming entices a plant to put forth new growth that may be killed by ensuing cold spells. Leave the dead leaves and branches alone. They provide some protection until the warm weather arrives. Once the plant begins to sprout, you can treat for cold damage. Starting at the end of a damaged branch, trim down until you come to fresh, healthy growth. Always paint the newly cut end of a branch with neutral copper and pruning paint to protect against infection and excessive sap drainage.

Remember the old adage: Prevention is better than cure. It is far easier and cheaper to plan ahead than to try to save your plants once they are withered by winter chill, scorched by summer sunshine or infested with insects.

CHAPTER TWO

Florida Trees and Palms

Florida is famous for many things, but most of all its abundance and variety of trees and palms. Our state truly is a growing paradise, with the widest range of palms, evergreens, and deciduous and flowering trees to be found anywhere in the U.S. Trees may be the slowest growing of all plants, but they are the most enduring, stately, and impressive elements in any landscape. They are an artistic investment that pays off over the years not only in beauty but also in increased value for your property.

SELECTING THE RIGHT TREE

Before purchasing any trees for your landscape, check the existing trees to determine if you want to keep them or replace them with other species of different sizes or shapes. Your plans may call for trees to balance the overall look you desire on your property. Or you may decide on trees that not only provide foliage but also offer blossoms to add color in the spring, such as the exotic royal poinciana with its exquisite orange-red flowers or the orchid tree with its multicolored blossoms that grow up to 6 inches across. Check with your nursery for recommendations.

You may imagine a large tree standing in stately majesty in the middle of your front lawn. But a mature tree can cost 10 times as much as a younger sapling that you can nurture and watch grow to its full size. Your decision, therefore, can be affected by the amount you wish to spend on a tree. Trees are the most expensive items in any landscape plan, but they endure the longest and give the richest rewards in protection, beauty, and improved value.

Some trees grow better than others in various parts of Florida. Knowing the high and low temperatures (micro-climate) of your location is helpful in making a decision about the types of trees to plant. And do not shop only for price; shop for quality, too. A cheap tree may save you a little now, but in time you may be dissatisfied and have to have it removed. Trees are like everything else — you get what you pay for. Cheap trees seldom are a satisfying or good investment.

Years ago, most trees were field-grown, in the ground. Transplanting resulted in shock, and often the transplanted tree did not survive. If you buy a

A slash pine exhibiting new growth.

field-grown tree, make sure it has a compact root system. Ask if the tree has been root-pruned to minimize transplant shock, then make sure the tree has been properly watered, cultivated, and fertilized.

These days, the majority of commercial nurseries grow trees in containers, which reduces transplant shock. A large metal or concrete ring surrounds the tree root system, holding the roots intact and allowing for expansion as the tree grows. Container-grown trees may vary from 10 to 25 feet in height. They may be transplanted without damage and will adapt to their new location at any time of the year.

Follow these guidelines before purchasing your trees:

1. Check your landscape plan. Make sure you have enough trees to complete the look you want.
2. Always deal with a reputable nursery that will guarantee its stock and replace any tree that does not survive.
3. Make sure each tree you select fits the height and width specifications in your landscape plan. Your nurseryman will be able to tell you the maximum height and width of any tree.
4. Buy only those trees that are vigorous and growing abundantly.

5. Check the leaves. They should be well formed and relatively free of insects and disease.
6. If the tree is dormant, scratch the bark to see if the cambium layer is green and moist. Also called the growth layer, the cambium layer is found just beneath the outer bark. And examine the buds (tips of new growth). They should be ready to swell and starting to grow.

TRANSPORTING TREES FROM THE NURSERY

Selecting the right trees for your landscape is one of the most important decisions you will make. Once you have decided on the right size and variety, you should also consider how to bring your trees home safely and without damage.

When carrying trees, hold them by the root ball, not by the trunk. If you use a truck or trailer, secure the plants and place them where they will receive the least wind abrasion. If you put them in the trunk of a car, place the root ball in first and secure the plant. Tie down the trunk lid. Always drive slowly and carefully. Wind will damage leaves.

If the tree is heavy, get help. Don't drag or pull the tree. Don't abrade the bark or crush the root ball.

Once you've selected the proper planting site where the tree will have a proper exposure and plenty of growing room, carry the tree by the root ball to the digging site.

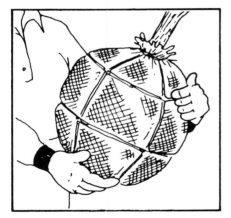

To avoid damaging the plant, always carry trees by the root ball, not the trunk.

To prevent damage in transit, secure the plant out of the wind as much as possible.

MR. GREEN THUMB RULE

Dig the planting hole about twice as wide as the tree's root ball. Add organic matter to the sand dug from the hole.

Dig the hole twice as wide as the root ball.

Place the plant upright in the center of the hole, without removing the burlap covering.

The top of the root ball should be level with the existing soil level that surrounds it.

PLANTING TREES

You may decide to have nursery personnel plant your trees, but if you prefer to do it yourself, here are some tips to help you guard against improper planting.

Generally, you should dig the hole twice as wide as the root ball. Place the plant upright in the center of the hole. Loosen the burlap at the top of the root ball, but do not remove it — the roots will grow through. Make sure the soil level does not come above the top of the ball or the top of the level of soil in the nursery container. Enrich with peat moss, refill soil, and water deeply immediately after planting.

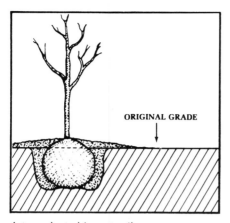

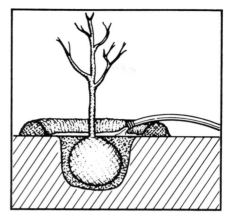

A tree planted in wet soil   A tree planted in dry soil

Young trees, in particular, need proper amounts of moisture to thrive and develop strong root systems. In dry soil, you may need to employ a system to ensure extra moisture. But in wet soils, especially in coastal regions, too much water can damage roots, and encourage diseases and insect problems. Here is how to deal with each situation.

In wet soil, plant the tree so that the root ball stands a few inches above the grade level. Build up soil around the trunk. This should hold roots above the water table, allowing proper growth and aeration of roots.

In dry soil, or during the summer months, build a 4-inch soil berm about 15 inches from the base of the tree all around the trunk. The berm will hold extra water and help provide adequate moisture for young roots.

STAKING TREES

Many new trees must be staked for the first year to support them against wind and weather, especially trees that may be top-heavy, with more foliage than the root system is able to support.

As shown below, place three wooden stakes in a circle, 3 to 5 feet from the hole in which you place the tree. Attach guide wires to the stakes and, before wrapping these around the tree itself, thread a 12-inch piece of old garden hose on the guide wires. Where the wire wraps around the tree trunk, slide the hose to this point so the wire does not cut into the bark. The hose protects the tree from injury.

Do not nail pieces of wood to the tree to protect the tree from being cut by the guide wires. While this may be effective temporarily, the damage to the tree can lead to fungus and borer infections. The pieces of hose are far more efficient.

If the tree is small enough, you may drive into the ground one heavy wooden stake a few inches from the trunk and attach the tree to the stake to help support it. However, the three-stake method is the best way to ensure that your newly planted tree remains upright until the root system has taken hold, usually after the first year.

Hammer notched stakes into the ground on three sides of the tree.

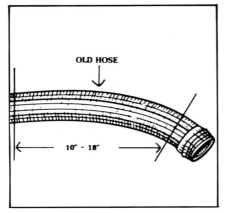

Cut strips of old garden hose or burlap to protect the tree.

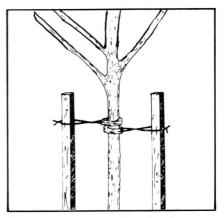

For some trees, two stakes placed as shown will give adequate support.

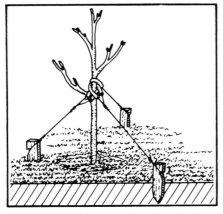

Run lengths of wire or twine through the hose and tie as shown.

Never drive nails into trees. This simply encourages diseases and insects. A single stake will help support larger trees.

CARING FOR YOUR TREES

The root system is the key to a healthy tree. After properly planting and staking your tree, water and fertilize it regularly to help build a good root system. Deep watering promotes a strong root system that makes a tree more drought-resistant and better able to withstand Florida's torrential rains and thunderstorms.

Trees should be fed at least three times a year. As a general rule, add fertilizer and soil builders in February/March, May/June, and September/October. Your nurseryman can advise you on a good tree-and-shrub fertilizer for your area. There are several ways to apply this very necessary supplement: by punch bar, watering rods, spikes, liquid fertilizer or by applying fertilizer on the ground around a tree.

The punch-bar method uses a steel rod that is hammered into the ground to a depth of 6 to 12 inches. Make 12 to 24 holes beginning 2 feet from the trunk of the tree and continuing every 2 to 3 feet to the drip line (the perimeter of the overhang of the branches), and 2 feet past the drip line. If your rod encounters a root, move the rod a few inches to avoid damage. When you have completed punching the holes, pour fertilizer into them and water thoroughly (to about ½ inch in depth).

The watering-rod method is the same principle as the punch bar, with the addition of water pressure. A watering rod is attached to the garden hose and inserted deep into the soil around the tree in the same manner described above. Some watering rods have an attachment for inserting a cartridge of fertilizer that dissolves in the water as it flows into the ground. This method will water and fertilize the tree at the same time.

Spikes are a relatively new product on the market and are most effective and easy to use. They are solid cores of fertilizer enclosed in a tube that is hammered into the ground. As the tree is watered, the moisture dissolves the fertilizer gradually, giving a long-term feeding to the root system.

Liquid fertilizers are the easiest method of fertilization for everything in your yard or garden. They can be applied by watering can, or they can be siphoned into the hose or into the sprinkler system. They do not leach away any quicker than other methods of fertilization, and are effective, economical, and easy to apply.

Broadcasting granular fertilizer around a tree also is simple. Start applying the fertilizer about a foot from the trunk and continue the application every foot until you're about 6 feet past the drip line. Normal watering will dissolve the fertilizer and carry it down to the root system.

MR. GREEN THUMB RULE

Remember to fertilize your trees at least three times a year, in February, June, and October, as a general rule.

TREE TRIMMING

Eventually, all trees must be trimmed, but this does not mean butchering or topping a tree. It usually is best to hire a professional to handle any large trimming chores, so that it is done safely and properly. For smaller branches, however, you should be able to do the job yourself, using a saw or a chainsaw.

When should you trim your trees? The following situations warrant attention. Branches may grow over the house or into power lines. Or your trees may suffer damage during the hurricane season. You may wish to eliminate heavy shade from part of your yard. Diseased limbs also should be removed.

If you see mistletoe growing in a tree, you should remove this parasite, which usually requires cutting off a branch. When cutting, remove the small leafy growth first, them trim branches in sections. Try to retain the aesthetic balance of the tree so that you do not wind up with a lopsided appearance. Try to retain the natural "look" of the tree: balanced on all sides under normal growing conditions.

If you have to remove a major branch, determine where you will make the cut, then undercut a "V" a few inches closer to the trunk. Next, proceed with your top cut. The weight of the branch will cause it to break evenly at the point of the undercut. Sometimes, you may need to attach a rope to the branch to hold it in place while cutting and to prevent it from falling into flower beds or shrubbery. The branch then can be lowered gently to the ground.

During the hurricane season, it is advisable to check trees for diseased areas that denote weakened limbs. These could fall during high winds and damage your property. Sawdust and blackened areas on the bark can indicate questionable parts that need attention. It is well worth a horticulturist's fee to have your trees examined periodically so you can maintain them in top condition.

SHAPING AND PRUNING OF YOUNG SHADE TREES

Shaping and pruning will help give young trees their distinctive shape and encourage growth. Newly transplanted trees should be pruned to compensate for

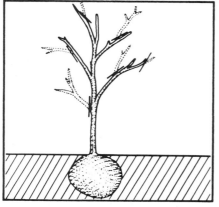

Example A   Example B

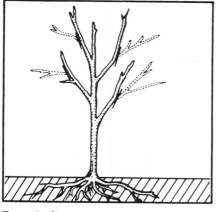

Example C

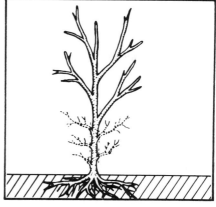

Example D

roots lost in transplanting (see example A). About 25 percent of top growth should be trimmed if the tree was balled-and-burlapped; about 40 percent should be trimmed if the tree was transplanted bare-rooted.

Trimming from the top, as in example B, will encourage lateral growth and outward spread, for best shade.

For vertical, upward growth, trim limbs and branches facing outward above buds, as in example C.

Growth at the base of the trunk encourages thicker trunk development, but this also creates a bushier shrub-like appearance. For shade trees with a tall, erect trunk, trim lower growth, as shown in example D, once the tree has become established.

Normally, pruning paint is not required for stripling trees, but limbs of an inch or more in diameter on larger trees should be painted to prevent loss of sap and possible insect or disease damage.

TRANSPLANTING TREES

A good initial landscape plan will eliminate the need to transplant a tree, such as when you install a patio or pool in your yard. If at all possible, leave your trees where they are. Transplanting a large tree is equivalent to major surgery, and if improperly done, the "patient" may not recover. Call in a professional to move any large tree. You can move smaller ones yourself, remembering the following guidelines:

1. Transplant only in the dormant season from December through January.
2. Be sure you move the tree to a location large enough to accommodate the tree's mature height and width.
3. Dig the hole at the new location twice as wide and twice as deep as the root ball of the tree to be transplanted.
4. When digging the hole, save the topsoil and mix it with an equal amount of peat moss before filling it back around the roots of the transplanted tree. To

get the hair roots off to a good start, use a hose to water-in the mixture of peat moss and topsoil around the root ball and force it into the space between the roots. Make sure there are not air pockets beneath the root ball. After filling the hole, make a ring around the base of the tree using the leftover soil. This forms a basin where the water may be caught and allowed to soak the roots.

5. To minimize transplant shock, apply a root stimulator-type fertilizer, one high in phosphorus (the middle number on the bag). Place this, along with the peat-moss mixture, around the root ball. A good liquid plant food also may be used, but avoid high-nitrogen lawn fertilizers. These can burn the roots.

6. Prune the tree, both in height and width, unless you are transplanting a container-grown tree. These rarely need pruning after being moved. Bare-rooted trees should be pruned 30 to 50 percent. Balled-and-burlapped trees should be pruned 25 to 30 percent.

7. If the transplanted tree is taller than 5 or 6 feet, you should stake it for the first year until the roots grow out and are able to support the tree.

8. To prevent sun scald on certain trees, wrap the trunk with tree-wrap, obtainable at your nursery. Ask nursery personnel which trees need this added protection after transplanting.

9. Water is the most vital factor to a newly transplanted tree. Be sure to water every day for the first two weeks, then once every two days for the following two weeks.

TREE VARIETIES FOR FLORIDA

You may choose from the following list of suggested trees for Florida, noting the climatic restrictions where applicable. (Not all of these trees are viable in all areas of the state.)

Acer rubrum
RED MAPLE
Height: 75 ft.   Areas: North, Central, and South Florida (N,C,S)

For wet areas, the Florida swamp red maple is ideal. It looks a lot like the northern maples, with three-lobed leaves that turn red in November, then drop. Growing in full sun to partial shade, the red maple flowers from December through January. However, it is not salt-tolerant and is prone to borers.

Bauhinia sp.
ORCHID TREE
Height: 25 ft.   Areas: C, S

This deciduous tree is grown in central and south Florida. It is admired for its orchid-like flowers, which can grow up to 3 to 4 inches across in shades of white, red, purple, and pink. Some varieties have flowers as large as 6 inches across. As a specimen or a small framing tree, the orchid tree is superb.

White orchid tree

Red maple

Callistemon rigidus
BOTTLEBRUSH

Height: 15-20 ft.   Areas: N, C, S

This tree has super spikes of red flowers in spring that resemble the old-fashioned bottlebrushes. It makes an outstanding, small specimen tree (or shrub). In a corner planting or as an accent plant, it is an excellent accent in the landscape. The bottlebrush has only moderate salt-tolerance but grows throughout the state.

Bottlebrush

Redbud

Deodar cedar

Cedrus Deodara
DEODAR CEDAR

Height: 40-50 ft.   Areas: N, C, S

Resembling the northern spruce and hemlock, the deodar cedar grows moderately into a blue-green pyramid of foliage. It can be planted anywhere in Florida.

Cercis canadensis
REDBUD

Height: 20-30 ft.   Areas: N, C

Native to Florida, the redbud is cold-hardy and grows mostly in the northern and central parts of the state. A deciduous tree, the redbud bursts into an umbrella of rose-pink flowers in spring, followed by the leaves that replace the blossoms and remain until they fall at the end of autumn. Also available with white flowers.

Cinnamomum Camphora
CAMPHOR TREE

Height: 40-50 ft.   Areas: N, C, S

The camphor tree does best in north and central Florida, although it can be grown throughout the state. This magnificent tree grows to mammoth size.

A large, thriving camphor tree

Cornus florida
DOGWOOD

Height: 20-30 ft.   Areas: N, C

The flowering dogwood is a traditional spring delight for nature lovers, with silvery white bracts its main attraction more than the actual flowers, which are relatively inconspicuous. The dogwood enjoys being shaded by other trees and protected from excessive heat, and grows well in enriched soil. An azalea-gardenia fertilizer is recommended for improved growth and appearance. Even though it is deciduous, the dogwood retains its attractive appearance in winter because of its beautifully formed branches.

Dogwood tree   Dogwood blossoms

Indian rosewood

Green ash tree

Dalbergia Sissoo
INDIAN ROSEWOOD

Height: 40-45 ft.   Areas: C, S

This tree is considered semi-evergreen or semi-deciduous. It has an upright, rounded head and can be used for avenue planting or as a specimen tree in the landscape. In central Florida, it is sometimes totally bared of its foliage by a hard frost, but will bounce back. In northern Florida, it may suffer severe injury.

Delonix regia
ROYAL POINCIANA

Height: 30-40 ft.   Areas: C, S

Best adapted to lower protected areas in central and south Florida, the deciduous royal poinciana is covered with exquisite orange-red blossoms in May and June. It is one of the most beautiful trees to use as a backdrop for your landscaped garden, and grows as tall as it is wide.

Fraxinus pennsylvanica
GREEN ASH

Height: 40 ft.   Areas: N, C

Growing in north and central Florida, the green ash is a tall, upright tree with beautiful, dark-green leaves during the warm months. Still, it loses its foliage for longer periods than most deciduous trees.

Grevillea robusta
SILK OAK

Height: 50-60 ft.   Areas: C, S

Despite its name, this is not a true oak tree but belongs to the *Proteaceae* family that originated in Australia. A rapid grower, it flourishes in central and south Florida with an attractive display of golden orange flowers. Because it drops a lot of leaves and small twigs, the silk oak is considered a messy tree. Allow plenty of room for its mature growth.

Ilex Cassine
DAHOON

Height: 30-40 ft.   Areas: N, C, S

Native to swamps, including the Biscayne Bay area, the dahoon has more salt tolerance than most other hollies and displays the traditional red berries during the Christmas season. Ideal as a small tree, it grows well in moist soil.

I. cornuta
CHINESE HOLLY

Height: 20 ft.   Areas: N, C, S

Although it usually grows to tree size, the Chinese holly often is used as a shrub. Not very salt-tolerant, it grows well in full sun and will tolerate partial shade. The dark, shiny leaves are edged with sharp spines. One popular and very common variety is Burford.

I. opaca
AMERICAN HOLLY

Height: 30-50 ft.   Areas: N, C

There are several varieties of this plant: the East Palatka, which has large, beautiful berries; the Howard; Taber #4; Savannah; Fort McCoy; Croonenberg; and the Dupre. Used for centuries for bordering avenues, the American holly grows well in north and central Florida.

American holly

Jacaranda

Jacaranda acutifolia
JACARANDA

Height: 50 ft.   Areas: C, S

Growing in central and south Florida, the jacaranda is a beautifully balanced tree, often as tall as it is wide. Its pale-blue, trumpet-shaped flowers appear in May and June, making it one of the most appealing landscape trees. However, because of its size, it may not be suitable for smaller gardens. A deciduous tree, it sheds its graceful, feathery leaves in winter. It enjoys full sun and will tolerate sandy — but not salty — soils.

Juniperus silicicola
SOUTHERN RED CEDAR

Height: 25-40 ft.   Areas: N, C, S

Cone-shaped when young, the red cedar gains a flat top at maturity. It grows throughout Florida and is quite salt-tolerant. It can be grown as a landscape specimen or used as a hedge. As with other junipers, mites can become a problem for the red cedar.

Koelreuteria formosana
GOLDEN RAIN TREE

Height: 20-30 ft.   Areas: N, C

An exceptionally beautiful specimen for landscaping, the golden rain tree is one of Florida's most popular trees. It is best adapted to northern and central areas of the state. It sometimes grows in a graceful, irregular pattern, with brilliant yellow panicles on the tips of the branches in October, followed by attractive pink seed pods almost 2 inches across. A deciduous tree, the golden rain tree can be planted on the east and west sides of the house, providing leafy shade in summer and allowing sunshine to reach the house in winter after the leaves have fallen.

Golden rain tree

Liquidambar Styraciflua
SWEET GUM

Height: 50-70 ft.   Areas: N, C, S

Where an upright, tall tree is desired, the sweet gum is an excellent choice. It spreads its foliage 30 to 40 feet across and is colorful. Its leaves turn red, orange, and yellow in the fall before they drop in the winter. Be warned, however. The sweet gum produces spiny fruit that is most painful to bare feet! A well-drained spot is best for the sweet gum.

Sweet gum tree

Sweet gum foliage

Magnolia grandiflora blossoms   Magnolia, just prior to blooming

Magnolia grandiflora
SOUTHERN MAGNOLIA

Height: 40-75 ft.   Areas: N, C, S

This Florida-native tree is a large, stately evergreen with big, white, fragrant blossoms in late spring. Like most flowering trees, the magnolia does best in full sun. Large amounts of peat moss and cow manure are recommended for maximum growth.

Melia Azedarach
CHINABERRY

Height: 40 ft.   Areas: N, C, S

Like the weeping willow, this tree is prone to spreading its roots into sewer lines, so be careful where you plant it. An excellent shade tree with dense foliage, the chinaberry has blue blossoms in summer but drops its berries and leaves in winter. Many people regard the chinaberry as a messy tree. It is salt-tolerant and grows in every part of Florida.

Wax myrtle

Peltophorum

Myrica cerifera
WAX MYRTLE

Height: 30 ft.   Areas: N, C, S

This Florida native is being used more often in our state because it's hardy, will take salt well, and is tolerant of conditions throughout the state. Because of its size, it is sometimes kept as a shrub or small tree; it is a nice screen and hedge plant.

Peltophorum inerme
PELTOPHORUM

Height: 40-50 ft.   Areas: C, S

Sometimes called the yellow poinciana or the yellow jacaranda because of similar foliage, this evergreen tree bears spikes of golden yellow flowers that bloom in early July.

Pinus Elliottii
SLASH PINE

Height: 70 ft.   Areas: N, C, S

Like the sand pine (*Pinus clausa*), the slash pine is native to Florida. If you have some of these trees on your property, and want to keep them, do not transplant them. The slash pine does not tolerate grade change. This tree also does not flourish with heavy equipment near the root system; barricades often are erected around slash pines to protect them from builders.

Slash pines

Platanus occidentalis
EASTERN SYCAMORE

Height: 125 ft.   Areas: N, C, S

    The sycamore has an open-headed appearance with a strong, straight trunk. The deciduous leaves have three to five palmate lobes and can be 3 to 4 inches across in small trees, and up to 10 or 11 inches across in mature trees. The bark often strips off in old trees, giving a mottled look. It is often used as a shade, avenue, or background tree.

Quercus laurifolia
LAUREL OAK

Height: 50-60 ft.   Areas: N, C, S

    Like the water oak, the laurel can grow in excess of 100 feet tall and also is partially deciduous. Its life span is at least 80 years, making it a permanent fixture in most locations. Its long, slender leaves (2-3 inches in length) create thick, robust foliage. Often used along public streets and avenues as well as in private landscapes, the laurel oak has only fair salt tolerance.

Q. nigra
WATER OAK

Height: 40-60 ft.   Areas: N, C, S

    Unlike the live oak, the water oak grows upright rather than spreading, sometimes to heights of more than 100 feet. A moderate-to-fast grower, it takes alkaline soils well though it may show some iron deficiency. In fall, most of the leaves drop, and the tree is nearly devoid of foliage.

Laurel oak

Live oak

Q. virginiana
SOUTHERN LIVE OAK

Height: 40-50 ft.   Areas: N, C, S

A moderate grower, the Southern live oak is considered the best tree for Florida, encountering few problems with diseases or insects and having a lengthy life span. It is salt-tolerant and, being evergreen, it maintains its leaves year-round. However, the live oak does spread as much as 50 feet, so allow plenty of room for it in your landscaping plans.

Salix babylonica
WEEPING WILLOW

Height: 25-40 ft.   Areas: N, C, S

Wet areas, ditch banks, and ponds are natural settings for this tree. Its graceful branches droop to the ground. Be sure to plant a weeping willow in a moist soil area. These trees are ravenous water consumers. Their roots have

Weeping willow
branches

Weeping willow

been known to spread immense distances in search of moisture. Never plant a weeping willow close to a house or sewer pipes. The hair roots will eventually clog the sewer line.

Sapium sebiferum
CHINESE TALLOW

Height: 30 ft.   Areas: N, C, S

Attaining a width of 30 to 35 feet, this fast-growing tree has orange, red, yellow, and wine-colored leaves in fall that drop during the winter. It prefers slightly acid soil.

Taxodium distichum
BALD CYPRESS

Height: 75-100 ft.   Areas: N, C, S

Some of Florida's famous gardens, such as Cypress Gardens, owe their unique beauty to this impressive tree that grows throughout the state, in water as well as on dry land. Young trees are pyramidal in shape, shooting up and out into a flat top that can reach more than 100 feet. This widely acclaimed tree is prized for its useful, long-lasting lumber and for its ''knees,'' which enable it to grow above water level in swampy terrain. The bald cypress is one of the few deciduous conifers. A very hardy tree, the bald cypress has few problems with insects or diseases.

Ulmus parvifolia
CHINESE ELM

Height: 20-35 ft.   Areas: N, C, S

Semi-evergreen and semi-deciduous, the Chinese elm has small, fine-textured leaves. It will grow in most soils in Florida but has only a fair salt-tolerance. It is an excellent choice where a small, fast-growing tree is needed. The Chinese elm is sometimes sold as weeping elm.

Bald cypress

Bald cypress knees in water

Even in a busy, tropical landscape, this graceful palm makes a significant visual statement.

FLORIDA PALMS

Florida is famous for many things, including its incredible variety and size of palm trees. Every visitor remarks on the majestic Washington palms that line our boulevards, the beautiful, curved elegance of the coconut palm, the stately royal palms standing like living concrete poles, crowned with green, glossy foliage. Easier to grow than other trees or shrubs, palms can be a picturesque addition to any yard, with a size and shape to satisfy your landscape requirements.

There are many palm varieties. Some are very tropical, others are moderate, and a few are cold-hardy, able to withstand near-freezing temperatures and survive in the coldest parts of Florida. For a lush, tropical look in your garden, you cannot choose any plant more suitable than a palm tree.

Study your available space and your proposed landscape plan before you choose your palms. Whatever size you select, the palms should remain in scale with your landscape and not upset the intended artistic balance. In some areas, a tall, slender palm will enhance the overall look you want. In other spots, you may need a palm with a short, fat trunk. Always remember the light requirements of the species you choose, as well as their tolerances to temperatures.

Most palms are tolerant of Florida's sandy soil. But you can improve the growth and appearance of your palms by adding peat moss, cow manure, chicken manure or wood chips to the soil.

Palm trees are like every other living thing: They need feeding. One pound of palm food or general fertilizer should be applied for every inch of trunk diameter. These applications should be done three times a year, in February, June, and October. In addition to a good palm food or general fertilizer, you should apply manganese and magnesium at the rate of ½ pound per inch of trunk diameter, up to 5 pounds.

Palms also need watering on a regular basis. Although mature palms are among the most drought-resistant plants, it is advisable to water them once a week. Newly planted palms, like other trees, need more frequent watering until they become established: daily for two weeks after planting, then once a week thereafter.

As a palm tree grows, it sheds its fronds at the bottom of the trunk. When you observe fronds turning yellow, it is advisable to remove them, using a palm saw. (This tool has a large curved blade on a long extension pole.) Trimming should be done when the fronds turn yellow and are still tender. Once they turn brown, they become hard and are difficult to cut.

Never try to trim the center of a palm. This is the bud from which new fronds emerge. Trimming the bud will kill a palm tree.

PALM VARIETIES FOR FLORIDA

The following palms are recommended for Florida. Please note climatic restrictions when selecting varieties.

Acrocomia sp.
GRU-GRU PALM

Height: 40-50 ft.	Areas: C, S

The large thorns on the leaf stalks and trunk of this palm give it a menacing appearance that causes a lot of comment, especially from tourists. It thrives in sandy soil and full sun. Look for it at nurseries specializing in unusual palms.

Adonidia Merrillii
MANILA PALM

Height: 20-25 ft.	Areas: S

This salt-tolerant, small palm has a green crown shaft and is sometimes called the baby royal palm. The foliage is elegant with bright-red clusters of fruit.

Queen palm   Queen palm with frizzle top

Arecastrum Romanzoffianum
QUEEN PALM

Height: 40 ft.   Areas: C, S

A straight-trunk palm requiring full sun for best growth, the queen palm is not very salt-tolerant. Once called the *Cocos plumosa,* it is the most popular palm in central Florida.

Caryota sp.
FISHTAIL PALM

Height: 40 ft.   Areas: C, S

A clump-type palm, the fishtail grows in southern and central parts of Florida, preferring protected areas. An impressive landscape addition, this palm gets its name from the shape of the fronds.

Chamaedorea elegans
HOUSEHOLD PALM

Height: 8-10 ft.   Areas: S

Here is one of the few palms that produces a variety of mature leaves after germinating from seed. Placed near a bright window, it will grow and flower indoors, and has both male and female plants.

Chrysalidocarpus lutescens
ARECA PALM or CANE PALM

Height: 20 ft.   Areas: S

Very salt-tolerant, this palm can be used in south Florida as a landscape specimen. In north and central parts of the state, it is best used as a potted specimen for patios and indoor plantings. With its long, arching feathery fronds, the areca is a very attractive and versatile palm for the landscape.

Areca palm

Cocos nucifera
COCONUT PALM

Height: 80-100 ft.   Areas: S

Best known for its fruit, the coconut palm has feathery fronds from 10 to 15 feet long, and the coconuts have a rough, fibrous husk. To avoid lethal yellowing (described in Chapter 12, "Insects and Diseases"), you should plant the dwarf Malayan variety, which is immune to this disease.

Livistona chinensis
CHINESE FAN PALM

Height: 20-30 ft.   Areas: N, C, S

Sometimes called the Chinese fountain palm, this one is only moderately salt-tolerant and should be grown in full sun to partial shade. A moderate-sized palm, the Chinese fan creates a nice effect with the ends of the palmation curling slightly on the edges. There are downward-pointing spines along the petiole, making this palm easy to identify.

Paurotis Wrightii
PAUROTIS PALM or SAW CABBAGE PALM

Height: 30-40 ft.   Areas: C, S

A native of the Florida Everglades, the paurotis palm loves wet areas but also will grow on higher, dry ground. It has good salt tolerance and grows well in full sun to partial shade.

Chinese fan palm

Paurotis (Saw cabbage) palm

> **MR. GREEN THUMB RULE**
>
> The queen, paurotis, and royal palms need special nutrients. Apply manganese and magnesium at a rate of ½ pound per inch of diameter of the trunk up to a maximum of 5 pounds.

Phoenix Roebelenii
PYGMY DATE PALM

Height: 8-12 ft.   Areas: C, S

Frequently grown in central and south Florida, this is a graceful, well-shaped dwarf palm with large, 3-inch thorns at the base of each leaf petiole. An excellent choice for a planter or entry, this small palm must be protected from hard freezes.

Roystonea sp.
ROYAL PALM

Height: 100 ft.   Areas: S

This stately palm requires a great deal of moisture to look its best. Its erect, white, cement-like trunk is topped with a 3-foot green shaft from which feathery fronds grow, often as long as 10 feet. It is the most widely grown palm from Sarasota to Miami. A native variety grows in the Everglades.

Royal palm

Pindo palm

Cold-Hardy Palms

Butia capitata
PINDO PALM or JELLY PALM

Height: 15-20 ft.   Areas: N, C, S

Sometimes incorrectly called *Cocus australis,* the pindo palm is one of the most cold-hardy palms in Florida, as well as being very salt-tolerant. It is a slow-growing, very attractive specimen palm with beautiful, blue-green pinnations and gracefully curved fronds. A jelly can be made from the fruit.

Chamaerops humilis
EUROPEAN FAN PALM

Height: 15 ft.   Areas: N, C, S

A native of southern Europe, this palm grows in north, central, and southern Florida. It is tolerant of many different soils and grows best in partial shade to full sun. A slow grower, the fan palm is considered a dwarf variety. It has fan-shaped fronds and often puts out several trunks at the same time.

Phoenix canariensis
CANARY ISLAND DATE PALM

Height: 50-60 ft.   Areas: N, C, S

This is one of our most beautiful specimen palms, often used to border avenues. In landscaping, it 'needs plenty of room because of its large size. With its straight, thick, bulging trunk and the diamond pattern formed where the fronds grow, it is sometimes called the pineapple palm.

Canary Island date palm

Rhapis excelsa
LADY PALM

Height: 8-10 ft.   Areas: N, C, S

Used as a foundation or container-grown plant, this is another clump palm with an abundance of fan leaves extending from the base. The lady palm prefers shade to partial shade, and is not salt-tolerant. But it can be planted on any side of a house that is protected from salt spray.

Sabal Palmetto
CABBAGE PALMETTO

Height: 60-80 ft.   Areas: N, C, S

The state tree of Florida, the cabbage palmetto is our most cold-hardy native palm. It grows in any part of the state and in any type of soil. It is so salt-tolerant that it will grow right down into salt water. From the southern Keys to Tallahassee, this palm can be seen growing wild.

Cabbage palmetto

Washington robusta
WASHINGTON PALM

Height: 60 ft.   Areas: N, C, S

For avenue planting, this palm is unequalled. It is too large for small properties, and its height makes it difficult to trim. It does best in full sun, has good salt-tolerance, and can be grown throughout Florida. When the old fronds begin to droop, they hang from the trunk like a petticoat.

Washington palm   Washington palm

PALMS FOR FLORIDA

COMMON NAME	SCIENTIFIC NAME	HEIGHT	SALT TOLERANCE	GROWTH RATE	SPECIAL CHARACTERISTICS	AREAS
Areca or Cane Palm	Chrysalidocarpus lutescens	20'	Excellent	Moderate	Bamboo-like	N,C,S
Cabbage Palmetto	Sabal Palmetto	60'-80'	Excellent	Moderate	State tree	N,C,S
Canary Island Date Palm	Phoenix canariensis	50'-60'	Moderate	Slow	Large pineapple trunk	N,C,S
Chinese Fan Palm	Livistona chinensis	20'-30'	Moderate	Moderate	Palmate leaves	N,C,S
Coconut Palm	Cocos nucifera	80'-100'	Good	Slow	Edible fruit	S
European Fan Palm	Chamaerops humilis	15'	Moderate	Slow	Clump grower	N,C,S
Fishtail Palm	Caryota sp.	40'	Fair	Slow	Foliage	C,S
Gru-Gru Palm	Acrocomia sp.	40'-50'	Fair	Slow	Spiny trunk	C,S
Household Palm	Chamaedorea elegans	8'-10'	Fair	Moderate	Household, dwarf	S
Lady Palm	Rhapis excelsa	8'-10'	Poor	Moderate	Matte clump	N,C,S
Manila Palm	Adonidia Merrillii	20'-25'	Good	Slow	Baby Royal	S
Paurotis or Saw Cabbage Palm	Paurotis Wrightii	30'-40'	Good	Moderate	Clump grower	C,S
Pindo or Jelly Palm	Butia capitata	15'-20'	Excellent	Slow	Edible fruit	N,C,S
Pygmy Date Palm	Phoenix Roebelenii	8'-12'	Good	Slow	Small, date	C,S
Queen Palm	Arecastrum Romanzoffianum	40'	Poor	Slow	Straight trunk	C,S
Washington Palm	Washingtonia robusta	60'	Good	Moderate	Tall-pole	N,C,S

N — North Florida   C — Central Florida   S — South Florida

FLORIDA'S FINEST TREES

COMMON NAME	SCIENTIFIC NAME	HEIGHT	SHAPE
Acacia, Banana-Leaf	Acacia auriculiformis	20'-30'	Upright
Ash, Green	Fraxinus pennsylvanica	40'-60'	Upright
Bottlebrush	Callistemon rigidus	15'-20'	Upright
Camphor Tree	Cinnamomum Camphora	50'-60'	Upright to Spreading
Cedar, Deodar	Cedrus Deodara	40'-50'	Upright
Cedar, Southern Red	Juniperus silicicola	25'-40'	Upright (young) Flattened (old)
Chestnut, Moreton Bay	Castanospermum australe	40'-50'	Upright
Chinaberry	Melia Azedarach	40'	Rounded, Spreading
Coral Tree	Erythrina crista-galli	20'-30'	Upright to Spreading
Cypress, Bald	Taxodium distichum	75'-100'	Pyramidal
Dahoon	Ilex Cassine	30'-40'	Upright
Dogwood, Flowering	Cornus florida	18'-30'	Upright
Elm, Chinese	Ulmus parvifolia	20'-35'	Spreading, Upright
Flame Tree	Brachychiton acerifolius	25'-30'	Upright
Fringe Tree	Chionanthus virginicus	20'-30'	Upright
Geiger Tree	Cordia Sebestena	20'-25'	Upright, Rounded
Golden Rain Tree	Koelreuteria formosana	20'-30'	Irregular
Golden Shower	Cassia alata	20'-35'	Upright to Spreading
Grape, Sea	Coccoloba Uvifera	20'-25'	Upright to Spreading
Gum, Sweet	Liquidambar Styraciflua	50'-70'	Upright to Spreading
Holly, American	Ilex opaca	30'-50'	Upright, Pyramidal
Holly, Chinese	Ilex cornuta	20'	Compact
Jacaranda	Jacaranda acutifolia	50'	Upright to Spreading
Lipstick Tree	Bixa Orellana	20'-30'	Round-headed
Loquat	Eriobotrya japonica	15'-25'	Upright
Magnolia, Southern	Magnolia grandiflora	40'-75'	Pyramidal, Upright
Maple, Red	Acer rubrum	75'	Upright, Full

N — North Florida   C — Central Florida   S — South Florida

COLOR: (B) BLOOM, (L) LEAF, (F) FRUIT	SEASON (COLOR)	SALT TOLERANCE	GROWTH RATE	AREAS
Yellow (B)	Summer, Fall	Good	Fast	C,S
Greenish (L)	Summer	Poor	Moderate	N,C
Red (B)	Spring	Fair	Moderate	N,C,S
———	———	Fair	Moderate	N,C,S
———	———	Good	Moderate	N,C,S
Greenish (L)	———	Good	Moderate	N,C,S
Yellow (B)	Spring	Fair	Moderate	S
Purplish Blue (B)	Spring	Good	Fast	N,C,S
Red (B)	Summer	Fair	Slow	C,S
Incidental	Summer	Poor	Moderate	N,C,S
Red (L,F)	Spring	Fair	Slow	N,C,S
White (B)	Spring	Poor	Moderate	N,C
Incidental	Summer	Fair	Fast	N,C,S
Red (B)	Fall, Winter	Fair	Fast	S
Greenish White (B)	Spring	Fair	Slow	N,C
Orange-Red (B)	Spring, Summer	Excellent	Moderate	S
Yellow, Pink (B)	Fall	Poor	Fast	N,C
Yellow Gold (B)	Summer	Good	Moderate	C,S
———	———	Excellent	Moderate	C,S
Red, Yellow (L)	Fall	Fair	Fast	N,C,S
Red (F,L)	Winter	Fair	Slow	N,C
Red (L,F)	Spring	Fair	Medium	N,C,S
Violet, Blue (F)	Late Spring	Poor	Moderate	C,S
Pinkish Red (B,L)	Fall	Good	Fast	C,S
Incidental	Fall	Good	Fast	N,C,S
White (B)	Spring, Summer	Fair	Moderate	N,C,S
Red (L,F)	Winter, Spring	Poor	Moderate to Fast	N,C,S

FLORIDA'S FINEST TREES

COMMON NAME	SCIENTIFIC NAME	HEIGHT	SHAPE
Mimosa	Albizia Julibrissin	25'-35'	Spreading
Myrtle, Wax	Myrica cerifera	30'	Irregular, Spreading
Oak, Laurel	Quercus laurifolia	50'-60'	Upright
Oak, Silk	Grevillea robusta	50'-60'	Upright
Oak, Southern Live	Quercus virginiana	40'-50'	Spreading
Oak, Water	Quercus nigra	40'-60'	Upright
Olive, Black	Bucida buceras	25'-40'	Upright to Spreading
Orchid Tree	Bauhinia sp.	20'-30'	Upright to Spreading
Peltophorum	Peltophorum inerme	40'-50'	Upright to Spreading
Pine, Australian	Casuarina equisetifolia	60'-80'	Upright
Pine, Japanese Black	Pinus Thunbergiana	20'-100'	Upright
Pine, Slash	Pinus Elliottii	70'	Upright
Poinciana, Royal	Delonix regia	30'-40'	Spreading
Redbud	Cercis canadensis	25'-30'	Spreading
Rosewood, Indian	Dalbergia Sissoo	35'-45'	Upright
Shaving-Brush Tree	Bombax sp.	30'	Spreading
Sycamore, Eastern	Platanus occidentalis	25'	Broad, Open-headed
Tallow, Chinese	Sapium sebiferum	30'	Upright
Toog	Bischofia javanica	40'-60'	Round-headed
Willow, Weeping	Salix babylonica	25'-40'	Upright

N — North Florida   C — Central Florida   S — South Florida

COLORS: (B) BLOOM, (L) LEAF, (F) FRUIT	SEASON (COLOR)	SALT TOLERANCE	GROWTH RATE	AREAS
Pink (B)	Summer, Fall	Good	Fast	N,C,S
Incidental	Winter	Excellent	Slow	N,C,S
Incidental	Spring	Fair	Fast	N,C,S
Yellow (L,B)	Spring, Summer	Fair	Fast	N,C,S
Incidental	Spring	Good	Moderate	N,C,S
Incidental	Spring	Fair	Moderate to Fast	N,C,S
——————	——————	Excellent	Moderate	S
White, Pink, Red, Purple	Spring	Good	Fast	C,S
Yellow (B)	Summer to Fall	Fair	Fast	C,S
——————	——————	Excellent	Fast	C,S
Incidental		Fair	Slow	N,C,S
——————	——————	Fair	Moderate	N,C,S
Reddish Orange (B)	Spring to Summer	Good	Fast	C,S
Dark Pink	Spring	Fair	Moderate	N,C
——————	——————	Fair	Moderate to Fast	C,S
Red (B)	Winter	Fair	Moderate	S
Incidental	Spring	Fair	Moderate	N,C,S
Incidental	Summer	Poor	Fast	N,C,S
——————	——————	Fair	Fast	C,S
Incidental	Summer	Poor	Moderate	N,C,S

CHAPTER THREE

Landscape Shrubs

There are more evergreen and flowering shrubs in Florida than in any other state. While trees are important to your landscape plan, they take years to achieve their full height, width, and beauty. Shrubs, on the other hand, develop quickly and give almost immediate results in completing the picture you are trying to create in your garden. Similarly, lawns do not sprout into their ultimate rich carpet of green overnight. Shrubs can serve to screen the lawn area while it is growing, and they can shade your home and add overall beauty and charm to your yard or garden.

Shrubs are a versatile decorating item in completing your dream landscape. They soften the lines of a wide area, creating a natural balance between flower beds, lawn expanse, and trees. A tall shrub fills in a corner very well — the corners created by a fence as well as the corners of your home. Shrubs also constitute a break between separate areas, becoming a transition plant from lawn to walkways or between lawn and ground cover, allowing the eye to flow smoothly from one area to the next. Shrubs also can be planted as specimens by themselves in order to break up large areas of lawn. Ligustrum and viburnum are good for this purpose, grown as standard shrubs or trimmed as trees. Whether you use a shrub as a shrub or as a small tree depends on what you envision for your landscape design.

The same principle applies to vines, such as bougainvillea and allamanda. These can be left as vining plants or trimmed into shrubs. The ultimate use of shrubs in your garden depends on their placement and how you care for them.

BUYING SHRUBS

Nurseries sell shrubs in one of the following forms: container-grown, balled-and-burlapped, or bare-rooted.

Whether you select a young shrub or a full-grown variety, container-grown plants generally offer the best root protection and the best transplant success, since they remain in their natural soil. To plant container-grown shrubs, you merely slide them out of their plastic containers and lower them gently into the ground. (I'll explain specific planting steps later in this chapter.)

Shrubs, such as this blooming glory bush, can be planted as specimens to create focal points in a large expanse of lawn.

Balled-and-burlapped (b&b) shrubs are also popular, but will suffer some initial root damage. They must be trimmed by about 25 percent after planting, which should be done as soon after purchase as possible.

Occasionally, roses, crape myrtles, and some other plants are sold bare-rooted, but this is not a common practice in Florida. If you do purchase a bare-rooted shrub, know that it will lose most of its feeder roots, and should be trimmed by about 40 to 50 percent after planting.

Choosing your shrubs demands that you pay attention to the climate in your particular area. Crotons may be inappropriate for Tallahassee, but in central Florida, they can give an added burst of color in the landscape. Later in the chapter, I'll provide information on some of the best shrubs for Florida, and their viable growth areas. If you're not sure about a particular shrub's climate requirements, check with your nurseryman.

Container-grown sweet viburnum

Container-grown shrubs offer the best transplant potential.

Balled-and-burlapped shrubs will need to be pruned after planting.

Bare-rooted shrubs require major pruning after planting.

PLANTING SHRUBS

Shrubs look best and are easier to care for when planted in beds. It is important not only to select the appropriate shrubs, but also to select your site carefully; prepare the soil properly; plant correctly; edge effectively; and spray, water, fertilize, and mulch the area as needed.

After measuring and staking the area for your shrub beds, spray the site with a short-lived weed killer to get rid of established weeds. Wait two weeks for the herbicide to do its job completely.

Next, rototill the soil in the staked area to a depth of 8 to 12 inches. Remove any roots, rocks or other debris from the area.

Improving the soil is crucial to good shrub growth — before and after planting. Before you introduce the plants, add organic material, compost, peat moss

MR. GREEN THUMB RULE

Always select shrubs with their mature sizes in mind; that way, you'll buy the right shrub for the right spot.

or shredded bark and till again. If you need to fumigate the soil, use Vapam or a similar product, following label directions carefully. Wait four weeks after application before planting the shrubs.

When planting, pay attention to the depth of each hole *and* the spacing between each plant. A minimum of 2 feet is recommended between small shrubs, 3 to 5 feet for larger shrubs. (Your nurseryman can tell you the mature size and space requirements of each shrub you purchase.)

Dig each hole to the depth of the particular shrub's root ball or container, and wide enough to accommodate the roots. If the root ball is too wet or too dry, it may come apart. Make sure it is just moist.

Next, place the plants in the soil so that the top of each root ball is level with the surrounding grade. Cover the roots with good planting soil, plus peat moss, cow manure, and compost to ensure a nutritious base in which your plants can thrive. Then water immediately. Too, apply a root stimulator to the area for one or two months before beginning a fertilizer program.

Finally, you'll need to use some edging material to separate the lawn from the shrub beds. Brick may be used, as well as a variety of other materials: wood, plastic, metal, etc. While railroad ties, creosote logs, and metal and plastic edging will help delineate the growth areas in your garden, lawn grass may still creep into any of these materials.

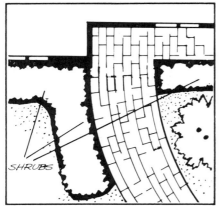

Measure and stake the area for your shrub beds.

Spray the beds with weed killer to eradicate established weeds.

Rototill the soil.

Add organic material, compost, peat moss or shredded bark.

Spacing counts; a minimum of 2 feet is recommended between small shrubs, 3 to 5 feet for larger shrubs.

Place the plants in the soil so that the top of each root ball is level with the surrounding grade.

Add edging material to separate the lawn from the shrub beds.

A bark mulch or other mulch will aid in water retention and temperature protection.

WATERING TIPS

Newly planted shrubs need plenty of water every day for the first two weeks; after that, twice a week is adequate. With established shrubs, it is better to water deeply twice a week than merely to sprinkle them daily. Daily watering may promote fungus growth on the leaves.

If you have a sprinkler system, any shrubs in the spray area will be watered at the same time as your lawn. However, the shrubs may not be receiving appropriate water with this routine — unless the sprinkler system is equipped with special adapters that water each shrub individually.

Drip irrigation allows a slow stream of water to trickle to the shrub's root system. The method is slow and reliable and provides uniform moisture to the soil.

Soaker hoses come in many types. Some are capped on one end with perforations around the entire hose; others are perforated on one side only, sprinkling directly into the soil. Both types are excellent for shrub beds.

If you select watering rods that penetrate directly to the roots, insert the instrument to a depth of 6 to 8 inches. Try not to damage roots or to pass the critical root area by going too deep.

Some automatic sprinkler systems come with special adapters for shrubs, sending a fine spray to the soil and lower greenery. These are generally effective and less time-consuming for the gardener.

To ensure that your shrubs are getting the right kind of watering — plenty at the roots, very little on the leaves (to discourage disease and blossom damage) — you may want to employ a more efficient system. Soaker hoses, drip irrigation, and watering rods are three good options.

FERTILIZING SHRUBS

Fertilizing shrubs is important because there is little natural fertility in Florida soils. Make sure you apply the right combination of elements. A fertilizer's elements are labeled on the package in the following order: nitrogen (N), phosphorus (P), and potassium (K).

Specific-application fertilizers for shrubs and flowering plants are available with chemical concentrations suited to specific types of plants. Explore the possibilities and consult your nurseryman before selecting one of these.

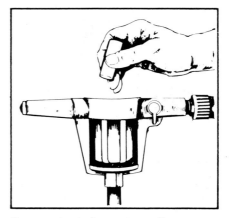

Some root-watering systems allow you to insert fertilizer cartridges that add nutrients directly into the root system. If you use one of these, be sure to keep the watering element—the spike—at root level—or about 6 to 8 inches deep.

Plant food spikes, available at most garden centers, allow nutrients to dissolve into the soil slowly and naturally over a period of time. These can be very beneficial for bedded shrubs.

Nitrogen promotes leaf growth, but too much will cause stress and possible shrub damage. Phosphorus aids root growth and flowering. Potassium helps in the overall strength of the plant.

Some gardeners prefer an evenly balanced formula such as 6-6-6 or 10-10-10. But, for best results in Florida use a 14-12-20, which offers a healthy and natural balance of needed nutrients. With some evergreens, especially if you desire heavy growth and dense foliage, use a tree-and-shrub fertilizer with a high nitrogen content (the first number in the analysis).

Fertilizing should be done immediately after planting and, thereafter, three times a year in spring, summer, and fall.

PRUNING SHRUBS

Immediately after planting, prune 25 percent of the top growth from b&b shrubs, and 40 percent from bare-rooted specimens. Too, all shrubs should be trimmed occasionally to prevent them from becoming untidy.

Power trimmers are useful for this purpose, making the job easier. But be warned: You can get carried away with power tools, to the detriment of your landscape plants. With power tools, you may remove large chunks of plant material unintentionally; this leaves unsightly scars that damage the plant. Hand trimming is far better for shaping a shrub, and helps you avoid stubs and notches that may mar the beauty of the plant.

Certain varieties of shrubs work better as hedges than others do. Most hedge materials, in their natural state, will remain full from top to bottom. By tapering the top slightly, you allow more sun to enter, promoting thicker growth below. Tapering the top is recommended for newly planted shrubs but, once a hedge has matured, you can leave it alone, allowing it to grow and form a living wall around your yard or patio.

Azaleas grown as a hedge make an attractive addition to the landscape.

COLD PROTECTION

The location of cold-sensitive shrubs is important. Some shrubs can be protected from the cold by positioning them close to water, such as a pond or lake, where the ground stays warmer. During a cold spell, you should protect all your shrubs by covering them with burlap or plastic sheets. When using plastic, always build a frame to hold the polyethylene away from the plant. If not, the cold will pass through the plastic and burn any leaves it touches. Too, cover the soil around the shrub in order to hold heat in the ground.

Mulching is a good way to prevent rapid changes in the soil temperatures around your shrubs and other plants. Mulch can be raked away from the plant base during the day to allow the sun's warmth to penetrate, then raked back at night to hold in the heat.

A plant can withstand extreme cold if the soil is moist. A well-watered and fertilized plant can withstand extremes of heat and cold far better than one that has been neglected. Even in periods of drought, plants can survive freezing temperatures if they have been watered adequately. While good soil and fertilizer contribute to the health and growth of a plant, it is water that is essential above all else, particularly in those areas of Florida where the temperature drops drastically in the winter.

MR. GREEN THUMB RULE

When buying dormant bare-rooted or packaged shrubs, you may want to scratch the bark with a knife to make sure the cambium layer (just under the bark) is a healthy green.

SHRUB VARIETIES FOR FLORIDA

You may choose from the following list of suggested shrubs for Florida, noting the climate restrictions where applicable. (Not all of these shrubs are viable in all areas of the state.)

Abelia sp.
ABELIA

Height: 3 to 8 ft.	Spread: 4 ft.	Areas: N, C

Useful as a border, hedge or screen plant, the abelia is a hardy evergreen seen mostly in the Gainesville area and the northern parts of Florida. During summer, this shrub is covered with white, tubular, bell-shaped flowers. The abelia can be propagated from seeds or cuttings, and has good salt-tolerance.

Abelia

Copper plant

Acalypha Wilkesiana
COPPERLEAF ACALYPHA

Height: 15 ft.   Spread: 5 ft.   Areas: C, S

Often used as a background plant in landscaping, the acalypha, or copper plant, grows best in full sun. This shrub spreads rapidly and needs trimming to keep it from getting out of hand. It is used mostly in protected areas in lower central and south Florida. Keep in mind that the copper plant's bright color may be too glaring for your particular landscape needs. Mealybugs and aphids occasionally are a problem. This shrub does suffer injury when the temperature drops to freezing, but it normally will grow back.

Agave americana
CENTURY PLANT

Height: 8 ft.   Spread: 7 ft.   Areas: N, C, S

This shrub grows only in sandy soil and does best in full sun, but do not plant a century plant in areas where children play. It has stiff, sword-shaped leaves with needle-like points at the end that can be quite dangerous. Every 6 to 12 years, the century plant grows a large, flower-topped stem 15 to 25 feet in

Variegated century plant   Century plant

Bird-of-Paradise

height that lives for several months, after which the plant dies. Then little plantlets will sprout around the base. These can be transplanted and about 98 percent of them will live.

Strelitzia reginae
BIRD-OF-PARADISE

Height: 4 ft.   Spread: 3 ft.   Areas: C (protected), S

This plant is often used for a tropical effect or as a conversation piece in the landscape. It grows in a large clump; the bird-like blossoms of orange and blue are spectacular. It needs protection below 30 degrees. Fertilize with a good liquid plant food in addition to a couple of applications of blood meal and bone meal during early and late summer.

Buxus sp.
BOXWOOD

Height: 6 ft.   Spread: 3 ft.   Areas: N, C, S

Flourishing from St. Petersburg to northern Florida, this evergreen shrub is extremely cold-hardy and will grow in full sun and partial shade. A versatile shrub for landscaping, it can be trimmed into virtually any desired shape. (The sister variety, English boxwood, is not well adapted to Florida's alkaline soils and heat.) This plant thrives best in rich, acid, organic soil. Disease problems include root rot and leaf spot.

Boxwood

Camellia blossoms

Camellia blossom

Camellia japonica
CAMELLIA

Height: 5-15 ft.   Spread: 5-10 ft.   Areas: N, C, S

The camellia's shiny, dark-green, toothed leaves are almost 4 inches long and create an interesting contrast to the brown twigs from which they sprout. During winter and early spring, camellia bushes make beautiful framing or accent plants. They grow best in north and central Florida. Like azaleas, these plants thrive in an acid soil and prefer partial shade during part of the day. They need to be sprayed regularly to prevent accumulation of tea scale insects on the foliage, and thrips and botrytis disease in the flowers. Mulching is especially important for your camellia plants. Florida's winters pose a special problem for camellia plants. The cool periods alternating with short heat waves produce a condition called "bull nosing" or "bud blast." When this occurs, flowers start to open and then simply fall off the branches. To avoid this condition, select varieties approved for use in Florida, particularly those that require shorter chilling times.

Carissa grandiflora
NATAL PLUM

Height: 15 ft.   Spread: 10 ft.   Areas: C, S

Natal plum is ideal for growing in central and south Florida. This plant has single, white flowers — that grow to more than an inch across — in spring, summer, and fall. The flowers are followed by dark red, elliptical berries that not only are decorative but also edible and can be used in making jellies. Natal plum has excellent salt-tolerance. It will freeze at 28 degrees, but grows back. It has two sharp-pointed thorns on each branch, dark green leaves, and a milky sap. Natal plum is best used as a background plant. A dwarf variety (Boxwood Beauty) can be used as a hedge. Natal plum does best in full sun. Disease problems include leaf spot, dieback, root rot, and sphaeropsis.

Codiaeum variegatum
CROTON

Height: 10 ft.   Spread: 6 ft.   Areas: C, S

A tender, colorful shrub, the garden croton does well in south Florida and in a few protected areas in central parts of the state. There are numerous combinations of leaf color, shape, and size. For best leaf color, crotons should be given full sun. Because they will freeze at 32 degrees, it is best to plant them against the house or fence for protection. Crotons exhibit eye-catching colors and should be used sparingly in your landscape. They may suffer from anthracnose and root rot.

Duranta repens
GOLDEN DEWDROP

Height: 18 ft.   Spread: 6 ft.   Areas: N, C, S

Golden dewdrop sometimes is known as the pigeon berry. This evergreen shrub has beautiful, lilac-blue, ½-inch flowers that hang from the branches like the Northern lilac. With its drooping habit, it can be used as a background shrub or espaliered on a wooden framework against a wall. It is susceptible to nematodes.

Elaeagnus pungens
ELAEAGNUS or SILVER THORN

Height: 12-15 ft.   Spread: 15 ft.   Areas: N, C, S

As a hedge or screening plant, this evergreen has a sprawling growth pattern, is quite tolerant of salt, and will grow in light shade to full sun. The leaves are dark green with a silver dot pattern underneath. Elaeagnus produces brown, drupe-like fruit from which jams and jellies can be made.

Croton

Euphorbia pulcherrima
POINSETTIA

Height: 10 ft.   Spread: 8 ft.   Areas: N, C, S

The poinsettia is a tender shrub that is killed back at 32 degrees. It will grow back and can be protected so it is seen growing in north, central, and south Florida. It is loved in the Christmas season for its bright red, floral leaves called bracts. It grows well in full sun, though it should be protected from night lighting. This plant will grow in any improved, well-draining soil. Normally, trim back about one-third after flowering. Do not trim later than September 1, as this may interfere with the timing of the Christmas blooms. Scab is an occasional problem and can be treated by trimming the infected area and spraying with a good general fungicide. The poinsettia has poor salt-tolerance.

Gardenia jasminoides
GARDENIA

Height: 8 ft.   Spread: 5-6 ft.   Areas: C, S

Like azaleas and camellias, these evergreen shrubs grow best in acid soil. They prefer filtered shade and cannot withstand temperatures below 20 degrees. Their exquisite white, double, waxy, fragrant flowers appear from April through early June, making an impressive show, especially against an all-green background in the garden. Particularly susceptible to nematodes, gardenias should be grafted on the *G. Thunbergia* root stock to minimize this threat. Other disease problems include leaf spot, algal leaf spot, and mushroom root rot.

Hibiscus Rosa-sinensis
HIBISCUS

Height: 10-15 ft.   Spread: 5 ft.   Areas: N (protected), C, S

One of central and south Florida's most popular plants is the hibiscus, a pleasant addition as an informal hedge or screen, foundation plant or background for other garden plants. Varieties often are selected on the basis of plant growth, habit, and size; the form and color of the flowers; and adaptability to specific environments. Six basic colors exist — red, orange, yellow, white, lavender, and brown — but many variations show up between varieties. Some of the newer varieties grow well only as grafted plants and are not widely available.

Given proper fertilization, hibiscus will grow in most of our sandy soils. A well-draining soil with a pH of 5.5 to 6.5 is preferred. Nutrient deficiencies may occur in alkaline soils.

MR. GREEN THUMB RULE

Keep the mulch a couple of inches from the hibiscus trunk. Mulching too close to the trunk increases the chances of root rot.

High Society hibiscus

Happiness hibiscus

Frisby hibiscus

Brilliant hibiscus

Hibiscus should be planted at the same depth as they were in their nursery containers. Staking may be necessary on the tree types. Most hibiscus should be spaced at a minimum of 4 to 5 feet apart. The planting hole should be at least 6 inches wider than the root ball. Add organic matter such as peat moss, dehydrated cow manure, or compost to the planting hole. This normally should be mixed one-third by volume with the existing soil. Plants should be watered thoroughly after planting. A mulch will conserve water, reduce weed problems, and give some control of nematodes. Mulches include cypress, oak leaves, pine bark, and pine needles.

Hibiscus should be watered heavily once a week during dry periods. A regular fertilization is essential. These plants do their best blooming when fertilized lightly and often — three to four applications per year, as a rule, in March, May, June, and November.

Hibiscus should be pruned to maintain a desired size and shape without disrupting their blooming or appearance by cutting only the longest third of the branches at one time.

Some hibiscus plants grow upright like trees or bushy like shrubs. They can be used in many ways: as an enclosing plant, as a background, a screening plant, an informal or formal hedge, even as a specimen. They grow best in full sun but can withstand partial shade. In either location, the soil should be well-drained. There are many different varieties, enabling you to have a hibiscus in bloom almost year-round. During cold snaps, protection is advisable. Freezing temperatures can injure these plants.

Hydrangea macrophylla
HYDRANGEA

Height: 4-5 ft.   Spread: 2-3 ft.   Areas: N, C, S

The hydrangea has long been admired for its enormous clusters of flowers that resemble pompons. The hydrangea is a natural pH indicator, exhibiting blue petals in acid soil, pink in alkaline soil, and off-white in near-neutral soil. By changing the pH of your soil, you can change the color of a hydrangea. This deciduous shrub grows best in shade or filtered sun. Moderate moisture is preferred, with a fairly high level of fertility in the soil. Hydrangeas, with their medium to dark-green leaves and large clusters of flowers, make an outstanding shrub against a wall or a fence or in the protected entranceway to your front door.

Hydrangea

Chinese holly

Burford holly

Ilex sp.
HOLLY

Holly usually is considered part of a northern landscape, but while it is not tropical, holly grows well in most parts of Florida. All types of holly prefer slightly acid soil and are moderate in their growth patterns. The varieties that bear the traditional red berries will do so only during winter. There are many hybrid varieties, with new ones being developed each year. Holly can be used as an ideal hedge, as well as along pathways and between areas within a yard.

I. Cassine
DAHOON

Height: 30-40 ft.   Spread: 6-10 ft.   Areas: N, C, S

Often considered a small tree, the dahoon's leaves are 3 to 4 inches in length, shiny on top and velvety beneath. Originally from Florida's swamplands, the dahoon has red berries in the winter and, sometimes, yellow berries as well.

I. cornuta
CHINESE HOLLY

Height: 10-15 ft.   Spread: 5-8 ft.   Areas: N, C, S (somewhat)

This is a large, compact shrub with glossy, dark-green leaves that have a sharp-pointed spine at the top of each leaf. Bright-red berries appear in late fall and winter. The Burford is a sport, or bud, variation of the *Ilex cornuta*. The dwarf Chinese holly *(Ilex cornuta* 'Rotunda') has similar leaves but grows to only 24 to 36 inches at maturity in a rounded shape.

Hetz Japanese holly

American holly (tree form)

I. crenata
JAPANESE HOLLY

Height: 3-5 ft.   Spread: 3 ft.   Areas: N, C, S

Japanese holly is grown mostly in upper central and northern Florida. It has medium to dark-green foliage and compact, shrubby growth. It grows best in shady locations and should be protected from afternoon sun.

I. hybrid
NELLIE R. STEVENS HOLLY

Height: 15-20 ft.   Spread: 5-8 ft.   Areas: N, C, S

One of the newer hybrids, this variety of holly is a very attractive, vigorous-growing plant with dark-green leaves and a rounded growth pattern. Disease problems include dieback, various fungi, leaf spot, and mushroom root rot.

I. opaca
AMERICAN HOLLY

Height: 40-50 ft.   Spread: 10 ft.   Areas: N, C, S

Normally grown as a tree because of its size, the American holly comes in many varieties, the most common being the East Palatka type, found throughout the state.

I. vomitoria
YAUPON HOLLY

Height: 20-25 ft.   Spread: 10 ft.   Areas: N, C, S

In regular or dwarf variety, this plant can be trimmed to any height and any shape, making it ideal for imaginative landscaping. Dwarf yaupon holly has become the most popular holly in Florida. Dwarf yaupon holly grows to 2 to 5 feet and can be kept trimmed in geometric shapes as low as 1 foot.

Illicium anisatum
ANISE TREE

Height: 15-20 ft.   Spread: 5-8 ft.   Areas: N, C

Grown in central and northern Florida, this hardy evergreen is an ideal accent or enclosure plant for full sun or partial shade. It grows best in improved, organic soil, so mulching is a definite asset for this plant. It needs trimming once a year, immediately after flowering in spring.

Ixora coccinea
IXORA or FLAME-OF-THE-WOODS

Height: 6 ft.   Spread: 4 ft.   Areas: C, S

Grown mostly in central and south Florida, this shrub has glossy green foliage with 2½-inch leaves and masses of brilliant red, orange, and yellow flowers from May through July. The ixora requires full sun for best flowering and will freeze at 30 degrees, but normally grows back. It can be used as a hedge. Set plants about 24 inches apart. Disease problems include leaf spot, stem gall, and mushroom root rot.

Jasminum sp.
JASMINE

Many species of jasmines flower and grow well in Florida, in full sun as well as partial shade. Jasmines can be trimmed as standard shrubs or grown as vines. Their height will vary depending on how they are used. Jasmine can suffer from algal leaf spot, anthracnose, and mushroom root rot.

Yaupon holly

Ixora

J. gracillimum
AUSTRALIAN JASMINE

Height: 4-5 ft.   Spread: 5-6 ft.   Areas: N, C, S

Often used as a background or enclosing plant, Australian jasmine is a slow-grower requiring full sun. It has glossy, dark-green leaves about 2 inches long and an inch wide, and freezes at 30 degrees.

J. multiflorum
DOWNY JASMINE

Height: 20 ft.   Spread: 4-5 ft.   Areas: N, C, S

This variety has dark-green hairy stems and leaves. Downy jasmine will freeze at 26 to 28 degrees but grows back fast. Like other jasmines, it can be started by misting soft wood cuttings in the summer.

J. nitidum
SHINY JASMINE

Height: 4-6 ft.   Spread: 3-6 ft.   Areas: C, S

Grown as a shrubbery border in central and south Florida, shiny jasmine can be trimmed as a shrub. But is more often used as a vine because of its strong, twining, sprawling growth pattern. In fact, the branches have to be trimmed to keep them under control.

Juniperus sp.
JUNIPER

This useful and dependable evergreen grows best in full sun. Junipers are ideal for Florida. They can withstand the heat, the dry spells, and the lowest temperatures without damage. They do not like very wet soil and need to be fertilized every two months with a good liquid plant food, or every three months with a tree or shrub fertilizer. Junipers can be started from cuttings in the summer. For excellent ground cover, try the Blue Rug or Blue Carpet cultivars, as well as the shore juniper (*Juniperus conferta*), which grow to 2 feet, and the Torulosa juniper (*Juniperus chinensis* 'Torulosa').

Spreading junipers with ilex plants

Bar Harbor juniper

Italian cypress juniper

Pfitzer juniper

Torulosa juniper

J. chinensis 'Columnaris'
JAPANESE JUNIPER

Height: 20-30 ft.   Spread: 6-10 ft.   Areas: N, C, S

With a straight trunk and a columnar growth, this juniper has scale-form and needle-form growths on every branch. This shrub is one of the best tall evergreens with dark-green foliage. Disease problems include twig blight, rust, and leaf spot.

Crape myrtle

J. chinensis 'Pfitzerana'
PFITZER JUNIPER

Height: 5 ft.   Spread: 8-10 ft.   Areas: N, C, S

This juniper is a horizontal-spreading plant with branch tips that point outward.

Lagerstroemia indica
CRAPE MYRTLE

Height: 20-25 ft.   Spread: 6-8 ft.   Areas: N, C, S

One of the few consistently beautiful deciduous shrubs, crape myrtle is attractive even without leaves because of its smooth, light-brown bark. A fast grower, it does best in full sun, is hardy, and flourishes in all parts of Florida. With attractive flowers (pink, red, and white varieties), it can be grown as a freestanding specimen or used to highlight evergreen plantings. Locating the crape myrtle where the morning sun can dry its leaves will lessen any potential powdery mildew problems. Pruning branches after flowering will help increase the following year's yield of blossoms. Mushroom root rot is a potential problem if the crape myrtle is planted in poorly drained soil.

Lantana Camara
YELLOW SAGE LANTANA

Height: 10 ft.   Spread: 3 ft.   Areas: C, S

This is a versatile shrub that can go wild if not kept under control. In fact, it is regarded as a weed in California. Nevertheless, the lantana can be a colorful addition to any landscape, flowering 10 months out of the year with small blossoms

Lantana

in red, lavender, orange, yellow, pink, or white. Lantana can be used in hanging baskets, as ground cover, or allowed to grow into a dense, rather prickly bush. It will freeze at 28 degrees, but will grow back. It has few disease problems.

Ligustrum lucidum
GLOSSY PRIVET

Height: 40 ft.　　Spread: 15-20 ft.　　Areas: N, C, S

Grown throughout Florida, this very popular shrub is sometimes called the wax-leaf ligustrum. The ligustrum grows very fast, especially when fed regularly, and can be used as a background plant, screening hedge, or enclosure. The leaves are pear-shaped, dark green, and glossy, reaching 4 inches in length. Glossy privet produces cream-colored flowers in panicles during the spring. This evergreen shrub is very hardy and has become one of the most popular landscape items in the state. It will self-sow, and the dozens of small seedlings can be

Ligustrums are available in tree and shrub forms.

transplanted easily, growing to 4 or 5 feet within two years with very little care. With regular fertilizing, growth and foliage improves rapidly. The ligustrum is one of the easiest shrubs to grow and one of the most rewarding. Disease problems include anthracnose and leaf spot.

L. japonicum
JAPANESE PRIVET

Height: 15 ft.   Spread: 5 ft.   Areas: N, C, S

The Japanese privet can be grown in full sun and partial shade, and often needs heavy pruning to keep it from growing too large. It can be used as an enclosure plant or as a sheared hedge. It is a very versatile plant for any landscape.

Nandina domestica
NANDINA

Height: 8 ft.   Spread: 4 ft.   Areas: N, C

Used from Orlando in central Florida to Pensacola in the north, nandina grows in an upright, compact shape. This deciduous shrub has small, white terminal flowers that give way to strikingly bright red berries in the fall and winter. It can be used as a background shrub against a fence, or to break up green borders and provide color in the winter. Caution: A rather slow grower.

Oleander

Nerium Oleander
OLEANDER

Height: 20-30 ft.   Spread: 10-15 ft.   Areas: C, S

The oleander has pink, white or red flowers on long, straight stems with stiff, green leaves 8 inches long. It has been a very popular shrub for centuries. The oleander can be grown as a specimen or as an informal hedge. Left alone, it grows into a tree and needs pruning to be kept under control. Oleander has excellent salt-tolerance but needs spraying with diazinon to control caterpillars. A dwarf variety grows from 3 to 5 feet in height. Disease problems may include bacterial gall and leaf spot.

Photinia glabra 'Fraseri' *x serrulata*
RED-LEAF PHOTINIA

Height: 20 ft.   Spread: 15 ft.   Areas: N, C

Found mostly in north and central Florida, the photinia grows best in full sun and should be used inland because of its moderate salt-tolerance. It needs organic-enriched soil upon planting. This shrub is greatly admired for its leaves, which are 3 inches long and about ¾ of an inch wide. They change from bright red to green as they mature. The cooler winters in northern Florida tend to bring out better color in this plant.

Pittosporum Tobira
PITTOSPORUM

Height: 15 ft.   Spread: 10 ft.   Areas: N, C, S

This hardy evergreen is very popular, with glossy, oval, leathery leaves that are dark green. A variegated variety offers white, marbled, cream-colored leaves. Pittosporum grows well in full sun, though the variegated variety has a better mixture of coloring when grown in partial shade. The plant has a thick, compact growth habit and does well near salt water. As a hedge plant or for an informal shrubbery area, the pittosporum is an excellent choice. Disease problems include angular leaf spot, crown gall, and dieback.

Pittosporum

Leadwort plumbago blooms

Plumbago capensis
LEADWORT PLUMBAGO

Height: 4-5 ft.   Spread: 6-8 ft.   Areas: C, S

The plumbago is a shrub that tends to sprawl. It looks like it wants to vine but doesn't vine much. It has very attractive, tubular, baby blue flowers that are 1 inch across; the plant flowers throughout the warm season. The plumbago grows mostly in central and south Florida because it tends to be killed back to the ground by temperatures below 28 degrees; however, it can grow back quickly. It is sometimes used as a color mass, a transition plant, or an informal flowering hedge. It flowers best in full sun and has fair salt-tolerance. It should be planted in a nematode-free soil. There is also a fine but less commonly grown white variety called *P. auriculata* 'Alba.'

Podocarpus sp.
PODOCARPUS

For a sheared hedge, podocarpus is one of the best choices. This very hardy shrub can be used anywhere in the state.

P. gracilior
FERN PODOCARPUS

Height: 30 ft.   Spread: 15 ft.   Areas: C, S

Fern podocarpus is more cold-sensitive than its relatives and should be planted in protected areas in central or south Florida. It makes an excellent corner plant or an outstanding accent plant. It also is used as a screening plant or espaliered on a frame against a wall or fence. It can be air-layered or started from cuttings.

P. macrophyllus
YEW PODOCARPUS

Height: 25 ft.   Spread: 10 ft.   Areas: N, C, S

One of the best for hedge plantings, the yew podocarpus has dense foliage from the ground up, with long, flat, linear leaves up to 3 inches in length. It grows well in full sun to partial shade and is salt-tolerant. It should be planted in well-drained soil; it does not thrive in wet soil. Yew podocarpus has a purple, edible aril attached to a green drupe. It can be started from soft wood cuttings in summer. This podocarpus suffers from angular leaf spot, crown gall, and dieback.

P. Nagi
BROADLEAF PODOCARPUS

Height: 25 ft.   Spread: 10-15 ft.   Areas: N, C, S

A strong accent plant, this podocarpus has large, green leaves 3 inches long and almost an inch wide, with parallel venation. The broadleaf can be grown in full sun or in shade and has good salt-tolerance. It has a strong central growing habit and does well as a large hedge. It can be propagated from seed or from cuttings in the summer.

Prunus caroliniana
CHERRY LAUREL

Height: 40 ft.   Spread: 15 ft.   Areas: N, C, S

Clipped or unclipped, the cherry laurel can be used as a hedge or as a large shrub where a screening plant is desired. Like the boxwood, it can be cut into almost any shape. A member of the true cherry tree family, it grows best in a slightly acid soil. Do not allow water to settle around this plant. It does not thrive in very wet soil. Caution: The cherry laurel foliage is poisonous.

Podocarpus

Pyracantha

Pyracantha coccinea
FIRE THORN or PYRACANTHA

Height: 20 ft.   Spread: 15-20 ft.   Areas: N, C, S

A large, spreading shrub, this hardy evergreen usually is espaliered, making a very attractive display against a wall with its small, white fragrant flowers followed in the fall and winter by bright, orange-red berries. Fire thorn flowers best in full sun but has some problems with fire blight, especially when over-fertilized. A low-spreading variety called "low dense" grows to only 6 feet in height. Fire thorn has good salt-tolerance and always attracts birds, which enjoy the "berries" — actually, pome-like fruit. It suffers from mushroom root rot.

Raphiolepis indica
INDIAN HAWTHORN

Height: 5 ft.   Spread: 4-5 ft.   Areas: N, C, S

Ranging in size from dwarf to standard, the Indian hawthorn is a popular landscape shrub with good salt-tolerance. The foliage is similar to that of the pittosporum, with small, rose-like flowers ½ inch across in pink, white, and rose. The blossoms are fragrant, and the fruit is drupe-like in shape, with a purplish black color. This plant can suffer from fire blight.

Rhododendron sp.
AZALEA

Height: 10-15 ft. (standard); 2 ft. (dwarf)	Spread: 1-3 ft.	Areas: N, C, S

The azalea is the queen of the garden from January through April. Azaleas come in a wide range of sizes and color variations: white, red, pink, purple, orange, and all shades between. Flowers can be single or double and often vary in the way they open. Azaleas are not salt-tolerant and must have an acid soil. A 50/50 mixture of peat moss and existing soil is helpful in promoting good growth and a healthy plant. Shallow-rooted, azaleas need frequent watering — at least every two days. They are used for masses of color, as an informal hedge, or as bedding and background plantings. Pruning the shrubs after they flower promotes the formation of more flower buds and prevents the branches from growing out of control and from looking straggly.

Caution: Do not trim after July 1. This is when azaleas set buds for the next season's flowers. Mulching is of utmost importance in growing good-looking azaleas.

Indian Hybrids:

These plants produce an abundant display of color in late winter and early spring.

Duc de rohan — An early, compact, spreading azalea that is semi-hardy and grows about 2 feet high.

Elegans — An abundant flowering shrub that reaches 10 feet in height, is quite hardy, and produces blossoms that are single, medium-sized, and pink.

Formosa — A vigorous, long-lived, hardy azalea with large, singular lavender blossoms. Grows from 10 to 15 feet in height and blooms early to mid-season.

Azalea shrubs

Formosa azalea bloom

Duc de rohan azalea bloom

White azalea blooms

Rhododendron Nova Zembia

Azaleas

Rhododendrons

Kurume Hybrids:

Kurumes are a Japanese species of azalea, with leaves and flowers smaller than those of the Indian variety. For best blooms, the kurumes need cooler weather. They do best in rich, acid, organic soil in partial shade, and are prone to petal blight.

Coral Bells — A hardy bloomer during mid-season, this hybrid grows to 4 feet in height and produces small, shell-pink flowers.

Hexe — This hardy hybrid grows to 2 feet in height with an abundant display of violet-red flowers.

Snow — As its name implies, this hybrid produces small, white flowers in mid-season. A dense grower, the plant matures to 2 feet in height.

Viburnum sp.
VIBURNUM

This popular shrub has a number of varieties that do well in Florida. The following are two of the most popular:

V. odoratissimum
SWEET VIBURNUM

Height: 40 ft.   Spread: 30 ft.   Areas: N, C, S

Often used as a hedge or as a screening plant, this shrub has white, fragrant flowers in the spring. It can be grown in full sun or partial shade, with medium- to bright-green oval leaves 4 to 6 inches long. It has fair salt-tolerance and is considered a fast grower that makes a nice, thick privacy hedge.

V. suspensum
SANDANKWA VIBURNUM

Height: 8-12 ft.   Spread: 4-8 ft.   Areas: N, C, S

A moderate grower, this shrub has dark-green, 4-inch-long leaves, and small white and pink flowers from late winter through early spring. It grows as well in full sun as shade and is often used in shady areas around a house. Sandankwa viburnum also makes an excellent hedge plant and can be used as a foundation plant. It has good salt-tolerance and withstands wet soil.

Viburnum screen planting

SHRUBS FOR FLORIDA

COMMON NAME	SCIENTIFIC NAME	HEIGHT	SPREAD
Abelia	Abelia sp.	3'-8'	3'-5'
Allamanda	Allamanda sp.	4'-10'	3'-6'
Anise Tree	Illicium anisatum	15'-20'	5'-8'
Azalea	Rhododendron sp.	2'-8'	2'-8'
Bird-of-Paradise	Strelitzia reginae	4'	3'
Bottlebrush	Callistemon rigidus	10'-20'	20'
Boxwood	Buxus sp.	6'	3'
Camellia	Camellia japonica	4'-15'	8'
Candlestick	Cassia alata	5'-10'	10'
Century Plant	Agave americana	8'	7'
Copperleaf or Acalypha	Acalypha Wilkesiana	15'	5'
Croton	Codiaeum variegatum	10'	6'
Elaeagnus or Silver Thorn	Elaeagnus pungens	12'-15'	15'
Elder, Yellow	Stenolobium stans	3'-6'	3'-5'
Gardenia	Gardenia sp.	2'-8'	8'
Glory Bower	Clerodendrum speciosissimum	5'-10'	8'-15'
Glory Bush	Tibouchina semidecandra	3'-10'	2'-10'
Golden Dewdrop	Duranta repens	18'	6'
Hawthorn, Indian	Raphiolepis indica	2'-8'	10'-15'
Hibiscus	Hibiscus Rosa-sinensis	2'-12'	2'-5'
Holly	Ilex sp.	6'-30'	6'-15'
Honeysuckle	Lonicera sp.	5'-8'	5'-10'
Hydrangea	Hydrangea macrophylla	4'-10'	2'-3'
Ixora or Flame-of-the-Woods	Ixora coccinea	3'-6'	3'-5'
Jasmine	Jasminum sp.	4'-8'	3'-8'
Juniper	Juniperus sp.	3'-20'	3'-5'

N — North Florida   C — Central Florida   S — South Florida

COLOR: BLOOM (B), LEAF (L), FRUIT (F)	SEASON (COLOR)	SALT TOLERANCE	GROWTH RATE	AREAS
White (B)	Spring, Summer, Early Fall	Poor	Moderate	N
Yellow (B)	Spring, Summer, Fall	Fair-Slight	Fast	C,S
Green, Yellow (L)	Spring, Summer	Poor	Moderate	N,C
Pink, Red, White, Purple (B)	Spring	Poor	Moderate	N,C,S
Orange-Blue (B)	Much of the year	Fair	Slow	C,S
Red (B)	Spring, Summer	Fair	Moderate	N,C,S
Green (L)	——————	Poor	Moderate	N,C,S
White, Pink, Red (B)	Late Fall, Winter, Spring	Poor	Slow	N,C,S
Golden Yellow (B)	Summer, Fall	Good	Fast	C,S
Green (L)	——————	Excellent	Moderate	N,C,S
Red (L)	Year-round foliage	Fair-Slight	Fast	C,S
Yellow, Red, Green (L)	Colorful leaves	Fair	Moderate	C,S
Silvery (B)	Winter	Good	Fast	N,C,S
Yellow (B)	Fall, Winter	Poor	Moderate	C,S
White (B)	Spring	Poor	Moderate	N,C,S
Red (B)	Most of the year	Fair	Fast	C,S
Purple (B)	Spring, Summer, Fall	Poor	Moderate	C,S
Lilac, Yellow eye (B)	Summer	Good	Fast	N,C,S
White, Pink (B)	Spring	Good	Moderate	N,C,S,
Red, Pink, White, others (B)	Most of the year	Fair	Moderate to Fast	N,C,S
Green-Red (F)	——————	Poor	Moderate	N,C,S,
White, turn Yellow (B)	Spring, Summer	Fair	Moderate	N,C
White, Blue, Pink (B)	Spring, Summer	Poor	Moderate	N,C,S
Red, Orange, Yellow (B)	Late Spring, Summer, Fall	Fair	Slow	C,S
White, some Yellow (B)	Spring, Summer	Good	Moderate to Fast	N,C,S
Blue-Green (L)	——————	Excellent	Slow	N,C,S

SHRUBS FOR FLORIDA

COMMON NAME	SCIENTIFIC NAME	HEIGHT	SPREAD
Lantana, Yellow Sage	Lantana Camara	2'-5'	3'
Laurel, Cherry	Prunus caroliniana	40'	15'
Leadwort Plumbago	Plumbago capensis	2'-5'	3'-10'
Ligustrum	Ligustrum sp.	15'-20'	5'-10'
Myrtle, Crape	Lagerstroemia indica	3'-20'	15'
Nandina	Nandina domestica	8'	4'
Oleander	Nerium oleander	5'-20'	5'-25'
Olive, Sweet	Osmanthus fragrans	5'-20'	5'-10'
Pampas Grass	Cortaderia	5'-8'	8'
Photinia, Red Leaf	Photinia glabra x serrulata 'Fraseri'	20'	15'
Pittosporum	Pittosporum Tobira	15'	10'
Plum, Natal	Carissa grandiflora	8'-18'	10'
Podocarpus	Podocarpus sp.	30'-50'	8'-10'
Poinsettia	Euphorbia pulcherrima	10'	8'
Pomegranate	Punica Granatum	2'-12'	2'-5'
Powderpuff, Red	Calliandra haematocephala	5'-8'	15'
Pyracantha or Fire Thorn	Pyracantha coccinea	20'	15'-20'
Quince, Flowering	Chaenomeles sp.	3'-6'	6'
Rain-of-Gold	Thryallis glauca	2'-8'	2'-3'
Scarlet Bush	Hamelia patens	3'-7'	10'-12'
Senna	Cassia Bicapsularis	5'-10'	10'
Shrimp Plant	Beloperone guttata	2'-5'	3'
Spirea, Reeves	Spiraea cantoniensis	2'-5'	2'-6'
Viburnum, Sweet	Viburnum odoratissimum	5'-35'	5'-20'

N — North Florida   C — Central Florida   S — South Florida

COLOR: BLOOM (B) LEAF (L) FRUIT (F)	SEASON (COLOR)	SALT TOLERANCE	GROWTH RATE	AREAS
Lilac, Red, Yellow, Purple (B)	Most of the year	Excellent	Moderate	C,S
Cream white (B)	Spring	Good	Fast	N,C,S
Blue (B)	Most of the year	Poor	Fast	C,S
White (B)	Spring	Excellent	Moderate to Fast	N,C,S
White, Red, Pink, Purple (B)	Summer to Early Fall	Fair	Moderate to Fast	N,C,S
Red (L)	Fall	Poor	Slow	N,C
White, Yellow, Red, Pink (B)	Most of the year	Excellent	Fast	N,C,S
White (B)	Fall until Spring	Poor	Moderate	N
White, sometimes Pink (B)	Spring, Summer, Fall	Excellent	Fast	N,C,S
Red (L)	Spring	Moderate	Fast	N,C
Cream yellow (B,L)	Spring	Excellent	Moderate to Fast	N,C,S
White (B)	Spring, Summer, Fall	Excellent	Slow	C,S
Green (L)	Summer	Good	Slow to Moderate	N,C,S
Red, White (B)	Winter	Poor	Moderate	N,C,S
Cream, Orange, Red (B)	Spring, Summer	Poor	Moderate	N,C,S
Red (B)	Spring, Summer, Fall	Poor	Fast	C,S
White (B), Red (F)	Fall, Winter (Berries)	Good	Moderate to Fast	N,C,S
Red (B)	Late Winter	Poor	Moderate	N
Yellow (B)	Most of the year	Fair to Good	Moderate	N,C,S
Red (B)	Most of the year	Fair	Moderate	C,S
Golden Yellow (B)	Summer, Fall	Good	Fast	N,C,S
White/Yellow, Reddish (B)	Most of the year	Fair	Fast	C,S,
White (B)	Spring	Poor	Moderate	N,C
White (B)	Spring	Good	Fast	N,C,S

CHAPTER FOUR

Fruits and Nuts

Thanks to the Florida Citrus Board, many people believe that the only fruit that grows in Florida is the orange! Although oranges and other citrus fruits are important to area landscapes (see "Citrus Trees" on page 113), our state has much more to boast about. Avocados, mangoes, and litchis grow better here than anywhere else; several other fruits do very well, too, including apples and peaches. Although Florida is not a major nut-producing state, pecans and macadamias do well here.

In actuality, Florida is a tropical-fruit paradise, and the secret to having a successful orchard is selecting the trees that do best in the state's climate. All fruit and nut trees have basic but vital growing requirements. Care should be taken in buying the best stock, planting the trees properly, then nurturing and feeding them so you will reap a consistently good harvest.

Always buy from a reputable Florida nursery and discuss your purchases with the nurseryman, making sure you get the right species for your area. Get advice on the best location and the proper care of the tree. Mail-order catalogs may have cheaper prices, but the results usually are not as good as buying from a local nursery.

Always buy fruit trees that are at least two to three years old. Not only will you get fruit quicker, but you eliminate going through the potential troubles that can afflict a tree in its early stages of growth. A tree 2 to 3 years old usually will be 3 to 5 feet tall. To achieve good pollination, you may need to plant more than one tree of the same variety. Your nurseryman can advise you on this matter. Normally, though, it is good to have several trees of the same species. One apple or peach tree can look rather lost on its own. Two or three can create a lush, full appearance that enhances the look of your garden. Plus, you get more fruit at harvest time!

PLANTING FRUIT AND NUT TREES

Planting fruit and nut trees must be done carefully to ensure proper growth. As with other plants, it is important to start with an enriched soil, one that has been amended with organic material such as peat moss, compost, manure, or straw. This enrichment should be applied to a depth of 2 feet below the soil surface. The organic material raises the pH of the soil to an ideal (slightly acid) reading of between 5.5 to 6.5.

Selecting the correct site for your trees is also important. Make sure you plant your fruit and nut trees in a bright, sunny location. Too, make sure that the roots of the trees remain moist, but not wet, while you're planting them.

Now you're ready to actually begin planting your trees. The following step-by-step guide will help ensure healthy trees and a bountiful crop of fruits and nuts.

1. Dig the hole large enough to accommodate the entire root system, but keep the top of the root system at ground level — the same depth at which it was grown in the nursery. (For a tree with a 2-foot-wide ball, dig a 3-foot-wide hole.)
2. Prune any damaged or broken roots from bare-rooted trees.
3. Make sure the trunk points upright; if necessary, stake the tree during its first year of growth.
4. Immediately after planting, fill the hole about halfway with enriched soil made up of dirt from the hole mixed with the aforementioned organic material/compost. Water thoroughly.
5. When the water has drained away, fill the hole to ground level and pack the soil lightly.
6. Since some roots have been lost in transplanting, prune 25 to 40 percent of the tree's top growth. You may also begin to shape the tree for vertical or lateral growth at this point, as described on page 40.
7. To protect the young trees from sunscald or other injury, you may choose to wrap the trunk to a point just below the first bud union. While this is merely a precaution, it can be helpful to new trees; the wrap should be removed two to six months after planting.
8. During the growing season, it helps to apply a root stimulator about once a month. Too, keep the tree well-watered, and begin a regular fertilization program during the second year of growth.

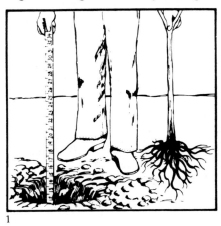

1

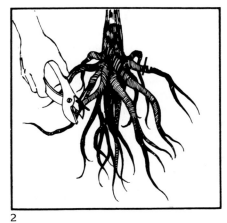

2

3

4

PRUNE
HERE →

5

6

7

8

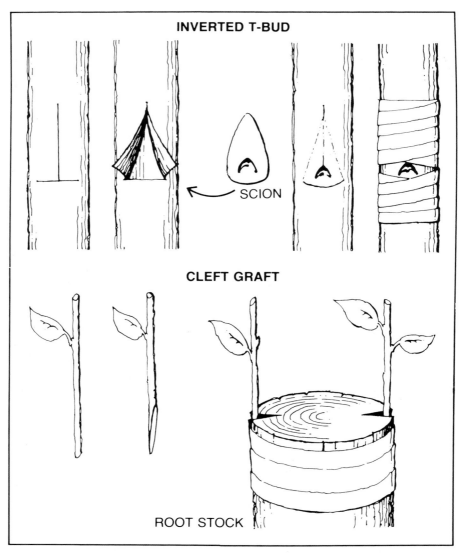

INVERTED T-BUD

SCION

CLEFT GRAFT

ROOT STOCK

The most common methods of propagating fruit and nut trees are budding and grafting.

MR. GREEN THUMB RULE

When planting fruit and nut trees, do so carefully to ensure proper growth. If a tree has a 2-foot root ball, you should dig a 3-foot-wide hole to allow proper positioning.

PROPAGATION

Some gardeners enjoy propagating their own plants rather than buying them from the nursery. There are various methods used to accomplish this, including propagation from seed and cuttings (as described in Chapter 5, "Annuals"). The two most common ways to propagate fruit and nut trees, however, are budding and grafting.

The T-bud and the cleft graft are the nonprofessional's two easiest ways to bud and graft. Budding, normally used for citrus trees, is usually done during the spring — the most active growing period — or when the bark will slip easily. Grafting, usually used for avocados, mangoes, camellias, and roses, is done during the early part of the growing season or during the dormant season. Grafting, in particular, may yield a tougher root stock that is resistant to cold and nematodes, and that produces larger flowers or better-quality fruit.

Inverted T-Bud

This common method is used on some ornamentals and citrus trees. Make a vertical slit in the bark of the stock or seedling plant about 1½ to 2 inches long. Make a horizontal slit in the form of an inverted T on the lower part of the vertical slit. The slit must be deep enough to peel back the bark to form flaps. Cut a bud from a twig of the plant to be propagated and slip this beneath the bark of the stock. Make sure that the cambium or inner bark of the stock and scion (bud) come together. Without this contact, the graft will not take. Tie the bud in place with waxed cloth, rubber bands, or another binding material. When the bud tissues have united with the stock (usually within 3 to 4 weeks), remove the bindings and prune off the stem above the bud. It's a good idea to bud more than you will need to allow for the buds that do not take.

Cleft Graft

Here's the nonprofessional's favorite method. Cut off the root stock close to the ground, squarely. Trim the cut surface smooth, using a sharp knife, then make a cut across the diameter of the stock. Place the knive blade on the face of the cut stock and hit it sharply with a wooden mallet. Usually, the knife is removed and reversed to hold the cleft open.

Select a scion from the parent plant. This can be a tip cutting 1½ to 3 inches long, having several pairs of leaves, or a cutting from farther down the stem. Make two sloping cuts about ¾ of an inch from a bud. These cuts should make the outer side of the scion wider than the inner side. Insert the scion into the cleft and line up the cambium or inner bark. Remove the wedge and tie and wax the scions in place.

Wraps for the T-Bud and the Cleft Graft

Cotton cloth strips — from ½-inch to 1-inch wide and soaked in grafting wax — make excellent wraps. Similar strips of rubber or another binding material may be used. Apply the wax on top of the bindings. To make grafting wax, heat 4 pounds of resin, 1 pound of beeswax, 1 pint of raw linseed oil, and 1 ounce of lampblack. Or forget all that and buy a mixture at your local nursery or garden supply store.

Protection of the Grafts

After the plants have been budded or grafted, keep them watered to prevent drying. Protect these plants, especially broadleaf evergreens, from the sun's direct rays. Cloth shade is ideal protection.

Commercial growers use cleft grafts, mound sand around the grafted area, and then cover the plant with a wide-mouthed jar. Of course, this type of special treatment may not be possible with grafts on larger plants and trees. In these instances, use the proper wrapping and waxing to prevent the scion and the adjacent part of the stock from drying out.

Another less-common but viable propagation technique is called air layering or Chinese pot layering; this method creates hormonal changes in a plant and forces it to put out new roots. To air layer: Using a knife, girdle the bark of a tree branch and remove the outer bark (cambium layer) until the white wood underneath is exposed. Then, cover the exposed white wood with wet sphagnum moss, topped by a layer of plastic wrap or aluminum foil. The tree branch will put new roots into the moss, creating a brand-new plant.

TREE WATERING

The most important element of all is water. Proper watering ensures that you will get higher grades of fruit at harvest time and maintain the overall health of your trees. Lack of water will result in dry fruit. The Florida climate can change drastically, with heavy rains at times and long dry spells between.

When planting your trees, don't scrimp on the water. Although you may plant a tree in a dry hole and water later, it is a good idea to fill up the hole with water and sink the tree into it. This ensures plenty of water around the root system and gets rid of air pockets in the soil. A root stimulator or liquid fertilizer can be added to the water at planting. If you add peat and cow manure as well, there will be additional small amounts of fertilizer in this material.

After planting, your trees will need watering daily for the first two weeks. A half-inch at a time is recommended. After two weeks, check the soil moisture before watering. You should apply 1 to 2 inches at each application. For juicier fruit, water on a regular basis.

MR. GREEN THUMB RULE

When buying a citrus tree, make sure there is a good graft union. It should be smooth, clean, and well-healed. Make sure there is no dead wood in the tree.

> **MR. GREEN THUMB RULE**
>
> Always buy your fruit trees from a reputable Florida nursery and discuss your purchases with the nurseryman.

After a tree has three months of growth, a "citrus special" fertilizer can be applied. Use 1 pound the first year, increasing to 1 pound per foot of tree spread in spring, summer, and fall. Do not use a high-nitrogen fertilizer for the fall feeding. This would produce a lot of new growth that could be injured by freezing temperatures in the winter.

COLD WEATHER PROTECTION

Florida winters can be a problem for fruit trees. The frequent cold days often are followed by warm, tropical days with temperatures in the 80s. When this occurs in December, many plants and trees suffer unless they are protected from the cold.

Follow weather reports closely. When a cold spell is predicted, take steps to guard your plants. Small trees can be covered with a sheet or blanket reaching all the way to the ground. Placing a small electric light bulb under the cover will help raise the temperature a few degrees and provides additional protection from the cold.

As an emergency measure only, you can ice your trees with a continuous spray of water, maintaining the flow until the temperature rises above freezing again. As the ice forms and thaws, latent heat is released. However, the weight of the ice can break delicate limbs. This method should be used only in extreme cases of bad weather when no other form of protection is possible.

Freezing temperatures damage all plants in varying degrees, but low temperatures also are a factor in promoting buds and blooms in the spring. Most deciduous fruit crops have a "biological clock-thermostat" that measures dormant-season exposure to cold. Fruit growers call this clock the plant's "chilling requirement."

Specifically, the plant measures its exposure to cold below 45 degrees and above 32 degrees. Each fruit variety has its own needs, a minimum number of hours of exposure to low temperatures that it must have before it can bud and bloom in the spring. This is true especially of peaches, apples, nectarines, and certain other varieties.

CHILLING REQUIREMENTS

The following map indicates the chilling hours received in each area of Florida. Locate your area on the map to determine its average winter exposure and plant only fruit varieties that coincide with that figure. This is essential to achieve best results. If you plant a tree with a much higher chilling requirement,

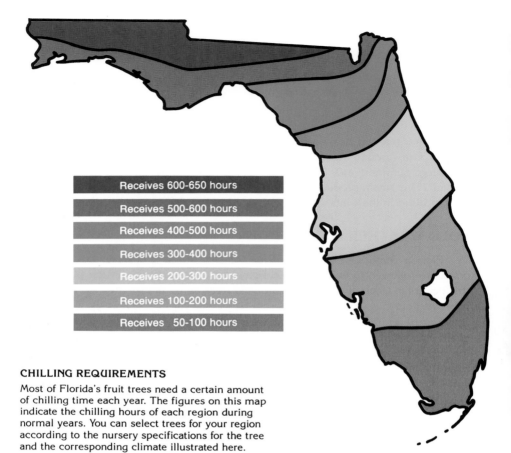

Receives 600-650 hours
Receives 500-600 hours
Receives 400-500 hours
Receives 300-400 hours
Receives 200-300 hours
Receives 100-200 hours
Receives 50-100 hours

CHILLING REQUIREMENTS

Most of Florida's fruit trees need a certain amount of chilling time each year. The figures on this map indicate the chilling hours of each region during normal years. You can select trees for your region according to the nursery specifications for the tree and the corresponding climate illustrated here.

it usually will fail to bud and bloom properly. It may not even leaf out and grow. Plant a variety with a much lower chilling requirement, and it will bloom too early almost every year and be frozen when cold weather hits again.

Chilling requirements of fruit crops vary, even within the same type of fruit. Peaches once needed as many as a thousand hours of chilling, but in the last few decades, varieties have been developed that need only 250 hours of chilling. Check with your nurseryman to find the varieties most suitable for your particular area of Florida.

HARVESTING TIPS

To make the most of your flavorful fruit crops, you must harvest the fruit at the right time. For most varieties, you should leave the fruit on the tree until it is of mature size, has good color, and has a smooth texture. In many cases, the fruit will be soft to the touch (except harder-skinned varieties such as the pineapple, sugar apple, jack fruit, and tamarind).

If you allow your fruit to mature on the tree, it will be sweeter and more flavorful. In fact, some varieties, such as the citrus fruits, *must* ripen on the tree.

However, if picked prior to ripening, the avocado may be placed on a windowsill for about a week to complete the ripening process.

When you do harvest your fruit, grasp each specimen and give the stem a firm twist. This action should be enough to release any *ripe* fruit from its tree.

CITRUS TREES

Citrus trees not only grow well in Florida, but they have helped the state establish itself as the nation's leading producer of orange juice. Florida growers also supply the country with grapefruit, lemons, tangerines, tangelos, kumquats, and limes. Whether you live in the Panhandle of northwest Florida or as far south as the Keys, there is an adaptable citrus tree for your area that can be included in your landscaping plans.

Citrus trees are easy-to-grow evergreens with a lush look to their foliage. When covered with ripe fruit, they are one of the most rewarding sights for any gardener. The beauty they add to a landscape is supplemented by the joy of picking and eating your own fruit as the years go by.

Most citrus trees available in nurseries range from 3 to 6 feet in height, with a trunk diameter of 1 to 2 inches at the base. Select a tree with a good, straight trunk and healthy, dark-green leaves. The graft union should be smooth, clean, and well-healed. Make sure there is no dead wood and that the union is sound. Be sure the roots are not protruding from the base of the container. Citrus trees tend to become root-bound, so before planting, pull the roots apart gently to allow them to continue growing out and down into the ground.

A bountiful orange grove

Stone fruit trees, such as peaches, are thinned by a method called the modified leader system. But citrus trees require very little thinning to maintain continued good production of fruit. Compared with some fruit trees, citrus trees need very little care, though they do need spraying to control insect problems. Citrus trees are moderate in their water needs, but the soil should not be allowed to dry out. A moist, but not wet, soil is ideal. They need fertilizing with a "citrus special" — a formula higher in the minor elements. The analysis will be lower in nitrogen such as 4-6-8, or with equal amounts of nitrogen and potassium, such as 6-4-6.

Citrus trees always should be planted in well-drained soil. If your garden does not have natural drainage, you should plant your citrus trees on a raised mound of soil 6 inches high and 8 feet across, into which you have mixed peat and dehydrated cow manure.

Your selection of citrus trees will depend on the type of fruit you prefer and the area of the state in which you live.

MR. GREEN THUMB RULE

Black, sooty mold indicates an insect problem such as whiteflies, aphids, or scale. Spraying should be done before the problem gets out of hand.

CITRUS VARIETIES FOR FLORIDA

Citrus aurantiifolia
LIME

Height: 15 ft.	Spread: 10 ft.	Areas: C, S

The Key lime fruit is small and lemon-yellow in color; it ripens from October through December. The Tahiti, sometimes called the Persian lime, bears year-round but offers most of its fruit in early spring and fall. This is not a cold-hardy variety.

Citrus Limon
LEMON

Height: 15 ft.	Spread: 10 ft.	Areas: C, S

The largest lemon fruit, often called the Florida pie lemon, is the Ponderosa, bearing from December through February and sometimes, during the rest of the year, too. The most common Florida lemon is the Meyer, maturing from December through April. Lemons are not cold-hardy, though they are more tolerant of cold temperatures than limes.

Citrus x paradisi
GRAPEFRUIT

Height: 30 ft.   Spread: 20 ft.   Areas: N, C, S

The Duncan is considered the best variety for Florida, with only one major drawback: It is seedy. It matures early, from October through January, and has the best flavor of all the grapefruits.

For a seedless variety, the Marsh is recommended. It matures from December through April.

For lovers of pink grapefruit, try the Thompson, a bud sport of the White Marsh. As flavorful as the Duncan, the Thompson has a pink flesh that enhances its appeal.

Citrus reticulata
TANGERINE

Height: 20 ft.   Spread: 15 ft.   Areas: N, C, S

Large in size and sprightly flavored, the Robinson tangerine is a hybrid of the Clementine tangerine and the Orlando tangelo. It produces fruit from September through October.

The Dancy tangerine bears from December through February, with easy-peeling skin typical of tangerines, and flesh that easily separates into sections.

One of the best hybrids is a rather new variety called Lee, which is another cross of the Clementine tangerine and the Orlando tangelo; the Lee produces flavorful, large fruit from October through November.

For colder areas of the state, the Satsuma tangerine does well, though the fruit is smaller than average. The fruit appears from October through December.

Citrus sinensis
ORANGE

Height: 15-25 ft.   Spread: 20 ft. (maximum)   Areas: N, C, S

There are a number of different varieties of oranges that can be grown in Florida. The most popular is the Valencia.

The Valencia has only a few seeds; a good, rich color; and a nice fragrance when cut. The fruit has an oval shape. The tree itself is rather upright, as are

Oranges are not only one of Florida's most famous fruits, but also are one of the most attractive varieties of trees.

most orange trees. The Valencia is the most popular orange (for its juice) in the state. It ripens from March through July.

The less-popular Naval has few seeds and is a great fruit for peeling and eating by hand. Often yielding large oranges, this early variety is harvested from September through January.

The Hamlin is a rather early variety; it ripens in early October through December. The fruit has a smooth skin, few seeds, and is one of the popular early (juice) oranges.

Pineapple orange is quite seedy, but makes a delicious raw fruit or juice. It ripens from December through March.

The Parson Brown is another tasty orange that can be used for its juice. It has a rather rough skin and ripens from October through December.

The Temple orange has a delightful, reddish orange color. It is one of the most popular oranges for its raw fruit. It matures from January through March.

The Queen is excellent for juice, and for eating by hand. It is rather seedy, and ripens from December through March.

The Jaffa has few seeds, but is not grown as much as some other varieties. Still, it is a terrific (juice) orange and ripens from December through March.

Citrus x Tangelo
TANGELO

Height: 20 ft.	Spread: 15 ft.	Areas: N, C, S

The Orlando tangelo is a hybrid of the grapefruit and the tangerine. It is large and easy to peel. The Orlando fruit appears from November through January.

The Minneola tangelo produces fruit from January through March. It has a pear-shaped neck and reddish orange flesh.

The tangelo is a delicious hybrid of the grapefruit and the tangerine.

Calamondin

Fortunella sp.
KUMQUAT

Height: 15 ft.   Spread: 10 ft.   Areas: N, C, S

Residents of the northernmost part of Florida may want to choose the kumquat for their gardens, since it is the most cold-hardy citrus variety. The nagami (*F. margarita*) kumquat is very tart, about 1 inch long, and oval in shape. It is used for making preserves and marmalade.

The Meiwa (*F.* hybrid) variety is rounded, sweet in flavor, and has edible flesh and skin.

Faguremsis loureiro
CALAMONDIN

Height: 10-18 ft.   Spread: 10-15 ft.   Areas: N, C, S

The calamondin looks like a small orange or tangerine. It is one of the most cold-hardy citruses. It has an acid flavor, and is used in marmalade and as a substitute for lemon. Some people leave the fruit on the tree, growing it as an ornament. The ripening period for this fruit is from October through January.

CITRUS PESTS AND DISEASES

Citrus trees are susceptible to a number of insects and diseases that can be controlled by regular spraying with malathion, diazinon, or a citrus spray.

Black soot (a black, sooty mold) indicates an invasion of insects such as white fly, aphids, and scale. Spraying should be done before the problem gets out of hand and your citrus trees suffer damage.

The *white fly* is closely related to the scale insects. The adult stage, which can be seen, is not harmful to citrus, but the transparent, silvery larvae insert their stylets into the leaf and feed on the plant's sap, causing damage. Any of the aforementioned sprays will control this dangerous pest.

Aphids are tiny, pear-shaped insects (often called plant lice) with very small, soft bodies no more than 1/5 of an inch in length. Aphids suck the sap from new leaves and stems, producing a secretion called honeydew, on which sooty mold will grow. These pests can be controlled by spraying with the chemicals recommended above.

Scale is found in several different types. The cottony cushion scale is really an egg sac and looks like a ½-inch long cocoon. The actual scale is reddish brown in color, about ¼-inch long. The hemispherical scale (sometimes called round scale) is 1/12-inch high and dark brown in color.

All these pests problems can be controlled by regular spraying. Your nursery can advise you on the best chemicals to use for each particular problem on your citrus trees.

The following chart specifies treatment for your citrus trees:

CITRUS SPRAY SCHEDULE*

When to Spray	Description	What to Use
March-April	Use a pre-bloom spray if scab or greasy spot has been a problem.	Neutral copper, nutritional spray, malathion, Ethion
May	Use a pre-summer spray if mites, white fly, and/or aphids have been spotted.	Ethion (for mites), malathion (for white fly and aphids)
June-July	Standard, summer spray; use according to temperature restrictions.	Ethion and oil or, with sustained temperatures above 85 degrees, malathion
October-November	Standard, fall spray.	Malathion
January	Use a dormant spray if scab or greasy spot has been a problem.	Neutral copper

*NOTE: When spraying, always coat upper and lower surfaces of all leaves and branches.

The pineapple develops large spiny leaves and thrives in full sun.

OTHER FRUITS FOR FLORIDA

Ananas comosus
PINEAPPLE

Height: 3-4 ft.   Spread: 4-6 ft.   Areas: C (protected), S

The pineapple has herbaceous leaves that resemble a long, narrow saw with little spines along the edges. The fruit grows out of the center of the plant on a long stem. The plant is damaged at 32 degrees and will be killed at 28 degrees, so protection is needed during cold spells. Sterilizing the soil with Vapam is recommended before planting because of nematode problems. Pineapples do well in full sun and can tolerate partial shade. This delicious fruit can be grown by planting the leaves and top ½ inch of a store-bought pineapple in a good potting soil. New plants also can be grown from ground suckers and suckers on the stem. Mulching and weed killers are recommended as the spiny leaves make weeding difficult. Plants should be placed 18 inches apart. As soon as they become established, place some organic material, such as well-rooted compost, in the buds to keep out sand and fertilizer, which will kill the plants. To force bloom, drop 10 to 12 grains of calcium carbide into the bud in July, but only after plants are at least 18 months old. This method, known as "gassing," will speed up fruit production by 5 to 7 months. Spraying with malathion will control mealybugs, which are the worst insect pests for pineapples. Red spiders also are a problem, controllable with a miticide. When planted in March, pineapples take 17 months for suckers, 26 months for slips, and 29 months for crowns to fruit.

Averrhoa Carambola
CARAMBOLA or STAR FRUIT

Height: 20-30 ft.   Spread: 15-25 ft.   Areas: C (protected), S

Several varieties of the carambola — the Golden Star, Pei Sy Tao, Newcomb, and Thayer — are all admired for their yellow, wax-like fruit. When cut across, the fruit resembles a star; hence the common name for the plant: star fruit. These trees of small to medium size have beautiful, alternate, compound leaves with larger leaflets at the end of each odd pinnation. Fruit is produced on the branches and the trunk of the tree.

Carambola (Star fruit)

Like most fruit trees, the carambola grows best in full sun but will thrive in partial shade. Older trees withstand temperatures as low as the mid-20s, though young trees are damaged in 32-degree weather.

Carica Papaya
PAPAYA

Height: 15-20 ft.   Spread: 5-10 ft.   Areas: C (protected), S

The papaya's herbaceous trunk grows straight up, and the fruit emerges from a cluster of leaves on the top. The fruit varies from ¾ pound to as much as 20 pounds. It looks like a melon, with firm, orange flesh that is delicious. The papaya does best in improved, organically enriched soil. Young plants are killed at 32 degrees, and the tree will die if the roots sit in water for too long. Sterilize the soil with Vapam before planting because the papaya has severe problems

Papaya tree

with nematodes. Another potential hazard is the papaya fruit fly, which can be held off by bagging the fruit after it emerges. A dwarf variety, the Hawaiian Solo, also can be grown in Florida.

Eriobotrya japonica
LOQUAT or JAPANESE PLUM

Height: 20-30 ft.	Spread: 15-20 ft.	Areas: N, C, S

The loquat has large, leathery leaves 10 to 12 inches long, with a fluffy white underside. The fruit is 1 to 2 inches in length, golden-yellow to orange in color, and egg-shaped, with a distinctive taste. The loquat, found throughout Florida, is a moderate grower with excellent salt-tolerance. Like most fruit trees, it must be watered during dry spells and responds well to regular fertilizing. Good varieties are the Fletcher, Oliver, Premier, Wolfe, and Golden Nugget. It suffers from fire blight. Over-fertilization tends to increase bacterial disease. Trim off diseased wood and spray with streptomycin.

Ficus carica
FIG

Height: 10-12 ft.	Spread: 10 ft.	Areas: N, C, S

Growing in full sun very rapidly, the fig tree can be planted in all parts of Florida. Fruit is from 1 to 3 inches in length and yellow, green, brown, or black in color, depending on the variety. The two best types are the Celeste and the Brown Turkey. Fig trees suffer from nematodes, which can be controlled by sterilizing the soil before planting. Vapam is very good for this purpose. Fig trees also should be mulched regularly with 3 to 4 inches of a quality mulch. This will conserve moisture and help deter nematodes. Rust, a fungus, can be a problem. Spraying with zineb or Dithane M-45 should control rust.

Fragaria sp.
STRAWBERRY

Height: 8-10 in.	Spread: 12-15 in.	Areas: C, S

Set out in October, strawberries will fruit in December, January, and February. It is advisable to purchase new runners each year from your nurseryman, who can advise you on the best variety for your area, such as the Florida 90, Tioga, or the Sequoia. These will bloom not only in winter but also in early spring. Diseases include anthracnose and leaf spot.

Litchi chinensis
LITCHI

Height: 20-30 ft.	Spread: 20-30 ft.	Areas: C, S

A native of China, the litchi tree has a beautiful, rounded head with leathery leaves that are shiny and dark green. The fruit (called the litchi nut) has a hard, leathery skin that turns bright red when ripe, with white flesh that has an excellent flavor and can be eaten fresh or frozen. The tree flowers in January and produces fruit in June and July. Mulching is recommended, plus extra watering when fruiting. Tender young trees suffer damage at 28 degrees and must be protected in central and south Florida. Older trees survive down to 20 degrees. The most popular variety is the Brewster. Litchi is susceptible to spider mites.

Malpighia punicifolia x glabra
BARBADOS CHERRY

Height: 10-12 ft.   Spread: 8-10 ft.   Areas: S

Thriving in partial shade or full sun, the Barbados cherry has one of the highest concentrations of Vitamin C known, making this delicious fruit a favorite with health-conscious dieters. The fruit grows 1 inch across with a bright-red, thin skin and yellow flesh. The flowers are rose-colored and appear intermittently throughout the year, followed in 60 to 90 days by the fruit. The plant is thick-growing and spreads in all directions. It is grown mostly in southern Florida because it cannot stand temperatures below 32 degrees. Sterilizing the soil before planting is recommended because nematodes are a problem with Barbados cherry. Plenty of organic matter should be added to the soil before planting to ensure beautiful fruit and a large, healthy crop.

Malus domestica Borkh
ANNA APPLE

Height: 15-20 ft.   Spread: 8-12 ft.   Areas: N, C

Many residents of Florida have tried and failed to grow apples, but three new varieties do very well: the Dorset Golden, the Ein Shemer, and the Anna. The Anna grows to 2½ inches in diameter, with a shape similar to the Red Delicious. The flesh is firm, and the skin is about 40 percent reddish blue color. This apple can be eaten fresh or frozen for later use. The trees last a minimum of 15 to 20 years with good production. Flowering mid-February through mid-March, the Anna grows best in well-drained soil. But if the soil is sandy, you will have to water more frequently to retain sufficient moisture for growth and juicy apples. The Anna does best in full sun but tolerates partial shade. Spraying with captan is recommended to control bitter rot.

The mango is a perennial favorite, but is relatively cold-sensitive.

Mangifera indica
MANGO

Height: 40-50 ft.   Spread: 30-40 ft.   Areas: C, S

Called "the apple of the tropics," the mango tree is available in many different sizes, and has fruit colors ranging from green to red, orange, purple, and yellow. Its delicious flesh is yellow to golden orange around a large seed about 3 inches long. Tender young trees will freeze at 28 to 30 degrees. The fruit ripens normally from July through late September. As this tree is a moderate grower, and very sensitive to temperatures when young, grafted trees are recommended and well worth the additional cost. A good citrus fertilizer will improve growth and hardiness. The original variety, the Haden, is good, but the improved varieties are excellent for Florida, including the Edward, Kent, Tommy Atkins, and Parvin. Problems include anthracnose, scale, and mites.

Musa hybrid
BANANA

Height: 15 ft.   Spread: 20 ft.   Areas: C, S

Several varieties of banana do well in Florida. The best is the Apple banana (Manzana), which grows to a height of 15 feet, and has very flavorful fruit about 4 inches in length. Another good choice is the Cavendish, a dwarf type similar to

Banana tree

the large bananas available in the supermarkets. Large banana varieties do not grow well in Florida. The Cavendish grows from 6 to 8 feet tall, with good quality, thin-skinned fruit. The leaves are fairly wind-resistant, and the plant is more cold hardy than others. The Ladyfinger offers thin-skinned fruit 3 to 4 inches long. The Red Jamaica banana has fruit 4 inches long and 2 inches wide, with an attractive pink skin. The Red Jamaica makes a striking plant in the garden but is quite sensitive to cold.

All bananas thrive in good, enriched moisture-retentive soil. They are heavy feeders and need light fertilizing once a month except in December and January. This herbaceous plant suffers damage below 32 degrees, with both leaves and stems showing injury below 26 degrees. Bananas require two years without frost to bear fruit that, once set, takes 120 days to ripen. After a stem has produced fruit, it should be trimmed back to the ground to allow suckers to emerge. Once bananas have appeared on a stalk, the bottom male bloom, called the "tail," can be cut off. While the fruit will ripen naturally on the plant itself, a stalk of mature green bananas may be cut off and hung upside-down in a cool, dark place indoors to ripen.

Myrciaria cauliflora
JABOTICABA

Height: 10-15 ft.   Spread: 5-10 ft.   Areas: C (protected), S

Growing well in full sun to partial shade, this small tree — a large bush, really — has round, tough-skinned fruit similar to the older Muscadine-variety grapes and with similar flavor. The fruit is dark purple and can be eaten fresh, or made into jelly or wine, or frozen without losing much flavor. Jaboticaba grows in most protected areas of central Florida and in all southern parts of the state. It will tolerate temperatures down to the low 20s. It often suffers from nutritional deficiency, needing an application of Perk, Essential 6, or Minor-El.

Persea americana
AVOCADO

Height: 30-60 ft.   Spread: 20-35 ft.   Areas: C, S

Introduced in 1833, the avocado is one of the oldest trees in Florida as well as one of the major tropical fruits in the state. Leaves are 6 to 10 inches long, tough and leathery, making the tree a beautiful evergreen for any landscape. The pear-shaped fruit may weigh as much as 2 pounds. Blooming normally from January through April, the avocado has fair salt-tolerance and grows best in full sun.

Grafted trees are best for their true-to-type fruit, though they can be grown from seed. Many people start avocado seedlings indoors, supporting the seed with three toothpicks, and the root end about ½ inch below the surface in a glass of water. The stem grows up rather rapidly. Then the seeding can be transplanted to soil outdoors.

The most cold-hardy avocado varieties are Gainesville and Young; these will tolerate temperatures as cold as 18 degrees. The Brogdon, Winter Mexican, Lulu, and Choquette varieties will tolerate freezing weather down to 25 to 26 degrees. Varieties for southern Florida, which will sustain injury at 32 degrees or lower, are Pollack, Simmonds, Booth 7, Booth 8, and Hall.

Prunus Persica
PEACH

Height: 20 ft.   Spread: 15 ft.   Areas: N, C

This deciduous tree grows small and open. Its long, slender, light-green leaves have fine, serrated edges. The fruit is rounded, with a small peak at one end and fuzzy skin. The flesh is yellowish orange, with a large seed. Peach trees did not always do well in Florida. The Jewel and Red Ceylon varieties were the only ones that thrived. Today, trees are grafted onto the Okinawa or Nemaguard root stocks, which are resistant to nematode damage, one of the major problems with peach trees. Peach trees also suffer from San Jose scale. Peach trees should be thinned each year. Thinning allows more light to reach the center of the foliage and produce more vigorous growth. For peaches and nectarines, chilling time is very important. Plant only those varieties that match the chilling time for your area of Florida. The map on page 112 indicates the chilling hours received throughout the state.

Psidium Cattleianum
CATTLEY GUAVA

Height: 15-20 ft.   Spread: 10-15 ft.   Areas: C, S

The Cattley guava has deep-green, glossy leaves only 2 to 3 inches long, compared with the 5- to 6-inch leaf on the Guajava guava tree. More of a bushy

A young avocado

Pruning a young peach tree

shrub with hard seeds, the Cattley has rounded fruit 1 to 1½ inches across and purple-red in color. Mulching and a sunny location are recommended for good growth. The Cattley is more salt-tolerant than the common guava. Both the Guajava and the Cattley fruit can be eaten fresh or made into delicious jelly.

Psidium Guajava
GUAVA

Height: 20-25 ft.	Spread: 15-20 ft.	Areas: C, S

The guava is a pear-shaped (sometimes rounded) fruit from 2 to 3 inches across, with a waxy, smooth skin in various colors of pink, yellow, and white. Guavas grow quickly and flourish in full sun, flowering in early summer to produce fruit throughout summer and fall. They suffer damage at 28 degrees but grow back again. Mulching is recommended for best growth.

Pyrus Lecontei
PEAR

Height: 15-20 ft.	Spread: 20-25 ft.	Areas: N, C

Pear trees grow best in northern and central Florida. This upright, deciduous tree is self-fruitful. It flowers in late winter with white, showy clusters of blossoms, with fruiting in early fall. Pears are vigorous growers for the first 10 years and have very poor salt-tolerance. Mulching is beneficial, and judicious fertilizing with low nitrogen and high potash is recommended. Excessive fertilizing with high nitrogen can cause fire blight, a bacterial disease. The Baldwin and Orient varieties are best. They have a crisp, white flesh. The Pineapple or Sand pear is used more for cooking. Diseases include anthracnose and fire blight.

Rubus albescens
RASPBERRY

Height: 4-6 ft.	Spread: 4 ft.	Areas: C, S

Very similar to the blackberry, the raspberry has thorny canes, a bramble vining habit, and reddish purple fruit that can be eaten fresh or made into delicious jams, jellies, and juice. Fresh raspberries do not last long after picking, which is why they are scarce in stores. The Mysore variety is the only common raspberry available in Florida. It grows best in full sun and is killed at 28 degrees. Diseases and insect problems include anthracnose and stink bugs.

Rubus hybrid
BLACKBERRY

Height: 4-5 ft.	Spread: 4 ft.	Area: C, S

Blackberries are loved for their large, succulent fruit. The best variety for Florida is the Brazos, developed at Texas A&M University. Very thorny, vigorous-growing plants, blackberries can be used as a privacy hedge that definitely will keep out intruders. The berries are very tasty when eaten fresh, but they also make excellent jellies and jams. Only semi-tropical, Brazos grows best in full sun and can suffer damage at 26 degrees. This is a semi-fertile plant, meaning that just one plant is needed to produce fruit.

Vaccinium Myrtillus
BLUEBERRY

Height: 3 ft.   Spread: 3 ft.   Areas: C, S

Two varieties — Sharpeblue and Floridablue — do best in our state and are grown from Gainesville, Ocala, and Jacksonville to the south and central areas rather than in the northern parts of Florida. Blueberries grow poorly in alkaline soil, so add plenty of organic material and sulfur to the soil before planting. They thrive in acid soil with a pH of 4.2 to 5.2. To promote growth of strong, new wood, prune off the small, twiggy growth during the winter. Blueberries have no major pest problems, but be careful with watering. Too much water leads to root decay. The soil should be kept moist but not wet.

Vitis rotundifolia
MUSCADINE GRAPE

Height: 8-10 ft.   Spread: 20-40 ft.   Areas: N, C, S

Bunch grapes such as the Blue Lake, Lake Emerald, Norris, and Stover have been adapted to Florida, but the northern European bunch grapes suffer from Pierce's disease and usually die within a year or two. However, the Muscadine varieties such as Fry, Dixie, Cowart, Welder, and Southland all do well. Though they have thick skins and seeds, their flesh is sweet and juicy — great for eating as well as for juices, jellies, and wines.

Grapes

Grapes must have an arbor, fence, or trellis to grow along. They are vigorous growers and do best in full sun. They prefer a slightly acid soil with a pH from 6.0 to 6.5. Every winter the side shoots must be trimmed back, but there is no need to trim the main stem. Grapes suffer occasionally from fungus problems. Check Chapter 12, "Insects and Diseases," for treatment directions.

NUT TREES FOR FLORIDA

Carya illinoinensis

PECAN

Height: 40-50 ft.   Spread: 30-40 ft.   Areas: N, C

A large-growing, upright tree, the pecan flourishes in well-drained soil, is totally cold-hardy and can be grown in northern and central Florida. It is a slow grower and has poor salt-tolerance. Nuts are produced on the tip growth and appear between October and November. Spraying with a nutritional fertilizer containing zinc will eliminate zinc deficiency, a problem with pecan trees. Good varieties for Florida are the Moneymaker, Desirable, and Curtis, all of which thrive best in full sun. A mature pecan tree needs 30 to 60 pounds of 8-8-8 fertilizer each year to maintain good growth and a fruitful harvest.

FRUITS AND NUTS FOR FLORIDA

VARIETY	HARVEST	HEIGHT	SPREAD	SHAPE
Apple	May, June	15'-18'	10'-20'	Upright, spreading
Avocado	Varies	20'-60'	25'-35'	Upright, spreading
Banana	Varies; 3 mos from flower to fruit	5'-25'	10'-20'	Tall, thin
Blackberry	May, June	4'	4'	Semi-erect bush
Blueberry	May-July	3'	3'	Semi-erect
Calamondin	Oct-Jan	10'-18'	10'-15'	Upright
Carambola	May-July	25'	20'	Small, symmetrical
Fig	May-Oct	12'	12'	Low, spreading
Grape	May-July	8'	25'-35'	Climbing vine

One of Florida's favorites, the pecan can produce an abundant harvest.

Macadamia integrifolia
MACADAMIA or QUEENSLAND NUT

Height: 25 ft.   Spread: 15-20 ft.   Areas: C (protected), S

A semi-tropical fruit tree, the macadamia has dark-green, waxy leaves 8 inches long and 2 inches wide, with small spines along the edges. The nuts are ¾ inch in diameter, have very hard shells, and can be eaten fresh or roasted. The plants can be started by air-layering or from seed. They do best in full sun and are moderate growers.

COLOR (FRUIT)	SALT TOLERANCE	GROWTH RATE	SUGGESTED SPACE BETWEEN PLANTS	AREAS
50% Red Overcolor	Unknown	Fast under good conditions	20'-30'	N,C
Black or Green	Fair	Moderate	25'-45'	C,S
Green to Yellow	Poor	Fast when fertilized	5'-10'	C,S
Black	Poor	Fast	4'-8'	C,S
Blue	Poor	Fast	6'-10'	C,S
Orange	Fair	Moderate	15'-20'	N,C,S
Yellow	Poor	Moderate	15'-20'	C(protected), S
Green-Yellow-Pink Violet-Brown-Black	Poor	Fast	15'-20'	N,C,S
Purple	Poor	Slow, then vigorous	10'-15'	N,C,S

FRUITS AND NUTS FOR FLORIDA

VARIETY	HARVEST	HEIGHT	SPREAD	SHAPE
Grapefruit	Oct-April	30'	20'	Upright, spreading
Guava	June-Sept	25'	20'	Large bush
Guava, Cattley	June-Aug	20'	15'	Bushy shrub
Jaboticaba	May have 5-6 crops a year; 1 mo from flower to fruit	15'	10'	Small, bushy tree
Kumquat	Oct-Jan	15'	10'	Few seeds, upright
Lemon	Dec-Feb	15'	10'	Small
Lime	Oct-April	15'	10'	Small, thorny
Litchi	June-July	20'-30'	20'-30'	Upright, rounded
Loquat	Jan-April	25'	20'	Small, well-shaped
Mango	May-Aug	50'	30'	Large, variable shape
Macadamia Nut	Nov-March	25'	15'-20'	Upright, spreading
Nectarine	April-June	20'	15'	Small, open tree
Orange	March-July	15'-20'	12'-20'	Upright, spreading
Papaya	July-Oct	15'	7'	Stout trunk
Peach	April-June	20'	15'	Small, upright
Pear	Sept-Oct	20'	25'	Upright
Pecan	Oct-Nov	35'-50'	30'-50'	Large, upright
Persimmon, Oriental	May-Oct	25'	20'	Compact
Pineapple	May-Sept	4'	6'	Short, stiff
Raspberry	March-May	6'		Semi-vining bush
Strawberry	Feb-March	6'		Spreading
Tangelo	Dec-March	20'	15'	Upright
Tangerine	Dec-Oct	20'	15'	Upright

COLOR (FRUIT)	SALT TOLERANCE	GROWTH RATE	SUGGESTED SPACE BETWEEN PLANTS	AREAS
Yellow-Orange	Fair	Moderate	25'-30'	N,C,S
Yellow, White, Pink	Fair	Fast	20'-30'	C,S
Reddish	Good	Moderate	15'-25'	C,S
Purple	None	Slow	10'-20'	C(protected), S
Orange	Fair	Moderate	20'-25'	N,C,S
Yellow	Good	Moderate	20'-25'	C,S
Green	Good	Moderate	20'-25'	C,S
Red	Poor	Moderate	25'-35'	C,S
Yellow to Orange	Very Good	Moderate	20'-30'	N,C,S
Green, Yellow, Red, Orange, Purple	Fairly Good	Moderate	25'-45'	C,S
Dark Brown Nut Hard Shell	Poor	Moderate	20'-30'	C(protected), S
Red-Orange	Poor	Moderate	20'-30'	N,C,S
Orange	Good	Moderate	20'-25'	N,C,S
Orange-Red	Fair	Moderate	5'-10'	C(protected),S
Red, Yellow	Poor	Moderate	25'-45'	N,C
Green	Very Poor	Vigorous first 10 years	20'-30'	N,C
Light Brown Nut	Poor	Slow	30'-50'	N,C
Yellow to Red-Orange	Fair to Poor	Moderate	15'-25'	N,C,S
Yellow	Fair	Moderate	10'-15'	C(protected),S
Purplish Black	Poor	Fast	4'-8'	C,S
Red	Poor	Fast	3'-4'	C,S
Orange	Fair	Moderate	20'-30'	N,C,S
Deep Orange	Fair	Moderate	20'-30'	N,C,S

CHAPTER FIVE

Annuals

When Juan Ponce de Leon discovered our part of the world in 1513, he named it La Florida, which is Spanish for "the flowered place." As gardeners have realized since, Florida's climate is ideal for growing many of the most beautiful varieties of flowers in North America.

While temperatures in Florida may be more moderate than in many other parts of the country, there can be extreme fluctuations during the cooler months, November through April. In May through October, you may have all the heat problems of the tropics. Spider mites and other insects are a big problem during these times. Certain less-hardy flowers and shrubs may have to be protected during Florida's infrequent cold spells, but in general, a garden of flowers can survive year-round and provide color, beauty, and satisfaction for the homeowner, if he or she is aware of the changing seasons, and plants accordingly.

Admittedly, a flower garden of annuals and perennials does demand more care and attention than a landscape of evergreen shrubs. But considering the rewards, the time and effort spent is well worth it. Flowers are no more difficult to raise than vegetables. Both require some preparation of the soil, frequent watering, fertilizing, and spraying for insects and various plant problems. Yet the baskets of cut flowers for the home, and the canvas of color you create in your garden, are more than sufficient compensation. Framing your home with an imaginatively landscaped flower garden not only will enhance the appearance but also increase the value of your property. You also can realize a deep inner joy when you work with nature to produce a feast for the eyes and the soul.

If you feel apprehensive about planting a flower garden, start small, with perhaps one flower bed by the front door and some pots on the patio. Within a year, you likely will be eager to transform your entire property and enjoy the rewards inherent in painting your landscape with living color.

Just as you plan other landscape elements, you will have to plan flower beds. Four to six hours of good, direct sunlight are essential for most flowering annuals and perennials. Position your flower beds so that they are not shaded excessively by trees or buildings. Study the requirements of various flowers so that

133

Annuals do require more care than evergreens— but they're worth it.

Condominium and apartment dwellers can be gardeners, too, by using hanging baskets, window boxes, and planters.

you can plan certain areas, and choose only those plants that tolerate the existing ratio of sun to shade.

Apartment dwellers with an itchy green thumb can use planters and window boxes to fulfill their gardening desires. Flowering vines can be grown over balcony dividers or on a trellis to add color to apartments and condominiums. Remember to let your imaginations run wild when planning any gardening project, large or small. It is pleasantly surprising what some people have achieved on their properties — large and small.

SOIL ENRICHMENT

Whatever your situation, your initial concern must be for the soil in which you will be growing flowers. The ground in Florida is sorely lacking in nutrients and always must be enhanced with peat moss, manure, and compost. About the only annual flower that grows well in poor soil is the nasturtium, which experienced gardeners humorously refer to as "a masochistic plant." The more it is neglected, the better it seems to thrive!

A good beginning for a flower bed: Take 25 pounds of cow manure, 25 pounds of peat, 2 to 3 pounds of a good, general fertilizer, and 1 inch of colloidal

Another small-space
option: Plant pansies
in a birdbath.

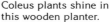

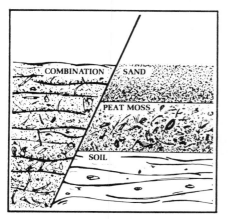

Coleus plants shine in
this wooden planter.

phosphate; rototill this mixture into the soil to a depth of 6 inches. This should
be sufficient for a flower bed approximately 10 feet by 20 feet.

After tilling, apply Vapam to kill nematodes, fungi, bacteria, and weed
seeds. Then rake the flower bed level and smooth, and let it sit for three weeks.
This will allow the Vapam to dissipate, preventing injury to your flowers and letting the new soil mixture settle. Be aware that Vapam is a toxic material and
should be used with care. If you decide not to sterilize, I recommend that you improve your soil, as described in Chapter 1.

A combination of soil additives should be
mixed with existing soil for maximum flower
performance.

Next, check the pH of your soil. Most annuals grow best with a soil pH of 5.5 to 6.5. If your analysis shows less than 5.5 pH, add dolomite. If the reading is above 6.5 add sulfur until the desired pH of the soil is reached.

PROPAGATION TECHNIQUES

Many gardeners derive added enjoyment from propagating at least some of their own plants, particularly annuals. Annuals may be propagated from seeds or from cuttings.

If you opt for planting seeds, buy them from a reputable seed company or from your nursery. Seeds from the dime store or supermarket aren't recommended, as they may be old or of poor quality.

When planting seeds, always follow directions on the particular seed package. You may choose to plant the seeds directly into the ground or you may opt to use jiffy pots.

Jiffy pots are compressed peat pots; to use them, simply put the seeds into the pots and, after the seeds have sprouted and grown a few inches, sink the pots into the ground. The pots dissolve into the soil and improve it at the same time.

Too, you can plant seeds in six-pack plastic containers filled with potting soil, or in large pots filled with prepared, sterilized soil.

Another way to propagate a plant is from a cutting. With many easy-to-root plants, you simply pinch off a 3- to 4-inch-long cutting of new growth and place it in good, sterile soil. The addition of rooting hormone, such as Rootone, helps to give the cutting the best possible start.

Nurseries and garden centers offer young annual plants in convenient, six-pack containers.

Impatient gardeners may want to plant annual seedlings, rather than starting with seeds or cuttings.

PLANTING WITH SEEDLINGS

If you aren't quite patient enough to plant from seeds or cuttings, you may purchase seedlings from your nursery, which will offer you the newest and best varieties. Seedlings are usually sold in four- or six-packs.

When you bring the seedlings home, be careful when removing them from the packs. An easy method of removal is to slit the sides of the plastic containers with scissors, thereby releasing the soil so that it slips out easily.

Now you're ready to plant. Prepare a hole in the ground slightly larger than the soil around the roots of each seedling. Gently lower each seedling into the

Space plants according to their mature height and width.

ground and press the soil around it firmly to hold it upright. As you're planting make sure you are allowing enough space between each seedling to allow for its mature size.

To minimize transplant shock, water each seedling immediately after planting with about a cupful of fertilizer, such as Nutri-Sol, which helps the plant get off to a good start. The next day, you can begin a regular watering schedule.

MR. GREEN THUMB RULE

In planting an annual bed, consider the particular variety's sun or shade preference, and the length of its growing season. Too, consider whether the variety will tolerate existing soil, or whether it prefers improved soil.

A water breaker system sprays a fine mist that helps protect delicate plants.

Drip irrigation

Soaker hose system

WATERING FLOWERS

Flowering plants are delicate bloomers that require plenty of moisture, especially if planted in well-drained soil.

A breaker-bar watering device minimizes possible damage to flowers and is used by many nurseries. A soaker hose or drip tubing is excellent and a very effective method of watering.

Annuals should receive at least 2 inches of water per week. If you are unsure whether your soil needs watering, press your fingers into the ground around the flowers to test for moisture. Depending on the needs of the particular flower, you may need to water or allow the soil to remain moist, but not dry. Dried-out soil can kill a flower quicker than an overnight freeze.

Improper watering can be fatal to your flowers, or it can cut down the potential number of blooms on a plant. Check the requirements for your flowers, and water accordingly. Watch for any plants that may turn gray and withered-looking. This denotes either a pest or a watering problem. If you are unsure of the cause of any condition, ask your nurseryman for advice.

Almost all flowers are subject to some type of problem, either in the soil or from insects. Watch for any unusual conditions and take steps at once. Details of insect pests and diseases can be found in Chapter 12, along with recommended sprays and insecticides.

SELECTING ANNUALS

Many popular flowers are grown in Florida. Your choice should be determined by your artistic preference for color, size, and shape, which gets back to your original landscape plan. With flower beds, always place the tallest flowers at the back, such as hollyhocks and larkspurs, to provide a background for the smaller plants in the middle and at the edge of the flower bed.

Unlike some other varieties, petunias look splendid when planted in a bed all their own.

It is also more appealing to mix flowers (both for color and variety) in the same bed to create interesting (but not gaudy) patterns of shape and color. A bed with nothing but one variety tends to look too regimented and unimaginative. The only exceptions to this rule might be petunias and roses, both of which are very acceptable without other flowers mixed in. Study the colors of various flowers and the mature sizes of the plants, then plan the manner in which you will position them in the flower bed for maximum growth potential and maximum artistic effect.

Building multilevel flower beds makes for an interesting display and provides the opportunity for more versatile arrangements of flowers. Imagine a top level, perhaps 6 feet above the ground, dropping to a second level 4 feet high and a third 2 feet high, held in place by a low stone edging; here, your blooming flowers seem to cascade like a colorful waterfall of blossoms and foliage.

ANNUAL VARIETIES FOR FLORIDA

All of the following annuals may be grown in all parts of Florida; see the chart that begins on page 168 for particulars on planting dates, spacing, etc.

Ageratum sp.
AGERATUM

Height: 6-12 in.

This is a low, bushy plant 6 to 12 inches in height, with clusters of small, fuzzy, ball-shaped flowers of lavender blue (also pink and white). The ageratum is good for edging flower beds, for use in rock gardens, and for patches of contrasting color in a large flower bed. A slow grower from seed, it is better to buy seedlings. Plant in February through April for flowering in April through August. These are tender plants requiring full sun or partial shade, and they like improved, well-drained soil. Spray for aphids, red spiders, and leafhoppers.

Blue Puff ageratum

Ageratum

Hollyhock

Alcea rosea
HOLLYHOCK

Height: 5-7 ft.

With large, dark-green, coarse leaves and hairy, thick stems, the hollyhock grows 5 to 7 feet tall. It is ideal against a wall or fence and provides a colorful, stately background to a flower bed. Pink, dark-red, and scarlet flowers, both single and double, open from the bottom all the way up to the terminal spike. The hollyhock likes good soil and moisture in either sun or partial shade. Hollyhocks should be planted from August through January for flowering in March through June. Plant seeds in fumigated soil and mulch well to prevent root-knot. Placing hollyhocks next to a building allows the roots to grow under the wall. This is a protection against root-knot.

Antirrhinum majus
SNAPDRAGON

Height: 6-36 in.

For cut flowers and bedding plants, snapdragons are most attractive. They grow in all colors except blue and have tubular flowers growing up a tall spike

Snapdragons

that can reach 36 inches in height. The snapdragon is an excellent choice for backgrounds. Frequent cutting of the flower spikes encourages more blooms. Snapdragons like moist, rich soil and thrive in sun or partial shade. A hardy plant, they have been known to live through a winter and continue blooming a second year. Plant seed from September through December for flowering from January through June. Snapdragons do experience problems with nematodes, wilt, rust, and aphids.

Begonia sp.
BEGONIA

Height: 6-12 in.

Begonias do best during the cooler months, so they should be planted in partial and full shade. These are small, rounded plants suitable for low borders, hanging baskets, and patio pots. The foliage varies from bright green to waxy bronze, with variegated types available. Flowers are red, pink, and white. You should buy transplants, since begonia seed is very fine and difficult to germinate, even in a greenhouse. This is one of the best flowers for season-long bloomings. The wax varieties are popular plants for Florida. The variety called Non-Stop tends to flower much of the year.

Viva begonia

Bingo Rose begonia

Bingo Pink begonia

A white wax begonia

Champion Yellow begonias

Pink wax begonias

Calendula officinalis
POT MARIGOLD

Height: 12-15 in.

A favorite for cut flowers and bedding plants, calendulas have light-green, slightly sticky leaves and yellow to orange flowers that grow 12 to 15 inches high. They are hardy and prefer a good moist soil in sun or partial shade. Plant from seeds in September through January for flowers in December through June. Spray for aphids and caterpillars.

Dwarf calendula mixture

Cockscomb, Geisha variety

Apricot Brandy cockscomb

Cockscomb (crested type)

Golden Torch cockscomb

Cockscomb (plume type)

Cockscomb (plume type)

Celosia cristata
COCKSCOMB

Height: 2-4 ft.

The cockscomb is a constant favorite with gardeners. It offers an impressive display of background color in a flower bed. The cockscomb grows 2 to 4 feet high, with feathery flower clusters or compact, velvety heads in red, yellow, white, and purple. This tender plant enjoys rich, moist soil in sun or partial shade. The seeds are easy to grow and should be planted in February through April for May-to-September blooming. Dwarf varieties also are available. Watch out for root-knot and caterpillars.

Centaurea Cyanus
CORNFLOWER or BACHELOR'S BUTTON

Height: 2½ ft.

Cornflower produces papery, round blossoms in blue, white, pink, red, and dark purple. This hardy plant covers a large area with its grayish foliage and colorful blooms and is excellent for bedding and cut flowers. Tolerant of almost any soil, cornflowers thrive in full sun and grow to 30 inches in height. Plant seeds in September through January for December-to-June flowering. Treat for aphids and root-knot. Cornflowers will reseed themselves year after year.

Chrysanthemum x superbum
SHASTA DAISY

Height: 2 ft.

These attractive large daisies are usually white. Some are double bloomers; others are single with contrasting yellow centers. Growing 18 to 24 inches in height, they make a vivid display. A dwarf variety is also available. They should be planted in early spring for summer and fall flowering. Clumps can be divided in the fall for new plantings. Shasta daisies are very hardy but do best in moist, rich soil with full sun.

Shasta daisies

> **MR. GREEN THUMB RULE**
>
> For most annuals, it is best to add 25 pounds of cow manure, 25 pounds of peat, and 2 to 3 pounds of a good fertilizer for every 100 square feet of growing space. Fill this area to a depth of 6 inches.

Clarkia sp.
GODETIA or FAREWELL-TO-SPRING

Height: 1-1½ ft.

This is an upright plant with clusters of satin-like flowers in white, red, rose, and purple. The godetia grows to 18 inches in partial shade. A hardy plant, it likes any well-drained soil and has only one insect problem: stink bugs. Planting from September through January will give you a mass of double and single primrose-like flowers from December through June.

Coleus sp.
COLEUS

Height: 12-18 in.

An ever-popular plant for indoors or outdoors, coleus has inconspicuous flowers but breathtaking leaves in red, green, yellow, bronze, and variegations of these colors. Excellent for pots, planters, and mass displays in flower beds, the tender coleus needs well-drained, improved soil and does best in partial shade. Grown from seed or cuttings, it should be planted in February through July. New plants can be started by placing a stem in a glass of water until it roots, then transplanting to good potting soil indoors or outdoors. A fast grower, the coleus should be pinched to promote bushy growth. Treat for aphids, mites, mealybugs, and nematodes.

A mixture of coleus varieties

Saber pineapple coleus

Coleus, Wizard mixture

Rose Wizard coleus

Cosmos sp.
COSMOS

Height: 6 ft.

Cosmos are easy to grow. In fact, in some parts of the world, they grow wild. Reaching 6 feet in height in Florida, the cosmos can be found with white, pink, crimson, orange, or yellow daisy-like flowers atop thin, graceful stems. This tender plant likes plenty of moisture and soil that is not too rich. Plant seeds in February through April for a mass of flowers from May through August. Be warned: These tall plants blow over easily and may need to be staked. They also suffer from aphids, mites, and caterpillars.

Cosmos

Dahlias

Cynoglossum amabile
CHINESE FORGET-ME-NOT

Height: 1-1½ ft.

Blue, white, and pink clusters of tiny flowers atop long, sticky stems about 18 inches high make the Chinese forget-me-not an interesting addition to any garden. These tender plants withstand light frost and prefer moist soil in sun and partial shade. This is a very satisfactory plant for borders, beds, cut flowers, and rock gardens. Plant from September through April for blooming in December through July. Watch out for root rot.

Dahlia sp.
DAHLIA

Height: 3-5 ft.

An herbaceous plant with large leaf clusters and many branches, the dahlia grows from thick, potato-like roots. These roots should be dug up after the first frost and stored in peat or sawdust through the winter, then set out again 6 inches deep in February and March for summer flowering. Dahlia blossoms are profuse; large, daisy-like, single and double blossoms in red, white, yellow, pink, bronze, and combinations of these colors. Dahlias grow best in improved soil with good moisture and prefer sun to partial shade. Dahlias are tender plants, growing to 5 feet in height. Treat for nematodes, aphids, stem borers, and powdery mildew.

Delphinium ajacis
LARKSPUR

Height: 4-5 ft.

Larkspur is loved for its delicate dark-green leaves and erect branches, where blooms open from the bottom to the terminal spike. Larkspurs are as impressive a background plant as hollyhocks. Growing to 4 or 5 feet in height, larkspur spikes come in lavender, blue, white, violet, and pink, with single and double blooms. This hardy plant enjoys most soils, adequate water, and sun or partial shade. It will reseed itself and grows best if seeded in its growing location. Plant from October through December for flowers from March through May. Particularly tall larkspurs may need to be staked. You should treat for crown rot, mites, and caterpillars.

Eschscholzia californica
CALIFORNIA POPPY

Height: 1-2 ft.

These cup-shaped flowers on tall, gray-green stems make an impressive display in shades of yellow, white, orange, pink, and red. The hardy plants grow 2 feet high in well-drained, improved soil, and must have full sun. Plant the seed in November through January for a riot of color from March through May. Poppies last only a day on the stem but flower profusely. Spray for aphids.

Euphorbia sp.
MOLTEN FIRE or SUMMER POINSETTIA

Height: 1-4 ft.

Like the coleus, molten fire plants are grown for their brightly colored leaves rather than their flowers, which are inconspicuous. Growing to 4 feet in Florida, molten fire is striking: Its leaves are blotched with red, green, and yellow. Useful as a background or a bedding plant, molten fire likes fortified, sandy soil and full sun. If the soil is too rich, foliage color will be less brilliant. Too much water causes crown rot. Plant seeds or tip cuttings in February through May for a massive display all summer. Root-knot and caterpillars can be serious problems.

Gaillardia pulchella
GAILLARDIA or BLANKET FLOWER

Height: 18-24 in.

With soft, hairy leaves and stems and multicolored flowers in shades of red, orange, yellow, and white, the gaillardia is useful as a coastal planting. They are quite salt-tolerant. In fact, they will thrive almost anywhere. This hardy species does well in sandy soil and full sun. In many western states, gaillardia can be seen growing wild. They have few insect problems and are possibly one of the most rewarding flowers to include in your garden. Plant seeds September through January for blossoms from April through August. Pinching off spent heads will prolong the blooming period. There also is a perennial variety, which grows a little taller and offers a slightly different flower formation.

Geranium sp.
GERANIUM

Height: 12-24 in.

The geranium is an herbaceous plant with hairy, aromatic leaves and clusters of white, red, and pink blossoms. It is a Florida favorite indoors and out,

Geranium blossom

A blooming geranium bed

Pink geraniums

Vaughn's Trial geraniums

Cameo geranium

Rose Pac geranium

though geraniums do best in full sun. They thrive in any soil but need little water. In fact, the soil should be on the dry side to prevent root rot. For robust, thicker plants, geraniums should be pinched back. Otherwise they will grow tall and spindly, to more than 18 inches. Numerous varieties offer a wide range of colors. Flowers are long-lasting. The Crimson Fire, Cherry Blossom, and Sincerity varieties are good for pot plants. For hanging baskets, try Sugar Baby, a pink flower; Yale, a double lilac-white; or Cornell, a lavender flower. There are also fancy leaf and scented types.

Gerbera Jamesonii
AFRICAN DAISY

Height: 2½ ft.

This hardy plant may grow to 30 inches in height in Florida, with blue, white, violet, cream, yellow, bronze, and red daisies atop long thin stems. The African daisy has few problems and grows easily in full sun, with no particular preference for soil. Plant in August through January for March-to-June blossoms. Excellent for cut flowers or edging a flower bed, the African daisy will reseed itself year after year. Whether cut or still on the plant, the flowers will close at night.

Gladiolus sp.
GLADIOLUS

Height: 1-4 ft.

Gladioli grow from corms. They should be dug up six weeks following flowering, before the foliage becomes yellow or brown, and stored in dry peat or sawdust through the winter. Planting should be done after the last frost for future flowering, at anytime except midsummer. "Glads" can be planted every week to ensure a continuous display of their impressive flowers, which are multicolored on a tall, green spike. They prefer full sun and improved, well-drained soil. These

African daisy

Gladioli, Little Darling mixture   Globe amaranth

tender flowers are subject to thrips, caterpillars, foliage diseases, and corm rot, a condition that requires dusting with captan before planting and after digging up for storage. Often reaching heights of 3 to 4 feet, gladioli are elegant flowers, excellent in rows at the back of flower beds to provide a background for shorter flowers. They are also very effective around a patio in small circular beds about a foot across, in which a dozen corms can be planted for a compact display of the flowers. For added strength and growth, a handful of bonemeal should be placed around each corm at the time of planting.

Gomphrena globosa
GLOBE AMARANTH

Height: 20 in.

A favorite source of dried flowers, the globe amaranth has stiff branches with dense, clover-like heads in purple, red, pink, white, and muted orange. Excellent for borders, cut flowers, and dried flowers, this tender plant tolerates poor soil and grows to 20 inches in full sun. Plant seeds from March to April for flowers from May through July. It has few growth or insect problems.

Grevillea sp.
SPIDER FLOWER

Height: 4 ft.

A tall, hairy, and strong-scented plant, the spider flower produces many white, rose, and purplish blossoms with long stamens on short, strong spines. Sow the seeds where they are to grow. In Florida, these flowers will reach 4 feet in height. They thrive in sandy soil and full sun and are very hardy, with a long flowering season. Plant seeds from September to May for blossoms from April through September. The spider flower has few insect problems.

Gypsophila elegans
BABY'S BREATH

Height: 24 in.

Baby's breath has loose branching, bushy foliage, with many tiny white-and-rose flowers on wiry stems. Baby's breath grows to 24 inches in height and makes attractive floral arrangements when combined with other flowers in a vase. It quickly blooms and goes to seed. For continuous flowering, plant new seeds each month. This hardy plant likes rich, well-drained soil with sun and partial shade. Plant in September through March for flowering from October through May. It suffers from root-knot and aphids, and is available in a perennial variety.

Helichrysum bracteatum
STRAWFLOWER

Height: 30 in.

As its name indicates, the strawflower is crisp and dry-looking. Arrangements of dried strawflowers have been a favorite for years. Available in yellow, orange, red, pink, and white, this tender plant likes good soil and full sun, withstands some drought, and has few insect problems. Plant seeds from March to May for May-to-August blooming. In Florida, strawflowers will grow to 30 inches in height.

Iberis umbellata
CANDYTUFT

Height: 20 in.

Candytuft grows beautiful red, pink, lilac, violet, and white crowded clusters of flowers atop 20-inch stems. This flower is a favorite for cut flowers as well as edging and bedding plants. A hardy specimen, candytuft likes moist soil and full sun. Plant seeds in September through February for November-through-April blossoms. For continuous flowering, plant seeds every 10 days. Spray for aphids. A perennial candytuft also is available.

Baby's Breath

Candytuft

Impatiens sultanii
IMPATIENS or TOUCH-ME-NOT

Height: 6-15 in.

For borders and planter boxes, impatiens provide a beautiful splash of color. They have dark-green, succulent leaves and clusters of pink, white, and scarlet flowers. Easily grown from seed, impatiens also root from cuttings. Pinching the main stem will produce a stockier, bushier plant. Growing from 6 to 15 inches in height, impatiens are hardy, like well-drained, improved soil, and do best in partial and full shade. For a long time, impatiens have been the most popular plant for shade in Florida. Now some of the new varieties will take a little more sun. This is a blessing for Florida gardeners. The Super Elfin, Scarlet, and Super Elfin White are excellent varieties. Nothing is more attractive than a hanging basket of double-flowering impatiens. Plant seeds in February through July for flowers from April until frost. Watch out for aphids and leaf-feeding caterpillars.

New Guinea impatiens

New Guinea impatiens with variegated leaves

Impatiens, Sherbet mixture

Ipomoea purpurea
MORNING GLORY

Height: 5-10 ft.

Nothing covers a wire fence quicker than morning glories. Their lush, heart-shaped leaves and delicate, funnel-shaped flowers greet the morning with pink, blue, and deep red splashes of color. The blossoms close later in the day, but the leaves form a solid, living wall of privacy. Morning glory vines also can be used on a patio's trellis for glorious shade and eye-catching beauty in the morning. Soak the seeds in water for a few days, and plant them where they are to grow. Planting from February to April will give you a good show from March through November. Morning glories like sun or partial shade and are tolerant of any kind of soil and moisture. Be warned: Once planted, morning glories will reseed themselves prolifically, year after year.

Lathyrus odoratus
SWEET PEA

Height: 2-3 ft. (without support)

Few vines surpass the sweet pea for impressive appearance and fragrant, frequent flowering. Blooming in white, pink, lavender, blue, orange, and red, sweet peas turn any fence or trellis into an expanse of color and heady fragrance. They often grow 10 to 15 feet above the ground, depending on the height of the support. Most gardeners will make a fence 6 feet high and as long as desired, then prepare a trench at the bottom before planting. Sweet peas are considered difficult to grow, but with good preparation of the soil, including fumigation and frequent fertilizing, they can be no more trouble than any other flower. Although hardy, the flowers will freeze, and the plants do best in full sun or partial shade. Plant seeds in October through January for January-to-April blooming. The more flowers you pick, the more will grow, and nothing freshens up a room better than a large vase of sweet peas. There also is a dwarf bush sweet pea, as well as a perennial type, but the blossoms on these are not as impressive nor as large as the regular type.

Liatris spicata
GAYFEATHER or BLAZING STAR

Height: 2-3 ft.

Actually a perennial, this plant is grown in Florida as an annual. A sparsely branched species, its leaves are threadlike, with a clustered flower spike in purple and white. It can be used as a border or for cutting. Gayfeather has few problems, is hardy, and thrives in moist soil in sun or partial shade. Plant in fall and spring for summer and fall flowering.

Limonium sp.

STATICE or SEA LAVENDER

Height: 2 ft.

A bushy plant with rough, wiry stems, statice has small flowers atop a branching spike in lavender, blue, white, rose, and yellow. A hardy plant, statice likes good soil and moisture and full sun. In Florida, it grows to 2 feet in height and transplants easily. Plant seeds from September through January for flowering from February to August. Statice has problems with foliage diseases.

Lobelia erinus

LOBELIA

Height: 1 ft.

Lobelia grows into a small bush about 12 inches high and wide, covered with tiny, irregular, blue, white, and red blossoms. The lobelia is excellent for edging, bedding, pots, and planter boxes. This tender plant likes improved soil, adequate moisture, and thrives in sun or partial shade. It can be planted from seed or cuttings from September through March for flowers from November through May. Cutting back prolongs the flowering period. The lobelia does well during cool weather but will wither in freezing temperatures.

Lobularia maritima

SWEET ALYSSUM

Height: 8 in.

Alyssum is a very small, delicate bush about 8 inches high, with rounded clusters of fragrant white, lilac, and purple blossoms. Sweet alyssum is an outstanding winter-flowering annual. It makes a good ground cover for flower-bed edges and rock gardens. Sow seeds where plants are to grow, or buy seedlings. Plant in September through January for flowering in October through June. These hardy little flowers like moist, good soil and lots of sun in the summer. Keep them somewhat drier in the winter. Spray for aphids.

Sweet alyssum

Sweet alyssum

Machaeranthera tanacetifolia
TAHOKA DAISY

Height: 2 ft.

Very similar in appearance to an aster, the Tahoka daisy has long-lasting, frilly blossoms with lush, fern-like foliage. Useful as bedding plants and cut flowers, these daisies are violet-blue with yellow centers. These hardy plants like moist, good soil and grow to 2 feet in full sun and partial shade. Plant seeds from February through April for blooming from June through November. Tahoka daisies are easy to grow but suffer from wilt and aphids.

Matthiola incana
STOCK

Height: 2 ft.

Stock is even more fragrant than sweet peas. It is a firm, erect plant about 2 feet high, with single or double flowers in racemes. Stock comes in various colors and is best known for the wonderful scent it gives off. A hardy plant, stock likes rich soil with good moisture and thrives best in full sun. Plant from September to February for winter and spring flowering. Stock is not recommended for south Florida, since it will not flower well during mild temperatures or mild winters.

Mirabilis Jalapa
FOUR O'CLOCK

Height: 2 ft.

Easily grown from seed, this brightly colored, tuberous rooted flower comes in red, pink, white, yellow, and variegated varieties that do well in moist soil, with full sun or partial shade. Plant in the spring for a carpet of blooms 2 feet high from summer to the first frost. Four o'clocks are ideal for flower beds and large areas requiring color.

Molucella laevis
BELLS OF IRELAND

Height: 2 ft.

A 2-foot-high, thorny plant, Bells of Ireland has small, white flowers encased in a large bell-like green sheath. Used as a cut flower, and for dried arrangements, borders, and beds, this tender plant likes sun and partial shade and needs moist, rich soil. Plant in February through July for blossoms in April through summer. The seeds germinate in cool weather, at about 40 degrees. Spray for aphids.

Nicotiana
(Jasmine tobacco)

Nicotiana alata
JASMINE TOBACCO

Height: 1-2½ ft.

Nicotiana's coarse, bushy stems form a compact plant more than 2 feet high with many white, crimson, or cream flowers at the top. The flowers close during the day but open at night, emitting a heady perfume that is most pleasant. This hardy plant prefers well-drained, improved soil and thrives in sun and partial shade. Use where a dense, thick patch of foliage and flowers is desired. Plant seeds in August through November for blooms from March through June. Spray for aphids.

Petunia sp.
PETUNIA

Height: 10-20 in.

For years, the petunia has been one of Florida's most popular flowering annuals. Some outstanding varieties are Old Glory White, White Cascade, Red Baron, El Toro, Blue Flash, and, for a bright orchid color, the Sugar Daddy. Don't plant in the same site three years in a row — rotate to a different annual. For hanging baskets or trailers, try Pink Carousel or Linda. One of the most glorious displays in any garden is a bed of petunias in mixed colors. Pinching the center shoot of these plants promotes dense, bushy foliage from 10 to 20 inches in height, with endless single or double funnel-shaped flowers. Petunias are difficult to grow from seed (the seeds are microscopic). Buy seedlings from a nursery and mix your colors when you plant. August-through-January plantings will flower October through July. Petunias like good soil with adequate moisture and do best in sun, especially in winter, but they also will thrive in shade. They are excellent as bedding plants, but many people use them in planters and window boxes.

Nicotiana and petunias   Summer Madness petunias

Rose Picotee petunias   Ultra Red petunias

Phlox drummondii
PHLOX

Height: 12-24 in.

Phlox has smooth-edged and erect branches with clusters of blossoms at the tips. It is an excellent border plant that can be massed in a flower bed. Phlox has few insect problems and responds well to fertilization, growing 1 to 2 feet high with profuse blossoms of various colors. Although phlox can be transplanted, it does better if planted from seed where it is meant to grow. Plant from September through February for riotous color from December through May. The plants like dry, sandy soil and do well in sun or partial shade. A hardy plant, phlox will reseed, but the next germination will have poorer color.

Phlox

Portulaca grandiflora
MOSS ROSE

Height: 6-8 in.

A great summer bloomer, portulaca takes hot summer temperatures very well. A super bedding plant, the leaves of portulaca are thick, narrow, and succulent and grow no higher than 6 or 8 inches. The rose-like flowers open only in sunlight, and flowering time is short, requiring new seeding every six weeks to maintain the carpet of color they create. Use this flower as a border plant or on rock gardens, and plant from February through May for May-to-October blooms. A tender plant, portulaca does best in full sun, in enriched, well-drained soil. Its only problem is damping-off, if planted in a poorly drained area.

Multicolored portulaca blooms

Sunnyside portulaca (moss rose)

Scarlet sage

Blaze of Fire sage

Salvia farinacea
SAGE

Height: 3 ft.

Salvia does well in full sun or partial shade. This sturdy plant has two-lipped flowers 1 to 1½ inches long in racemes. The flowers are usually bright scarlet and grow to 36 inches. A tender plant, the salvia prefers enriched, moist soil in sun and partial shade. Plant seeds or cuttings from February through June for April-to-September blooming. Excellent for borders, bedding plants, and cut flowers. If cut back, the plant will bloom again. Although scarlet salvias are the predominant favorite, this plant does come in pink, purple, and white, as well as a blue perennial described in the following chapter. Other varieties you may want to try are Red Hot Sally and St. John's Fire.

Streptosolen Jamesonii
AMETHYST FLOWER or BROWALLIA

Height: 1-2 ft.

Growing to 1 to 2 feet in height, with tubular violet or white blossoms, the amethyst flower is easy to grow from seeds or cuttings. It can be used as a houseplant or for cut flowers. Plant in September through November for flowering in December through May. The tender plants require pinching to avoid staking the stems. They like rich, moist soil and will grow in sun or partial shade. Slug pellets around the base will ward off slugs.

Tagetes sp.
MARIGOLD

Height: 6-36 in.

Strong-scented foliage; double blossoms in orange, yellow, or maroon; and a compact, bushy shape make the marigold an ideal addition to any garden. Plant from seeds, clippings, or seedlings in February to May for lush foliage and endless flowers from May to November. Marigolds thrive in moist, good soil and in sun or partial shade. Spray for spider mites and serpentine leaf miner.

Marigold bed

Inca Yellow marigolds   Crackerjack marigolds   Spinwheel marigolds

Tropaeolum majus
NASTURTIUM

Height: 10-18 in.

    Known in England as "the poor man's flower," nasturtiums will grow virtually anywhere with little care. The nasturtium nevertheless is a very rewarding plant that flowers profusely. Available in dwarf bush varieties as well as climbers, nasturtiums are tender plants preferring light, moist soil and full sun to partial shade. Nasturtiums provide wonderful color for bordering a flower bed, as well as edging it with its thick, rounded leaves. They are resistant to nematodes but do suffer from aphids and serpentine leaf miners. Plant seeds where you wish them to grow in February to March for April-through-June flowering. The more flowers you pick, the more will appear. Caution: Do not fertilize nasturtiums. This leads to excessive leaf growth and very few flowers. The nasturtium is the one flower that seems to thrive on neglect, making it a popular item for lazy gardeners!

Nasturtiums

Periwinkles

Periwinkle blossoms

Vinca rosea
PERIWINKLE

Height: 6-24 in.

Periwinkles are among the easiest flowers to grow, and survive almost any amount of neglect. They are very salt-tolerant and grow in almost any soil, in full sun or partial shade, to a height of 6 to 24 inches. They are evergreen but become a little sparse in late fall and winter. Spring growth is bright green, with purple-blue flowers. Periwinkles should be sprayed for leaf rollers in summer. A new dwarf series is available called Magic Carpet; it requires more protection than the regular green trailing periwinkle. Because they reseed themselves and are relatively hardy, periwinkles may also be treated as perennials.

Viola tricolor hortensis
PANSY

Height: 6-10 in.

These low-growing plants are perennials but are used as annuals. For beds, borders, patio plantings, and cut flowers, pansies have an Old World charm. Their dark green foliage is about 8 inches high, and they produce masses of velvety, flat flowers in almost every color of the rainbow. The variegated flowers look like small, smiling faces staring up from the ground. A cold-weather plant, pansies should be planted from September to December for flowering from January through May. They are hardy and thrive in rich soil with good moisture in sun or partial shade. Mulching is advised, both for protection in cold weather and improved growth and flower protection.

Beconsfield pansies

Hybrid Show pansy blossom

Universal Orange pansies

Hybrid Show pansy blossom

Zinnias

Zinnia sp.
ZINNIA

Height: 6-36 in.

Zinnias are one of the most popular annuals in the world and one of the easiest to grow. The zinnia can flood a flower bed with double, semi-double, and single blossoms in practically every color of the rainbow except blue. From the dwarf varieties for borders and edging plants to the 3-foot-high plants for mass plantings and backgrounds, zinnias are unrivaled. Growing best in full sun, they can tolerate almost any soil and bloom profusely from April through November. Staggered plantings from February through August will ensure an ongoing selection for cut flowers. Zinnias are tender plants, suffering from powdery mildew, spider mites, caterpillars, and crown rot. Spraying will take care of these problems, but as a preventive measure, water only the soil around zinnias — not the leaves. Peat moss and organic matter added to the soil will improve growth and flower quality. So will a 6-6-6 or 8-8-8 fertilizer (2 pounds per 100 square feet of bed area).

Zinnias should be planted from seed where they are to grow. In warm soils, zinnias will germinate within one week. After the seedlings send out four leaves, they may be thinned to 10 inches apart for the smaller varieties, 12 to 18 inches apart for the larger types. Delayed thinning will result in stunted growth and few flowers. Zinnias need room to grow tall and bushy.

The main problem afflicting this flower is powdery mildew. If there is the slightest indication of a grayish white coating on the leaves, treat at once with sulfur dust, Karathane, Acti-Dione PM, or benomyl (Benlate). Some zinnia enthusiasts will cover the budding plants with cheesecloth. The filtered light results in increased insect protection as well as flowers of larger size and crisp, striking color.

Zinnias come in solid colors and in striped and variegated types such as Peppermint Stick and Ortho Polka. There are others, such as Dark Jewel, which have twisted and ruffled petals. The largest blossoms are California Giant and Super Giant, which have mammoth-sized blooms almost 6 inches in diameter. For patio or porch, try a pot of one of the Short Stuff varieties.

Zinnia

ANNUALS FOR FLORIDA

COMMON NAME	SCIENTIFIC NAME	COLOR (BLOOM)	SUN OR SHADE
Ageratum	Ageratum sp.	Blue, Lavender, White, Pink	Sun to Partial Shade
Alyssum, Sweet	Lobularia maritima	Violet, Purple, White, Lilac	Sun
Amaranth, Globe	Gomphrena globosa	Purple, Red, Pink, White, Soft orange	Sun
Amethyst Flower	Streptoselen Jamesonii	Violet, White	Sun or Partial Shade
Baby's Breath	Gypsophila elegans	White, Rose	Sun or Partial Shade
Begonia	Begonia sp.	Pink, Red, Orange	Some Sun to Shade
Bells of Ireland	Molucella laevis	White, Inconspicuous	Sun to Partial Shade
Candytuft	Iberis umbellata	Red, Pink, Lilac, Violet, White	Sun
Carnation	Dianthus Caryophyllus	White, Pink, Red, Yellow, Combinations	Sun to Partial Shade
Chrysanthemum (annual)	Chrysanthemum carinatum	All Colors Excluding Blue	Sun or Partial Shade
Cockscomb	Celosia cristata	Purple, White, Red, Yellow, Gold	Sun to Partial Shade
Coleus	Coleus sp.	Leaves — Various Blooms — Blue	Partial Shade
Cornflower	Centaurea Cyanus	Blue, White, Pink, Dark Purple, Red	Sun
Cosmos	Cosmos sp.	White, Pink, Crimson, Yellow, Orange	Full Sun
Dahlia	Dahlia sp.	Red, White, Yellow, Pink, Bronze, or Combinations	Sun to Partial Shade
Daisy, African	Gerbera Jamesonii	Blue, White, Violet, Cream, Yellow, Bronze, Red	Sun
Daisy, Shasta	Chrysanthemum x superbum	White with Yellow Center	Sun
Daisy, Tahoka	Machaeranthera tanacetifolia	Blue Violet with Yellow Center	Sun or Partial Shade

HEIGHT	HARDINESS	SEED TO BLOOM (DAYS)	PLANTING SEASON	SUGGESTED SPACE BETWEEN PLANTS	PROBLEMS
6″-12″	Tender	75-80	Feb-April	6″-2′	Red spider mites, Aphids, Leafhoppers
8″	Hardy	45	Sept-Jan	5″-7″	Aphids
20″	Tender	90	March-April	9″-12″	Few
1′-2′	Tender	60-75	Sept-Nov	6″-18″	Slugs
24″	Hardy	50-60	Sept-March	18″	Root knot, Aphids
6″-12″	Tender	75-90	Year-round	1′-3′	Mites, Scale, Aphids
2′	Tender	60-80	Feb-July	12″	Aphids
20″	Hardy	70	Sept-Feb	8″-12″	Aphids
12″-36″	Hardy	125-150	Aug-Jan	9″-12″	Aphids, Root rot, Mites, Rust, Wilt
2′-4′	Hardy	75-100	Feb-March	12″-18″	Nematodes, Mites, Thrips, Leaf spot
2′-4′	Tender	60-80	Feb-April	12″-18″	Root knot, Caterpillars
12″-18″	Tender	——	Feb-July	12″	Aphids, Mealybugs Mites, Nematodes
2½′	Hardy	90	Sept-Jan	12″-24″	Aphids, Root knot
6′	Tender	75	Feb-April	12″-24″	Plants blow over easily; Aphids, Mites, Caterpillars
3′-5′	Tender	50-60	Feb-March	24″-36″	Nematodes, Aphids, Stem borers, Powdery mildew
2½′	Hardy	90	Aug-Jan	12″-24″	Few
2′	Very Hardy	120	Aug-Dec	12″-18″	Root rot, Aphids, Caterpillars
2′	Hardy	90-120	Feb-April	24″	Wilt, Aphids

ANNUALS FOR FLORIDA

COMMON NAME	SCIENTIFIC NAME	COLOR (BLOOM)	SUN OR SHADE
Forget-Me-Not, Chinese	Cynoglossum amabile	Blue, White, Pink	Sun to Partial Shade
Four O'Clocks	Mirabilis Jalapa	Red, Yellow, White, Striped	Sun or Partial Shade
Gaillardia	Gaillardia pulchella	Red, Orange, Yellow, White	Sun
Gayfeather	Liatris spicata	Purple, White	Sun or Partial Shade
Geranium	Geranium sp.	Red, White, Pink	Sun
Gladiolus	Gladiolus sp.	White, Yellow, Red, Pink, Purple, Lavender	Sun
Godetia	Clarkia sp.	White, Rose, Red, Purple	Partial Shade
Hollyhock	Alcea rosea	Pink, Many other colors	Sun to Partial Shade
Impatiens	Impatiens sultanii	Pink, White, Purple, Red	Partial Shade to Shade
Larkspur	Delphinium ajacis	Lavender, Blue, White Violet, Pink	Sun to Partial Shade
Lobelia	Lobelia erinus	Blue, Red, White	Sun or Partial Shade
Marigold	Tagetes sp.	Yellow, Orange	Sun to Partial Shade
Marigold, Pot	Calendula officinalis	Orange, Yellow	Sun to Partial Shade
Molten Fire	Euphorbia sp.	Red (Foliage)	Sun
Morning Glory	Ipomoea purpurea	Pink, Blue, Deep Red	Sun or Partial Shade
Moss Rose	Portulaca grandiflora	White, Pink, Salmon, Red, Yellow	Sun
Nasturtium	Tropaeolum majus	Red, Yellow, Pink, Orange,	Sun to Partial Shade
Pansy	Viola Tricolor hortensis	White, Yellow, Blue	Sun to Partial Shade

HEIGHT	HARDINESS	SEED TO BLOOM (DAYS)	PLANTING SEASON	SUGGESTED SPACE BETWEEN PLANTS	PROBLEMS
1'-1½'	Will stand light frost	85-100	Sept-April	18"	Root rot
1½'-2'	Tender	60-75	Feb-May	12"-18"	Few
18"-24"	Hardy	60-75	Sept-Jan or all year	18"	Very few
2'-3'	Hardy		Sept-May	6"	Few
12"-24"	Hardy	85-100	Feb-June	12"	Nematodes, Mosaic, Aphids, Caterpillars
1'-4'	Tender	60-90	April-Nov or any time when frost safe	4"-6"	Thrips, Caterpillars, Corm rot
1'-1½'	Hardy	60-75	Sept-Jan	8"-12"	Aphids, Mealybugs, Mites, Nematodes
5'-7'	Hardy	150-175	Aug-Jan	2'	Red spider mites, Root knot, Rust
6"-15"	Tender	65-90	Feb-July	8"-12"	Caterpillars, Aphids
4'-5'	Hardy	80-90	Oct-Dec	12"-18"	Crown rot, Mites, Caterpillars
1'	Tender	70	Sept-March	8"	Few
6"-36"	Tender	45-60	Feb-May	6"-18"	Spider mites (bad), Serpentine leaf miner
12"-15"	Hardy	90-110	Sept-Dec	12"-18"	Caterpillars, Aphids
1'-4'	Tender	90	Feb-May	18"-24"	Root knot (can be serious), Crown rot
Vine	Tender	60-75	Feb-April	12"	Nematodes
6"-8"	Tender	45-60	Feb-May	6"	Damping-off
10"-18"	Tender	60-80	Feb-March	12"	Aphids, Serpentine leaf miners
6"-10"	Hardy	90	Sept-Dec	8"	Crown rot

ANNUALS FOR FLORIDA

COMMON NAME	SCIENTIFIC NAME	COLOR (BLOOM)	SUN OR SHADE
Pea, Sweet	Lathyrus odoratus	White, Pink, Lavender, Blue, Orange, Red	Sun or Partial Shade
Periwinkle	Vinca rosea	White, Pink, Lavender	Sun to Partial Shade
Petunia	Petunia sp.	White, Pink, Red, Purple	Sun
Phlox	Phlox drummondii	Red, Pink, Purple, White	Sun
Pinks	Dianthus chinensis	Combinations of Pink, Red, White	Sun to Partial Shade
Poppy, California	Eschscholzia californica	White, Yellow, Orange, Pink	Sun
Sage	Salvia farinacea	Violet Blue, White	Sun or Partial Shade
Snapdragon	Antirrhinum majus	White, Pink, Red, Yellow, Green	Sun to Partial Shade
Spider Flower	Grevillea sp.	White, Rose, Purplish	Sun
Statice	Limonium sp.	Lavender, Blue, White, Rose, Yellow	Sun
Stock	Matthiola incana	Various, including White and Rose	Sun
Straw Flower	Helichrysum bracteatum	Yellow, Orange. Red, Pink, White	Sun
Tobacco, Jasmine	Nicotiana alata	White, Crimson, Cream, White	Sun to Partial Shade
Wishbone Flower	Torenia Fournier I	Tube — Blue; Throat — Yellow	Sun to Partial Shade
Zinnia	Zinnia sp.	Yellow, White, Red, Gold	Sun

HEIGHT	HARDINESS	SEED TO BLOOM (DAYS)	PLANTING SEASON	SUGGESTED SPACE BETWEEN PLANTS	PROBLEMS
Vine	Hardy	70-85	Oct-Jan	6″-8″	Aphids, Thrips, Root knot
6″-24″	Tender	80-90	Feb	24″	Blight
10″-20″	Hardy	75-90	Aug-Jan	12″-18″	Crown rot, Aphids, Nematodes
12″-24″	Hardy	75	Aug-Jan	6″-8″	Few
10″-12″	Hardy	60-75	Sept-Dec	6″	Root rot, Crown rot, Aphids
1′-2′	Hardy	80-90	Nov-Jan	12″	Aphids
3′	Hardy	85-100	Sept-Jun	18″	Thrips
6″-36″	Hardy	90-120	Sept-Dec	18″-2′	Aphids, Rust, Nematodes
4′	Hardy	70-90	Sept-May	12″-24″	Few
2′	Hardy	60-75	Sept-Jan	18″	Foliage diseases
2′	Hardy	75-90	Sept-Feb	12″	Aphids, Crown rot
30″	Tender	60	March-May	12″-18″	Few
1′-2½′	Hardy	90-100	Aug-Nov	12″	Aphids
12″-18″	Tender	60-75	Feb-Sept	8″	Few
6″-36″	Tender	45-60	Feb-Aug	6″-30″	Powdery mildew, Spider mites, Caterpillars

CHAPTER SIX

Perennials

While annuals infuse a flower bed with eye-catching color, the sight is a passing joy. Annuals, by their very name, last only a season and then are gone. Perennials, on the other hand, can provide equally impressive visual rewards without fading so quickly. In fact, perennials, by *their* very name, bloom year after year.

Gardeners with limited landscape time find perennials a particular blessing. After all, they have to be planted only once, and require considerably less care than annuals. Too, in general, perennials are more convenient and are more adaptable to Florida conditions than their annual pals. Even perennials that are damaged by frost will emerge the following season, often with larger and more abundant blossoms.

Not only do perennials offer a variety of appealing flowers, but their foliage can also be more interesting in shape, size, and color than annuals. To improve the overall appearance of your landscape and to ensure year-round color, you should include an assortment of perennials in your annual beds.

Separate beds of perennials, however, can be breathtaking, permanent, "easy" spots in your garden. Here, hand weeding, watering, and insect and disease control will be much less taxing on your time than annual beds.

DRAINAGE TIPS

Just because perennial beds are easier to care for doesn't mean they don't have to be carefully planned. Perennials, as a rule, should be planted in well-drained areas. If your landscape doesn't offer optimum drainage conditions, it's a good idea to plant your perennials in raised beds, which encourage drainage and delineate landscape areas. A raised bed can be built by creating a square or rectangle with railroad ties, logs, or pressure-treated lumber. (I have used 8x8-inch railroad ties and 1x6-inch lumber with equal success.) Fill the delineated area with good potting soil up to the top of the ties (6 to 8 inches should suffice). Hall's and The Potting Shed offer quality soil for this purpose.

SOIL ENRICHMENT

Soil enrichment is just as important for perennials as it is for annuals. In fact, it's even more important, since a perennial bed, unlike an annual bed, won't be reworked every season. You should give your perennials added nutrients before you plant them, especially if you're planting them in your landscape's existing soil.

The first thing you need to do is check the pH of your soil, and, if necessary, adjust it to a slightly acid range of about 5.5 to 6.5. If it's a brand-new bed, you may wish to sterilize the soil with Vapam, which helps get rid of many of the insects and diseases found in Florida soils.

The next helpful step is the addition of 25 pounds of peat and cow manure per 100 square feet of bed. Too, you should fertilize with 2 to 3 pounds of 6-6-6 fertilizer per 100 square feet of space, or water-in the perennials with a good, liquid fertilizer.

Don't stop feeding your perennials when they become established and start to thrive. They continue to need added nutrients to perform their best. A 10-20-20 fertilizer is advisable, since a fertilizer high in phosphorus and potassium helps generate better bulb growth and more vigorous blooms. (Don't use a high-nitrogen fertilizer, as it promotes foliage rather than flowers.) And remember, the best time to fertilize is when a plant is actively growing.

WATERING TIPS

Watering, too, is crucial to your perennials' continued good health. Most need a good, weekly watering; in fact, I'd advise giving these perennial beauties 1/2 inch of water *twice* a week to ensure that their thirst is quenched. (For more information on watering techniques, see "Watering Flowers" on page 139.)

Chrysanthemums blooming in a greenhouse

Gerber daisies and other perennials continue to need nutrients after they become established in the garden.

MULCHING

Perennials benefit greatly from mulching, which makes a flower bed more attractive, discourages weeds, inhibits soil erosion, and helps conserve moisture in the soil. Cypress or pine wood chips, leaves, and grass clippings are excellent mulches. For perennials that are dormant in winter, mulching in late October and November is recommended. Some gardeners call this practice "putting the perennials to bed for the winter."

Many gardeners divide their landscapes into specific areas: some areas for perennials that become permanent parts of the layout of the garden; and other annual areas, which may change at the gardener's whim. Perennials, however, should be left where they are planted initially, so they can grow and mature without interruption, as do trees and shrubs. Relocating any plant will set it back and inhibit its overall growth and flowering capabilities.

Perennials—especially roses— should be planted and allowed to grow in the same spot without being disturbed; relocation may inhibit growth and flowering.

PERENNIAL VARIETIES FOR FLORIDA

Most of the following perennials may be grown in all parts of Florida; just make sure that the varieties you choose are viable in your area.

Alpinia speciosa
SHELLFLOWER

Height: 3-8 ft.   Areas: C, S

Commonly found from Orlando to south Florida, this attractive perennial grows from 3 to 8 feet in height, with unusual, shell-type flowers, one on top of the other, and pearly white in color. Plant the rhizomes about 2 inches deep in rich, moist soil, with full sun or partial shade. The plants can be used as backgrounds or as interesting specimens in large pots on the patio.

Caladium sp.
CALADIUM

Height: 1-2 ft.   Areas: N, C, S

Caladiums grow from tubers and produce large, heart-shaped leaves. The leaves show a variety of exotic colors and grow 1 or 2 feet high on long petioles. Shades of pink, red, white, and green make an unusual and provocative display in mass plantings or in pots and planter boxes. Caladiums prefer rich, moist, acid soil and do best in partial shade. These tender plants do produce flowers, but they are inconspicuous. Caladiums have few problems except for chewing insects. The tubers should be taken up if your winter temperature gets below freezing. In the warmer areas of the state, the tubers can be left in the ground all year.

Caladium

Canna sp.
CANNA

Height: 2-5 ft.   Areas: N, C, S

Cannas have large, paddle-shaped leaves, green or reddish green in color, with large, soft-pleated blossoms emerging from the center, very much like gladioli. Cannas can be used as patio plantings, or as backgrounds (they grow to 5 feet in height), and are wonderful in damp areas, such as around ponds or pools. Planting from December through February will result in a display of beautiful flowers through summer. Plant the rhizomes about 2 inches deep in an area where they can spread. They will spread prolifically, especially in fertile, moist soil with full sun. As the cannas spread, you can cut off the rhizomes and start new arrangements around the garden. Cannas are particularly effective scattered in clumps in a rock garden, or as a background for flower beds. These tender plants suffer during a frost, but recover. Spray regularly, using a systemic with Di-Syston granules; cannas are favorite targets for leaf-rolling caterpillars. A dwarf variety is available that will grow to about 24 inches in height. Both regular and dwarf varieties come in pink, yellow, rose, cream, and white, plus mixtures of these colors.

Centratherum sp.
MANAOS BEAUTY

Height: 2-2½ ft.   Areas: N, C, S

Manaos Beauty is prized for its blue-green, serrated leaves and soft, thistle-like blue flowers. This tender plant is an attractive addition to any garden. Growing about 30 inches tall, the Manaos Beauty can be planted all year, for continuous flowering in all seasons. Tolerant of all soil and moisture conditions as well as sun or shade, it grows well under difficult conditions and has only one problem: leafhoppers. Manaos Beauty can be used as a bedding or border plant, as well as around foundations and in pots.

Chrysanthemum sp.
CHRYSANTHEMUM

Height: 2-3 ft.   Areas: N, C, S

Available in many different sizes, shapes, and colors, the hardy chrysanthemum is one of the easiest flowers to grow and one of the most popular

Cushion mums

Garden mum

Chrysanthemums are readily available at area garden centers and nurseries.

Garden mums

because of its luxurious display of blossoms. Chrysanthemums grow to 3 feet in height and are quite bushy. They have aromatic, grayish green foliage, and their flowers are single, double, semi-double, and spider-type, in all colors except blue. Chrysanthemums can be used for cut flowers, bedding plants, or patio plants in pots or boxes. Pinching side shoots on a stem will result in one large flower at the top. Pruning will increase the density of the foliage and improve flower production. Plant cuttings from February to March for fall flowering. Chrysanthemums prefer improved, well-drained soil in sun and partial shade. Frost damages the flowers, but not the plant. Problems include nematodes, mites, thrips, aphids, leaf spots, stunt, and root rot.

Shasta daisies

Chrysanthemum x superbum
SHASTA DAISY

Height: 1½-2 ft.   Areas: N, C, S

This very hardy plant has long, narrow-toothed leaves. Its stiff stems hold 4-inch white blooms with yellow centers. Excellent for borders and unexcelled as cut flowers, shasta daisies are a perennial favorite with gardeners all over the world. Shasta daisies enjoy rich, moist soil and take full sun, sometimes growing to 2 feet in height. Plant seeds or divisions from August through December for January-to-May flowers. The plant is subject to root rot, aphids, and caterpillars.

Coreopsis sp.
TICKSEED

Height: 10-30 in.   Areas: N, C, S

A very hardy perennial, coreopsis has attractive, apple-green foliage and luxurious single and double, daisy-like flowers in yellow or yellow with maroon centers. This perennial grows to 30 inches and reseeds itself prolifically. In many parts of the Southwest it grows wild. Weeding out the seedlings around a coreopsis is essential if you want to keep growth under control in a flower bed. Plant seeds from October through May for a sea of yellow color from April through July. Coreopsis thrives best in any well-drained soil in sun or light shade. The plants suffer from aphids, leaf beetles, and mites. An annual variety called calliopsis (*Coreopsis tinctoria*) is available.

Delphinium sp.
LARKSPUR

Height: 3-5 ft.   Areas: N, C, S

This is one of the stateliest plants in any garden. The larkspur has rich, palm-shaped foliage and elegant single and double blossoms growing on a stalk as tall as 5 feet. For background plantings and cut flowers, larkspurs are outstanding. They come in dark or light blue, white, violet, and rose colors. A hardy plant, larkspur should be planted from seed from September through November for blooming in March through May. This plant needs rich, well-drained soil in sun or partial shade. It is prone to crown rot, mildew, mites, and caterpillars.

Dianthus Caryophyllus
CARNATION

Height: 1-3 ft.   Areas: N, C, S

Carnations are hardy, straggly plants with blue-gray, grass-like leaves on long stems. From the top of the stems, flowers emerge in a thimble-like calyx that opens into double blooms, with many ragged-edged petals. Pinching off side shoots will promote one large flower at the end of each stem, like those sold in florist shops. Carnations have a distinctive fragrance that makes them favorite cut flowers. Grown as borders or in planters, carnations thrive in improved, well-drained soil, in sun and partial shade. Plant seeds or cuttings in August through January for blooms from March through June. Carnations weather low temperatures without damage but suffer from aphids, root rot, mites, rust, and wilt.

Baby Doll carnations

Connecticut Yankee larkspurs

Gaillardia (Blanketflower)

Gazanias

Gaillardia sp.
BLANKETFLOWER

Height: 12-30 in.   Areas: N, C, S

Similar to the annual gaillardia, this hardy perennial has few problems and grows in almost any soil in full sun. If left alone, it can cover a field in a few seasons. Ideal for cut flowers and border plantings, gaillardias have hairy, light-green foliage and large red, yellow, and orange daisy-like flowers that grow to 30 inches. Plant seeds or clump divisions from September through January for flowering from April to August. Excellent for splashes of color in a rock garden.

Gazania sp.
GAZANIA

Height: 6-18 in.   Areas: N, C, S

Like the flowers of the African daisy, gazania blossoms close at night. By day, however, they make a colorful display as a border along flower beds or in planter boxes on a patio. Growing 6 to 18 inches in height, the gazania likes moist, rich soil, sun or partial shade, and is salt-tolerant. The small, daisy-like blooms are 3 inches across and come in yellow, brown, red, and white. Plant seeds, or divide the plant for new growth in early spring for summer flowering.

Gerber daisies

Gerbera Jamesonii
TRANSVAAL (GERBER) DAISY

Height: 6-18 in.   Areas: N, C, S

For cut flowers, beds, border plantings, and pots, the gerbera is one of the hardiest perennials. It grows in rich soil, and likes good moisture and sun or partial shade. The leaves are dark green and rough-looking, with large, slender-petaled, daisy-like blooms atop a long stem. The blooms come in shades of orange, red, white, pink, and violet. Plant seeds or divisions from September to January for continuous flowers all year long. The gerber flourishes as a wild flower on the veld (grassland) of South Africa. Here, it responds to good care. Do not plant too deep, and be careful to keep sand out of the crown; sand rots the plant. Treat for leaf-spot diseases, serpentine leaf miner, and nematodes. Gerber daisies also do well as indoor plants in a sunny location. A popular new variety is called Happy Pot.

Hemerocallis sp.
DAYLILY

Height: 1-2 ft.   Areas: N, C, S

Yellow and orange daylilies provide a handsome splash of color in any garden, and can be used for bedding or borders. These hardy perennials like full sun and tolerate almost any soil. They should be purchased when in bloom so you can select your preferred color. After flowering, they can be planted any time for blooming from February through October. As their name implies, they bloom for the day, but sometimes survive two to three days indoors after being picked. They multiply rapidly in the ground, and the divisions can be dug up and used to start new clumps of the flowers in other locations. Apart from its attractive flowers, which rise on single stems 2 feet high, the daylily's low, sword-shaped foliage makes an attractive edging along flower beds or beside pathways.

Daylilies

Blue lisianthus

Hunnemannia fumariifolia
MEXICAN TULIP POPPY

Height: 1-2 ft.   Areas: N, C, S

The Mexican tulip poppy has narrow, segmented, bluish green leaves and tulip-shaped, yellow flowers. It grows to 2 feet in height and can be used for cut flowers, borders, or bedding. This hardy plant has few problems, and enjoys full sun and good, moist soil. Plant seeds where they are to grow from November to December for April-to-June blossoms.

Lisianthus sp.
LISIANTHUS

Height: 1½-3 ft.   Areas: N, C, S

A relatively new perennial in Florida, this plant comes in blue (about 18 inches tall), white (about 2 feet tall), and pink (about 3 feet tall). Lisianthus grows well in fairly dry soil and should not be overwatered. It flowers well in the hot summer months, has few apparent insect problems, and is becoming very popular. Pinching young plants promotes bushy growth.

Sweet alyssum
grown as a border

Container-grown
sweet alyssum

Lobularia maritima
SWEET ALYSSUM

Height: 4-8 in.   Areas: N, C, S

Although sweet alyssum can be transplanted successfully, it is best to sow its seeds where they will grow. The seedlings are delicate and hard to handle. Growing low to the ground in small clusters, sweet alyssum has tiny lilac, white, and violet-purple flowers with a very pleasing fragrance. It is good for borders and as clumps of color in rock gardens. Plant seeds from September through January for blooming October through June. Spray for aphids. Watch for damping-off. Be careful not to overwater.

Rudbeckia hirta 'Gloriosa Daisy'
CONEFLOWER

Height: 2-3 ft.   Areas: N, C, S

With long, coarse leaves and hairy stalks, the gloriosa has 5- to 6-inch-wide daisy-like yellow and gold flowers with dark-red touches. As a border, clumps of color in a rock garden, or for cut flowers, gloriosa daisies are extremely rewarding. Hardy and easily grown, they like enriched, moist soil in sun and partial shade and grow to 2 to 3 feet in height. Plant seeds or divisions in late summer or fall for spring and summer blossoms. Watch for crown rot, aphids, and caterpillars.

Salvia azurea
BLUE SAGE

Height: 1½-3 ft.   Areas: N, C, S

One of the most enduring and trouble-free perennials, the blue salvia can be grown easily from seed. The mature plant will bloom year after year, an unending source of exquisite, delicate, violet-blue flowers on thin stems more than 3 feet long. Blue salvia will self-seed, producing many seedlings that can be transplanted to other desired areas of the garden. A hardy plant, the blue salvia likes good, moist soil in sun and partial shade. Plant seeds September through June for mature flowers from March through October. Thrips are about the only problem affecting this plant.

Coneflower (Rudbeckia)

Blue sage

Stokesia laevis
STOKES ASTER

Height: 10-12 in.   Areas: N, C, S

The perennial aster has purplish stems covered with short, whitish hairs. It grows to 12 inches in height, with 3-inch blooms on the end of each branch. The Stokes aster is hardy and likes well-drained soil in sun or partial shade. Flowers come in shades of lavender-blue, pink, white, and yellow. Plant seeds or root divisions from September through March for a mass of delicate flowers all summer long. As with many other perennials, it's better to introduce nurtured aster plants than to start from seed. If you divide established aster roots, you'll have more plants every three years.

Verbena sp.
VERBENA

Height: 6-8 in.   Areas: N, C, S

Growing only 8 inches high, verbena is excellent as a border plant, in rock gardens, and in planter boxes. This sprawling plant has hairy, fragrant, serrated leaves with tiny flowers compacted in globular heads. The red, pink, and white flowers often have "eyes" that make them interesting items in the garden. These hardy plants prefer good, moist soil in sun or partial shade. Plant seeds or cuttings from August to December for January-through-July blooming. Spray for red spiders and leafhoppers, a major hazard for verbena.

Verbena

Periwinkles

Vinca sp.
PERIWINKLE

Height: ½-2 ft.   Areas: N, C, S

Bush and creeping periwinkles have some similar characteristics: glossy, oblong, dark-green leaves with everblooming, small lavender-pink-and-white flowers that are tubular and flat-faced. The bush type can be used as a substitute for shrubs in landscaping, while the creeping type is an excellent ground cover. Both can be attractive in pots and planters, too. Seeds or cuttings should be planted in spring for year-round flowering. This tender plant does well in sun or shade, is tolerant of various soil and moisture conditions, and has few problems; the main disease is blight. Periwinkles are very salt-tolerant and will reseed.

BULBS

If you're new to the state, you might not think that Florida is a particularly "bulbous" place. Granted, you can't really grow jonquils and hyacinths here, and tulips require extra-special care in our state.

Still, there are a number of bulbs that do well in Florida. The following, with the exception of the finicky-but-popular tulip, are some of the best bulbs for our state.

Agapanthus africanus
AFRICAN LILY

Height: 1½-2 ft.   Areas: N (protected), C, S

If you like large, beautiful blue or white flowers, this bulb is ideal. The lily-like flowers may reach 2 inches in length. African lilies should be protected in north Florida, but do well in central and southern portions of the state. They seem to flower best in partial shade. The clumps are usually divided every 2 to 3 years for best results. Like many bulbs, the African lily seems to grow best in an improved, organic soil. They should be planted from October through March, and bloom during the spring.

Alocasia sp.
ELEPHANT EAR

Height: 3-8 ft.   Areas: N (protected), C, S

These plants — which grow from rhizomes and tubers — have humongous leaves that really do resemble elephant ears in size and shape. They do best in moist soil. They are vigorous growers that may overtake a garden if not kept in check; still, for a tropical look, they can add much to the look of your landscape. They should be planted in full sun to partial shade. Elephant ears may be killed to the ground in northern Florida, but they grow like weeds in central and southern parts of the state.

Crinum sp.
CRINUM

Height: 3-5 ft.   Areas: N, C, S

The crinum lily is a Florida native that has large, strap-like leaves similar to the amaryllis, but the crinum grows much larger, up to 3 to 5 feet in height. This hardy bulb is sometimes called the swamp lily. Crinums flower best in full sun and bloom in spring to early fall, about two months after planting. The flower, which looks like a string lily, is white with rose-pink tinges. Like amaryllises, crinums may have problems with red blotch and should be dug and sorted every few years; discard the diseased bulbs and replant the healthy bulbs in a new perennial bed of improved soil.

Eucharis grandiflora
AMAZON LILY

Height: 1½-2 ft.   Areas: N, C, S

Amazon lilies are not seen here as often as amaryllises, but they are worth the effort it takes to grow them. These lilies have star-shaped flowers that are waxy, white, and quite fragrant. Each flower may be up to 3 inches across at maturity. Amazon lilies normally grow to 2 feet in height, are planted in the spring, and flower in midwinter. Plant them 1½ feet apart and about 4 inches deep. They are rather tender; a heavy frost has been known to kill these plants. The Amazon lily, a native of South America, does have some problems with fungal leaf spot.

Gloriosa sp.
GLORIOSA LILY

Height: 3-6 ft.   Areas: N, C, S

The gloriosa is a tuber that is grown throughout the state. The flowers are striped crimson and yellow. Planting time for the gloriosa is usually January through April. Plant them about 1 foot apart and 4 inches deep. The gloriosa blooms from spring through fall. They may be dug up and reset each season, or left in the ground. Gloriosas normally need some type of trellis for support.

Haemanthus multiflorus
BLOOD LILY

Height: 2-3 ft.   Areas: N, C, S

The blood lily is a true bulb that should be planted with the tip just above the soil surface. It is grown throughout Florida. Planted in the spring, it will exhibit a bright red bloom during the summer. The blood lily seems to do best in partial shade. During the winter it should be kept somewhat on the dry side. Fertilization should be done during the growing season.

Hippeastrum sp.
AMARYLLIS

Height: 1½-2½ ft.   Areas: N, C, S

The amaryllis is one of the best bulbs for this state. It is planted from October through February, which prompts it to produce flowers from as early as March through May. (It usually takes about two months from the time of planting to the time of blooming.) Amaryllises have large flowers that can reach up to 6 to 8 inches in width. The flower emerges from the center of the bulb. Amaryllises perform best in partial shade.

The amaryllis should be planted with one-third to one-half of the bulb above the ground. Because of this exposure, some of the bulbs may develop red blotch; these diseased bulbs must be dug up and discarded. After a few years in one site, healthy amaryllis bulbs should be dug up and replanted in a new bed with improved soil.

Iris sp.
IRIS

Height: 1-2 ft.   Areas: N, C

Most of the irises grown in the northern part of the country do not do well here; still, there are some native irises and some Louisiana irises that seem to like our state; consult your nurseryman for specifics about these irises. They should be planted in semi-shade in the summer or fall for spring blooms.

Iris

Lilium sp.
LILY

Height: 1-2 ft.   Areas: N, C, S

There are a number of true lilies that do well in Florida, such as the Easter lily, madonna lily, regal lily, and the Formosan lily. Florida even has a native species called the pine lily, which is seen in the moist flatwoods during the end of summer and the beginning of fall. Lily flower colors include white, yellow, orange, and red. Most of these lilies will grow in full sun or partial shade. Plant them between 3 to 6 inches deep.

Narcissus Tazetta
NARCISSUS

Height: 12-18 in.   Areas: N, C

These bulbs, which bloom in hues of cream, white, yellow, and orange, are grown in full sun to partial shade. Narcissuses should be planted at a depth of 4 inches, and from 8 to 10 inches apart. True daffodils do not grow well in Florida; these look-alikes may be planted in September through December for spring blooms.

Sprekelia formosissima
AZTEC LILY

Height: 2-2½ ft.   Areas: N, C, S

This bulb is grown throughout the state and can be planted year-round. Normally, Aztec lilies are set 3 to 4 inches deep and spaced between 6 to 12 inches apart. The blood-red flower makes it a real attention-getter. This lily blooms during the spring and summer, and has been known to bloom more than once during the summertime. The Aztec lily makes an excellent potted specimen.

Narcissuses

Tulips

Tulipa sp.
TULIP

Height: 6-12 in.　　　Areas: N, C

Tulips flower poorly in southern Florida, but in north Florida and in some central parts of the state, the tulip bulb can be grown. Although they are considered perennials, tulips are more properly treated as annuals here. If you want to give these delicate bulbs a try, plant them from December through January, about 5 inches deep and 8 inches apart in improved soil. Prior to planting, the bulbs must be chilled for 60 days at 40 degrees, or for 120 days at 50 degrees.

Rosa sp.
ROSE

Height: 1-10 ft.　　　Areas: N, C, S

While the preceding perennials have been listed alphabetically, I have saved for last what some gardeners consider the best: the rose. Roses come in so many varieties, with new ones appearing each year, that it would be impossible to list them all. However, a visit to a nursery should help you make the best selections for your particular landscape.

Here, you'll find details about the different types of roses and hints on buying, planting, and caring for these plants.

Peace rose

Apollo yellow rose

Lavender Lace rose

Improved cultivars have increased the long-standing appreciation of roses. Because Florida has a year-round gardening climate, the rose is an evergreen shrub here that will continue to increase its flower yield for at least 5 to 10 years; some rose bushes have been known to grow for 20 years and still produce prize-winning blooms.

In central and southern Florida, roses grow and bloom all year. (Two recommended ever-blooming varieties are the Fortuniana and the Dr. Huey.) Even in northern Florida, roses bloom for nine months of the year and retain some of their foliage during the winter. A rose shrub can produce a greater abundance of blooms than other flowering shrubs. You receive five to seven bloom cycles per year with the average rose bush.

Roses are moderate- to high-maintenance plants in Florida, and caring for them properly is important. Also, the plants usually grow larger here and, therefore, should be allowed more growing space than is recommended for other parts of the country.

Banking is not necessary for winter protection, but trellising is necessary to reduce wind injury on climbing and tall varieties of roses.

Plant roses where they will receive direct sunlight at least six hours daily. Where shading is sometimes unavoidable, morning sun is preferred because it will dry the dew on the leaves and lessen the chance of black spot. Open areas

Rose gardens, such as this backyard expanse, require at least six hours of direct sunlight daily.

are also preferred so the roots of nearby plants will not compete for nutrients. Roses should be planted in well-drained soils, not in marsh areas. Sometimes by ditching or raising the bed levels, minor drainage problems can be improved. Our native sandy soils have low water-and-nutrient capacities, and nutrients are easily leached beyond the roots during heavy rains. Such soils can be improved with soil amendments; I recommend peat, dehydrated cow manure, wood shavings, or sawdust. Add as much as 4 to 6 inches of any of these materials, or any combination of two or more, to improve the soil.

Hybrid Tea Roses

When people think of roses, it is the tea rose that springs to many minds. The tea rose is very popular and grown throughout the world. Growing from 3 to 5 feet in height, hybrid tea roses produce flowers that are large and beautifully proportioned. Many of the flowers have a medium to strong fragrance. Tea rose plants have glossy, dark-green foliage. Literally hundreds of varieties are available, with new hybrids being introduced by major nurseries each year. A circular rose bed, from 12 to 20 feet in diameter, located in full sun and in the middle of a lawn, can become the focal point of any garden and a source of joy and admiration for many years. Most tea rose bushes can be spaced 3 feet apart. This leaves enough room for pruning and picking flowers and to allow the bush to branch out and make a compact, attractive display in your landscape.

Confidence (hybrid tea)

Royal Highness (hybrid tea)

Summer Sunshine (hybrid tea)

Olympiad (hybrid tea)

Grandifloras

Closely resembling the hybrid tea rose, the grandiflora grows 5 to 8 feet in height and flowers on long stems, singly or in clusters. These make excellent background plantings in a rose garden.

Floribundas

These are known as "landscaping" roses because of their neat, compact habit. They grow to only 2 to 3 feet in height. The roses appear in clusters and are ideal for low borders and massed plantings.

Climbers

Not actually vines, climbing roses usually are trained and tied to a fence or trellis. There are standard and miniature climbing varieties as well as climbers in every standard rose color. Don Juan is one of my favorite varieties.

Queen Elizabeth (grandiflora)

Europeana (floribunda)

Prominent (floribunda)

Pink Perfection (floribunda)

First Edition (floribunda)

Miniature roses

Miniatures

Planted in the ground or in pots around a patio, miniature roses are identical to standard varieties except for their smaller size. If grown in containers, miniatures require protection in sub-freezing weather.

How to Buy Roses

Always buy your roses from a reputable nursery to avoid disappointment and poor-quality bushes. Roses are graded with numbers: 1, 1½ and 2. Number 1 bushes are the best, with sound roots and vigorous canes. Number 1½ will be intermediate in quality, and Number 2 will be weak and slow to produce good blooms. Although Number 1 grade roses cost a little more, they are well worth it.

Packaged bare-rooted rose bushes demand greater care in planting and take longer to establish than roses already in containers. Bare-rooted roses are cheaper, but you will have to wait longer before you can pick your first rose.

Container-grown roses are the best buy. Not only can you see the rose in flower when you buy it, but you are assured a healthy and vigorous bush. For

MR. GREEN THUMB RULE

Make sure your roses will receive at least six hours of direct sunlight daily; morning sun is preferred.

best root development, select a bush in a 5-gallon container. The 2-gallon containers are also good, though not as advanced as those in 5-gallon pots.

The tag on the rose bush may read "All America Rose Selection." This is your assurance of a good rose bush. The designation means the rose has been tested and has out-performed other varieties in an assortment of soils and climates. Generally, AARS winners are good investments for your rose garden.

Planting Roses

The best planting seasons for roses are winter and spring, four to six weeks before the truly cold weather or the last freeze occurs. Position the plants in full sun. Shady locations promote lanky growth, poor flowering, and disease. If your garden suffers from poor drainage, plant your roses in raised beds. Use masonry or railroad ties as an edging to allow a rise of 6 to 8 inches above surrounding soil. Soil for a rose garden should be loose and well-drained, preferably a sandy loam. Add a 4- to 6-inch layer of peat moss, shreaded bark, compost, or other organic matter and mix with a rototiller to a depth of 10 to 15 inches. Rake out rocks and debris and treat the soil with Vapam to kill nematodes and weeds. Be sure to wait at least three weeks after using Vapam to allow the fumigant to dissipate. Otherwise, you will kill your roses.

The spacing between roses should be determined by the variety. Your nurseryman can advise you on this. In general, floribundas can be spaced 30 to 36 inches apart. Other varieties may need 4 to 5 feet of space between each plant. Roses are very selfish plants and do well with adequate room. Do not mix other types of flowers in your rose bed; you'll only be asking for trouble!

Roses in a field

Plant bushes so their bud unions are slightly out of the soil. This usually is the same height at which they were growing in the nursery. (Duplicate the same planting depth that is present in the container.) Remove any damaged roots and limbs and apply a root-stimulating fertilizer with plenty of water immediately after planting. To ensure that there are no air pockets in the hole you dig, fill the hole first with water, then sink the rose bush into it carefully, and thoroughly pack the soil. This will set your rose bush firmly in the ground and enable it to get a good start.

Roses should be watered well year-round. Spring and fall waterings ensure good blooming. Summer watering is essential to keep the plants alive, and mid-winter watering protects the roots against cold-weather injury. (Mulching helps, too.)

When watering, concentrate on the soil, not on the foliage. Moisture on the leaves promotes disease, especially black spot, for which you will need to spray with a good fungicide. Soaker hoses or trickle irrigation methods are excellent for watering roses.

Roses, like all other plants, need regular feeding. Apply a good rose fertilizer when the plants begin growing in the spring, and continue feeding every four to six weeks through late summer. A balanced formula such as 12-12-12, or one that is slightly richer in phosphorus, such as 12-10-20, is recommended. Apply ½ to 1 pound of fertilizer per 100 square feet of bed space, applying in four-to-six-week intervals except in the heat of midsummer. A systemic fertilizer/insecticide such as Orthene is highly recommended. It can prevent many of the numerous problems that afflict rose bushes.

While fungicides control black spot, prevention is easier than cure. Providing good air circulation and keeping water off the leaves are two ways to minimize black spot, a major problem in Florida.

Many roses develop powdery mildew, a white, crusty fungal organism that looks like flour dusted on the leaf surface. Some fungicides may help with powdery mildew. Consult your nurseryman for latest recommendations. It is best to change fungicides from time to time. Some suggestions: Karathane, zineb, and maneb.

Cooler weather can bring insect damage from aphids. In summer, leaf-cutting bees attack. Regular spraying with a good insecticide such as malathion can control these pests. Always spray in the evenings to minimize the chance of "burned" foliage.

MR. GREEN THUMB RULE

Prune roses during the dormant season, from December through late January.

Pruning Rose Bushes

Roses demand constant vigilance and pruning. The pruning should be done several times during the year. Most bush roses are pruned in mid-to-late winter, four to six weeks after the last frost. Climbing roses should be pruned immediately after their flush-of-spring blooms.

Prune hybrid tea and grandiflora roses (1) by removing all weak, spindly stems (canes), and (2) by reducing the overall height of the bushes to 18 to 24 inches. Always cut right above a bud that faces away from the center of the plant, so the branching that develops will spread away from the crown of the rose bush. Seal the cut ends with clear shellac or with white wood glue. You also should prune during the growing season, removing old flower heads and weak growth.

Floribundas should be pruned less severely. Remove weak growth and prune the entire plant down to a uniform height for better landscape appearance.

Climbing roses demand a different technique. Remove weak, spindly twigs that develop along the stems and prune back the most vigorous canes to about 4 or 5 feet. Climbers should be pruned only *after* they begin flowering. Pruning in winter before they flower will remove the flowering wood, and your climbers will not blossom.

PERENNIALS FOR FLORIDA

COMMON NAME	SCIENTIFIC NAME	COLOR	SUN OR SHADE
Alyssum, Sweet	Lubularia maritima	White, Lilac, Violet	Sun
Amaryllis	Amaryllis sp.	White, Pink, Red	Partial Shade
Aster, Stokes	Stokesia laevis	Pink, White, Yellow, Lavender, Blue	Sun
Beloperone	Beloperone sp.	Red, White, Yellow	Sun to Partial Shade
Blanket Flower	Gaillardia sp.	Orange, Yellow, Red	Sun
Caladium	Caladium sp.	White, Green, Red, Pink Stripes	Partial Sun to Shade
Canna	Canna sp.	Red, Orange, Rose, Yellow, White	Sun
Carnation	Dianthus Carophyllus	Red, Orange, Rose, Yellow, White	Sun to Partial Shade
Chrysanthemum	Chrysanthemum sp.	Red, Orange, Rose, Yellow, White	Sun to Partial Shade
Coleus	Coleus sp.	Lilac, Blue	Partial Shade
Coneflower	Rudbeckia hirta 'Gloriosa Daisy'	Gold, Yellow	Sun to Partial Shade
Crocus, Fall	Colchicum autumnale	White, Blue, Yellow, Purple	Sun to Partial Shade
Dahlia	Dahlia sp.	White, Yellow, Red, Pink	Sun to Partial Shade
Daisy, Shasta	Chrysanthemum x superbum	White, Yellow Center	Sun
Daisy, Transvaal (Gerber)	Gerbera Jamesonii	Red, Orange, Pink, White, Violet	Sun to Partial Shade
Daylily	Hemerocallis sp.	Yellow, Orange	Sun to Partial Shade
Garlic, Society	Tulbaghia violacea	Lavender	Sun to Partial Shade
Gazania	Gazania sp.	White, Red, Yellow, Brown	Sun to Partial Shade
Gladiolus	Gladiolus sp.	Yellow, Red, Lavender, White, Pink	Sun
Hyacinth	Hyacinthus sp.	Blue, White	Sun

AREAS	HEIGHT	HARDINESS	PLANTING SEASON	SUGGESTED SPACE BETWEEN PLANTS	PROBLEMS
N,C,S	4″-8″	Hardy	Sept-Jan	6″-8″	Aphids
N,C,S	1½′-2½′	Hardy	Oct-Feb	1′-2′	Red Blotch, Caterpillars
N,C,S	10″-12″	Hardy	Sept-March	1′	Aphids, Root rot
N,C,S	4′-8′	Tender	Year-round	3′-5′	Caterpillars, Aphids
N,C,S	12″-30″	Hardy	Nov-Jan	12″-24″	Aphids
N,C,S	1′-2′	Tender	March-June	6″-1′	Aphids, Nematodes
N,C,S	2′-5′	Tender	Nov-Feb	1′-4′	Caterpillars
N,C,S	1′-3′	Hardy	June-Jan	8″-12″	Aphids, Mites
N,C,S	2′-3′	Hardy	Feb-April	1′-2′	Mites, Aphids, Nematodes, Thrips
N,C,S	1′-1½′	Tender	Year-round	1′-2′	Mites, Mealybugs, Aphids
N,C,S	2′-3′	Hardy	July-Oct	12″-18″	Aphids, Caterpillars
N	4″-8″	Hardy	Nov-Jan	2″-3″	Dislikes excessive heat
N,C,S	2′-5′	Tender	Feb-April	2′-3′	Powdery mildew, Aphids, Nematode
N,C,S	1½′-2′	Hardy	Jan-May	1½′-2′	Caterpillars, Aphids
N,C,S	6″-18″	Hardy	Sept-Jan	10″-15″	Leaf miners, Crown rot, **Nematodes**
N,C,S	1′-2′	Hardy	Year-round	1½′-2′	Nematodes
N,C,S	8″-18″	Hardy	Feb-Oct	6″-2′	Aphids, Garlic odor
N,C,S	6″-18″	Tender	Feb-Sept	8″-2′	Mites, Aphids
N,C,S	1′-4′	Tender	Frost free; Year-round	6″-8″	Caterpillars, Thrips, Corm rot
N	4″-6″	Hardy	Fall, Winter	2″-3″	Dislikes excessive heat

PERENNIALS FOR FLORIDA

COMMON NAME	SCIENTIFIC NAME	COLOR	SUN OR SHADE
Larkspur	Delphinium sp.	White, Blue, Lavender	Sun to Partial Shade
Lily, Amazon	Eucharis grandiflora	White	Partial Shade
Lily, Calla	Zantedeschia sp.	White, Yellow, Pink	Partial Shade
Lily, Spider	Crinum sp.	White, Rose	Sun
Lily, Zephyr (Rain)	Zephyranthes sp.	Red, Yellow, Pink, White	Sun to Partial Shade
Lisianthus	Lisianthus sp.	White, Blue, Pink	Sun
Manaos Beauty	Centratherum	Blue	Sun to Partial Shade
Narcissus	Polyanthus Narcissus	White, Yellow	Partial Shade
Periwinkle	Vinca sp.	White, Pink, Lavender	Sun to Partial Shade
Poppy, Mexican Tulip	Hunnemannia fumariifolia	Gold, Yellow	Sun
Rose	Rosa sp.	Many colors	Sun
Rose, Climbing	Rosa sp.	Many colors	Sun
Rose, Floribunda	Rosa sp.	Many colors	Sun
Rose, Grandiflora	Rosa sp.	Many colors	Sun
Rose, Hybrid Tea	Rosa sp.	Many colors	Sun
Rose, Miniature	Rosa sp.	Many colors	Sun
Sage, Blue	Salvia azurea	White, Violet	Sun to Partial Shade
Shellflower	Alpinia Speciosa	Pink	Partial Shade
Tickseed	Coreopsis sp.	Yellow, Maroon Center	Sun to Partial Shade
Tulip	Tulipa sp.	Just about all	Partial Shade
Verbena	Verbena sp.	Pink, White, Red	Sun to Partial Shade

AREAS	HEIGHT	HARDINESS	PLANTING SEASON	SUGGESTED SPACE BETWEEN PLANTS	PROBLEMS
N,C,S	3'-5'	Hardy	Oct-Dec	1'-2'	Caterpillars, Mites, Crown rot
N,C,S	1½'-2'	Tender	Feb-March	12"-18"	Leaf spot fungus
N,C,S	2'-2½'	Tender	Feb-April	1'-2'	Thrips, Red spider mites
N,C,S	3'-5'	Hardy	Feb-Oct	2'-4'	Red spider mites, Red blotch
N,C,S	6"-10"	Hardy	Feb-Oct	6"-15"	Lubber grasshoppers
N,C,S	18"-3'	Hardy	Year-round	18"-3'	Aphids, Root rot
N,C,S	2'-2½'	Tender	All year	1'-2'	Leafhoppers
N,C	12"-18"	Hardy	Dec, Jan, Feb	2"-4"	Nematodes (Dig bulbs each season)
N,C,S	6"-2'	Tender	Feb-Aug	1'	Red spider mites, Leafhoppers
N,C,S	1'-2'	Hardy	Nov-Dec	12"	Aphids
N,C,S	See below	See below	See below	See below	See below
N,C,S	5'-10'	Hardy	Year-round	3'-8'	Black spot, powdery mildew
N,C,S	2'-3'	Hardy	Year-round	3'-5'	Black spot, powdery mildew
N,C,S	5'-8'	Hardy	Year-round	3'-5'	Black spot, powdery mildew
N,C,S	3'-5'	Hardy	Year-round	3'-5'	Black spot, powdery mildew
N,C,S	1'-2'	Hardy	Year-round	1'-2'	Black spot, powdery mildew
N,C,S	18"-3'	Hardy	Sept-July	1'-1½'	Aphids, Thrips
C,S	3'-8'	Tender	Year-round	3'-5'	Caterpillars
N,C,S	10"-30"	Hardy	Oct-May	6"-12"	Aphids, Mites, Leaf beetles
N,C	6"-12"	Hardy	Dec-Jan	6"-8"	Aphids, Root rot
N,C,S	6"-8"	Hardy	July-Dec	1'	Red spider mites

CHAPTER SEVEN

Orchids

The most exotic flower in the world is the orchid. Luckily, with our climate, these showy bloomers may be grown here easily. The orchid has a unique growth habit, breathtakingly delicate petals, and a wide variety of shapes and color combinations. Orchids are the second largest family of plants on Earth, exceeded only by grains and grasses in the number of varieties.

Orchids grow in almost every size, shape, and color, but still maintain certain common botanical characteristics. The orchid has a six-part flower with three sepals and three petals. One petal is always different in shape and color from the other two; it's frequently the lower part or the lip of the flower.

Both stem and pistil of an orchid are found in a fused column. The column produces tiny, dust-like seeds in a three-part seed capsule that contains as many as two million seeds. Essentially a tropical plant growing in jungles from South America to Hawaii and Africa, the orchid is as tough as many succulents and cacti. Still it needs certain conditions to flourish and produce its prized flowers.

TYPES AND VARIETIES

Orchids are divided into two overall types: sympodial and monopodial. The sympodial orchid normally grows on a rhizome or creeping stem. From these aerial branches will emerge both leaf and flower. The monopodial type has a swollen, bulbous tissue called a pseudobulb. Monopodial orchids grow from one erect stem that will lengthen each year, producing additional flowers and leaves in erect clusters.

Orchids are further divided into epiphytic and terrestrial types. Most of the showier orchids grown in Florida are classified as epiphytic, meaning they grow above the ground in trees, baskets, pots, and other containers, without the use of soil. Instead, these orchids are planted in a combination of organic materials, such as tree ferns; shreds or chunks of bark and osmundine fiber; or mixtures of bark, coconut husks, styrofoam chips, and porous rock.

Major epiphytic varieties include *Cattleya,* the most commonly grown orchid for the hobbyist; *Dendrobium,* with showy sprays of flowers that often last for weeks; *Epidendrum,* which has a wide array of beautiful colors; *Oncidium,* an American genus; and *Phalaenopsis,* sometimes known as the moth orchid.

Cattleya orchids

Terrestrial orchids are also grown here in Florida. For greatest success, you should plant this type in a well-drained mixture of soil and peat moss.

The most common terrestrial orchids in our state include the *Phaius,* or nun's orchid, which is easily grown; *Cymbidium; Calanthe; Terete* types of *Vandaceous* orchids; some *Epidendrums;* and several others that have exquisite combinations of colors and shapes.

CULTIVATION AND CARE TIPS

It takes five to seven *years* for an orchid to bloom from seed. Trying to grow your own plants is slow and tedious at best. Orchids are propagated in three ways: 1) by seed germination in sterile bottles containing nutrients; 2) by dividing mature plants into two or more divisions; and 3) by tissue culture, a reproductive technique that's also known as cloning. Cloning involves stimulation of a tiny propagation "eye" or tip in a sterile bottle; the tip must then be divided regularly as it grows in this artificial, hospital-like atmosphere. This last method is complicated, and is best left to the orchid experts.

Most orchid hobbyists start their collections with nursery-grown plants. Since there is such a wide variety of orchids available, it is best to buy a mature plant in bloom. That way, you can select the variety and coloration you prefer. A developed orchid plant bought at a nursery will yield flowers the following year.

In the central and southern parts of Florida, good shade trees are all that you need to grow orchids. *Cattleyas, Dendrobiums, Oncidiums,* and most of the *Vandaceous* types will thrive in the protection of oaks, citrus trees, and most other shady varieties growing near the house. Some of the *Vandaceous* orchids even do well in full sunlight.

On nights when temperatures drop to frost or freezing, you must bring your orchids inside. Almost all orchids can withstand temperatures down into the low 30s without damage, unless they are fully exposed to frost and unprotected from the sky. Still, they cannot withstand freezing temperatures of any kind.

In northern Florida, orchids can be grown outside during most of the year, but permanent cold protection must be provided during the winter. Some orchid hobbyists in the northern part of the state leave their orchids outdoors for the bulk of the year, bringing them into the house only when the temperature drops to freezing.

WATERING ORCHIDS

For the most part, orchids need a good deal of water. Most growers water their orchids every couple of days, allowing the plants to dry out a bit between waterings. During the warm months, orchids may require even more water, depending on the amount of heat and air flow to which they're exposed.

Since epiphytic orchids grow naturally in the trees of tropical jungles, they are accustomed to drawing moisture from the surrounding air. To approximate this atmospheric condition, many growers use a breaker-bar watering system for

Miltonia orchids

Epidendrum orchid   *Vandaceous* orchid

their orchids. The breaker bar is a long, metal bar that has a shower head on the end; this system allows the orchid hobbyist to water his or her plants in a gentle, economical manner.

Other growers water via a hose that serves a dual purpose. These gardeners syphon a liquid fertilizer into the hose, then water and fertilize their specimens simultaneously. Terrestrial orchids are often watered and fertilized in this manner.

FEEDING ORCHIDS

Whether you use the hose-fertilization method or not, these plants do need *some* enrichment on a regular basis. (Most orchids grow rather slowly and do not need a great deal of fertilizer.) One of the easiest ways to provide these extra nutrients is to feed the orchids with a liquid plant food — via hose or watering can — once a month during the growing season, from about March through October.

MR. GREEN THUMB RULE

During the winter season, be prepared to move your orchids to a protected area. If you're transferring them to a greenhouse, be prepared to turn on the heat. Most varieties get stunted or killed when exposed to temperatures below 32 degrees.

Phalaenopsis (moth) orchid

USING A GREENHOUSE

Some hobbyists build greenhouses for their orchids. But even though these plants are tropical, orchids cannot survive the high heat and light levels that often build up in enclosed-glass or plastic-covered greenhouses. Shade and ventilation are essential. Most of the better-known orchids will thrive on a *maximum* of 25 to 30 percent direct or filtered sun. Therefore, a greenhouse should have the capacity to provide shade for 70 percent of the daylight hours, with adequate ventilation on the sides and top of the structure.

Commercially built greenhouses usually come equipped with exhaust fans and radiator-like wet pads. Water drips through the pads, cooling and humidifying the air as it enters. Humidity is very important for proper orchid growth, and misting your orchids is recommended. Here, too, orchids should be fertilized lightly once a month during the growing season with a liquid plant food.

FOR MORE INFORMATION

Dozens of organized orchid societies in Florida have members who are willing to help and guide newcomers to the fascinating hobby of growing orchids. A nursery is a good source, too, not only for advice on cultivation, but also for information on an orchid society in your area.

CHAPTER EIGHT

Vegetables

Many people think of a garden as a space that is beautiful with flowers. But to just as many, the word "garden" means "vegetables." There is no reason why you cannot combine flowers *and* vegetables into an attractive picture that will please not only the eye, but the palate, as well. There can be just as much beauty in a well-laid-out array of plants that produce food instead of flowers, and, from an economics standpoint, a vegetable garden can contribute a great savings to your food bill, something not to be overlooked in today's society. For every dollar spent on a vegetable garden, you will reap a $5 to $6 return in value. Not only do fresh, home-grown vegetables save you money, they contain the optimum in health-giving nutrients. Plus, there are fringe fitness benefits to the gardener who *must* exercise in order to prepare, weed, and care for a vegetable garden.

Your first consideration should be the site. It will be determined by the quantity and types of vegetables you want to grow. Of primary importance is exposure. You need at least six hours of full sunlight daily for a productive vegetable garden. Determine which part of your property receives the most sun, then decide how to landscape the rest of the area around this spot. If the appearance of a vegetable patch offends the eye of a flower fancier, you can surround your crop with a 4-foot chain-link fence (or chicken wire). On the fence, vines may be grown to conceal the area behind it, thus maintaining the aesthetic integrity of your flower garden. A row of ligustrum bushes can serve the same purpose.

On the other hand, if your vegetable needs are minimal, you can intersperse flowers with certain types of vegetables, combining both types of plants into an appealing display that fills both your vases and your pantry.

The space allocated for vegetables should be gauged by the preferences of your family. Ask the members of your household which vegetables they prefer. There is no sense in growing bushels of eggplant if only one person likes to eat this vegetable! Once you have made a list of your family's preferences, do a little arithmetic to work out how many plants you will need to produce a sufficient crop during a season. This will help you decide whether you need 2 or 12 tomato plants, 1 or 10 rows of corn, a dozen summer squash plants — or none at all.

When it comes to a vegetable garden, site selection is crucial.

KIDDING AROUND

With the help of my son and daughter, I've found that gardening can be a family affair. Children take special pride in helping their parents cultivate, tend, and harvest a garden.

The best way to introduce kids to gardening is by starting them off with some of the tried-and-true vegetables: lettuce, cucumbers, tomatoes, beans, and radishes (which will sprout in only five days). To spark the children's interest even more, you might want to add a few flowers, such as zinnias or marigolds.

Since children are naturally inquisitive, be sure to explain what is happening in the garden as the flowers and vegetables grow and prosper. For instance, they'll be curious as to how a plant flowers, is pollinated, and then sets fruit. They'll be fascinated to realize that not all vegetables come wrapped in plastic from the grocery store! And it wouldn't hurt to explain to the kids that gardening can be not only a money-saving hobby, but it can also be a great way to relax.

MR. GREEN THUMB RULE

Your vegetable garden will grow that much better if you sit down and draw a plan for the garden first.

PLANNING YOUR GARDEN

Having decided on the number and type of vegetables you will plant, continue your arithmetic and work out the amount of space you need to raise your desired crop. Small as it may sound, an area 6 feet wide and 20 feet long can produce a remarkable amount of food. You do not have to give over half your yard to vegetables. For example, one tomato plant grown in a tub on the patio can produce enough tomatoes for two people for two months or more. A relatively small-sized bed, tucked away at the back of your property, often can be ample space for growing all the vegetables you desire.

Make sure the area you select has easy access to water and is far enough away from trees to avoid problems from roots. Be particularly careful to position your vegetable garden away from living fences, such as honeysuckle, whose roots can extend 6 to 10 feet from the hedge and sap the soil of nutrients.

If you are going to grow vegetables for the first time, start modestly with a small space. A compact, well-maintained, thriving vegetable garden will be far more rewarding and less frustrating than a large, sprawling area that winds up being a backbreaker and produces far more food than you need.

SOIL IMPROVEMENT

Once you know where you will start your vegetable garden, the next step is to prepare the soil. Remember: To grow anything, flowers or vegetables, the results always depend on the quality of the soil.

Make sure your vegetable garden is the right size, has access to water and at least six hours of sunlight daily, and is far enough away from trees to avoid competing with their large, demanding root systems.

Before being planted, your vegetable plot must be cleared of rocks and debris, and rototilled thoroughly.

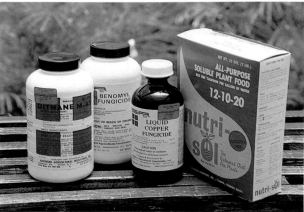

Liquid fertilizers and various fungicides are essential parts of a successful vegetable garden.

Check the pH of your soil and take whatever corrective measures may be necessary to achieve the proper balance for your intended crops. Clear out any rocks and debris, then begin rototilling the soil, adding the following mixture: 25 pounds of peat moss, 25 pounds of cow manure, 25 pounds of colloidal phosphate, 3 pounds of super phosphate, and 3 pounds of quality fertilizer for every 100 square feet of ground space.

After tilling, rake the surface smooth and apply Vapam at the rate of 1 quart for every 100 square feet. Use either a hose-end sprayer or a watering can, applying 1 inch of water over the entire area, then covering the soil with heavy plastic or visqueen. Leave the ground covered for at least 48 hours, then remove the plastic and allow the fumigant to dissipate for at least three weeks before planting.

Once you are ready to plant, your ultimate needs will determine how many plants to start, either from seed or seedlings obtained from your nursery or garden shop. Seeds are most useful if large quantities are desired. Otherwise, purchase plants and position them the correct distance apart according to seed-packet directions. Most nurseries carry six-packs of vegetable seedlings. These often are more than enough for the average family.

VEGETABLE PLANTING

Careful planting will help get the vegetables off to a good start. Make a hole just large enough for a seedling, fill it with water to which you have added liquid fertilizer, such as Nutri-Sol, and sink in the seedling, packing soil gently around the edge until the plant is firmly set in the ground. The liquid fertilizer lessens the possibility of transplant shock.

Once planted, your garden will need watering, fertilizing, and weeding, plus spraying for insects and diseases if and when they appear.

Sixteen essential elements are needed for optimum growth of any living plant. Some fertilizers contain only nitrogen, phosphorus, and potassium, which are the three most important feeding elements. For vegetables, use a 12-10-20 fertilizer that contains the major *and* minor elements, such as calcium, sulfur, magnesium, zinc, and copper. Fertilize every two weeks when your seedlings are small, then taper off as the plants grow. Mature plants need to be fertilized every three to four weeks unless a particular vegetable calls for heavier feeding.

COMBATING PESTS AND WEEDS

Several common insect pests undoubtedly will attack your garden, including the mole cricket and the cutworm. Mole cricket bait should be applied to the soil before planting. Aphids, stink bugs, and leafhoppers succumb to Diazinon or malathion sprays. Dipel (Thuricide) and sevin will control caterpillars, aphids, and worms. Many insect problems appear only after the plants are growing because, obviously, these critters are going to attack only if there is something there for them to eat! However, sterilizing the soil before planting usually gets any garden off to an insect-free, disease-free start.

With all insecticides, be sure to follow label directions. Most of these sophisticated chemicals do a wonderful job of eliminating unwanted insect pests. But, if they are mixed too generously, the chemicals can set back growth, harm leaves, or even kill a plant.

MR. GREEN THUMB RULE

It is important to check the pH of the vegetable-garden soil. Most vegetables grow best with a pH of 5.0 to 7.0. Seven to ten pounds of sulfur will lower the pH one unit; 40 to 65 pounds of dolomite will raise the pH one unit.

Weeding your vegetable garden is necessary not only for looks, but also to avoid wasting soil nutrients on unwanted growth. Watch for weeds between your plants, and remove them as soon as they appear.

WATERING TIPS

As with all other living things, water is of paramount importance to your veggies. People often ask, "How often should I water my vegetables?" Normally, you should water seedlings twice daily because if the seed dries, it dies. This holds true for transplants, too. Most vegetables need at least 1 inch of water per week, but this varies according to the time of year and the amount of actual rainfall we receive.

To make sure you're watering your vegetables properly, you may want to place a rain gauge in your garden, as I have. Check it on a weekly basis, and adjust your watering schedule accordingly. Too, watering with a drip-irrigation system may help lower your water use in the garden by as much as 50 percent.

Many vegetables, such as tomatoes and squash, are more susceptible to fungi and mildew if you water them in the late afternoon, especially if you give their leaves a good spray. This is because, instead of evaporating, the water tends to sit on the foliage all night, creating the perfect breeding ground for these problems.

MULCHING

Mulching helps ensure a bumper crop of vegetables. This practice is particularly important in Florida, where the hot sun can wreak havoc on tender

Different vegetables must be harvested at different times; be sure to keep track of the various maturity dates.

vegetation. Mulching not only conserves moisture and deters weed growth, but it also reduces the soil temperature during the heat of the day. Too, as the mulch breaks down, it improves the organic make-up of your garden soil. Many people use shredded bark, wood chips, well-rotted compost, and even old newspapers; each makes a fine mulch.

HARVESTING YOUR CROP

Once your plants are growing, check the calendar and keep a record of the recommended harvest time for each vegetable. Any edible plant should be harvested just when it reaches the height of maturity, except those vegetables that are designed for earlier harvest. Remember, if crops are allowed to remain on the plant after full maturity, the plant will stop producing and die. To keep a plant producing, you must pick the crop; don't let it linger on the stalk. Your seed-to-harvest times, therefore, are very important if you want your vegetable garden to continue producing all through the season. If you have more vegetables than you can eat, continue picking, and give away the extra veggies instead of leaving them on the plants.

USING GROW BOXES

Growing your vegetables in a ground-level plot is not the only way to raise fresh food. For instance, you might enjoy trying a "grow box." This is a vegetable bed enclosed by 1 x 8-foot boards, concrete blocks, or railroad ties, and filled with near-perfect soil.

A grow box is a great way to cultivate vegetables in a relatively small, controlled environment. You'll encounter fewer problems with weeds here than in the typical vegetable garden.

MR. GREEN THUMB RULE

Some "salad garden" vegetables, such as leaf lettuce, radishes, and cherry tomatoes, require little space. Other vegetables, such as corn, require a lot of space. For best pollination, corn must be planted in blocks.

Grow boxes provide the opportunity to develop the best possible soil in a small area. Ideally, a grow box should contain one-fourth water, one-fourth air, one-fourth mineral, and one-fourth organic material.

Because a grow box does not fit tightly on the ground, excess water easily can drain from beneath the frame. The soil inside remains airy and easy to work, since you do not walk between the plants and compact the ground above the plant roots, as usually happens with ground-level gardens. In addition, plants can extend their root systems below the depth of the soil in the grow box.

And grow-box soil will hold more moisture because of its texture, thereby reducing your watering needs. Building and filling a grow box adds to the initial cost of your vegetable garden, but in the long run, it is well worth it.

A trellis can be built at one end of the grow box and attached to the frame, for climbing vegetables such as beans, pole lima beans, cucumbers, and some melons. A grow box should be placed where it receives at least six hours of full sun daily. Preferably, it should run north and south. Place the trellis, if you build one, at the north end to receive the best light.

Grow boxes are compact gardens, but do not fall into the trap of placing your grow-box plants too close together. Stunted growth and intensified insect problems can result. A regular program of feeding is necessary. Raising vegetables in a grow box is exactly the same as if you plant them in the ground, with the added advantage of having superior soil and better drainage.

As with regular vegetable beds, you can *interplant* crops in a grow box. This refers to placing faster-growing plants between slower-growing varieties. The faster-growing plants can be harvested while the slow crop is still half-grown. Also, planting every two weeks gives you mature vegetables for picking over a longer period of harvest.

A minor variation of the grow box is the "raised bed." The raised bed has an extra layer of porous rubble beneath the soil, which raises the bed even higher off the ground and ensures good drainage. Some gardeners, particularly those with back problems, find the raised beds a great convenience.

OTHER GROWTH METHODS

Container gardening is a great alternative for "green thumbers" who live in townhouses, condominiums, and apartments. Small-space dwellers may not have yards, but that shouldn't stop them from raising a respectable crop of vegetables. In fact, such container gardens are actually easier on the gardener, allowing him or her to provide the vegetables sun, shade, and cold-protection at will. (Simply pick up the pot and move it indoors or out!)

Some vegetable varieties are particularly suited to containerized growth. Sugar Lump tomatoes and Sugar Baby watermelons may be grown in large containers on a porch or balcony. I have used whiskey barrels to grow everything from strawberries and tomatoes to lettuce, scallions, and parsley. For more information on vegetables designed for use by small-space gardeners, look through seed catalogs and check with your nurseryman for his advice.

When planting a balcony vegetable garden, use 5- or 10-gallon containers filled with a quality potting soil. Make sure there is adequate drainage at the bottom of each container; vegetables need a well-drained environment. Too, maintain a regular watering and feeding schedule, and allow your plants to get at least six hours of sunlight each day.

Some ambitious vegetable gardeners build "Japanese rings," ideal if growing space is limited. A Japanese ring is built with two concentric rings of construction-gauge wire, which, when placed in position, make a low circle of soil on the outside of the structure like the imprint of a bundt pan. The inside circle is higher, from 4 to 6 feet tall, and is used as a compost pile. Plant your vegetables in the soil and organic material in the lower, outside ring. Cucumbers or beans are perfect for this type of planting. They will climb the wire on the inside cage for support. Lower-growing vegetables, such as broccoli, cabbage, radishes, and lettuce, can be grown on top of the inside ring containing the compost. As the compost breaks down, it provides valuable nutrients to feed the root systems of the lower, outside ring.

GROWING PLANTS ORGANICALLY

Organic gardening has received much publicity in recent years. The term refers to growing crops without the use of certain chemical insecticides or fertilizers. For the avid environmentalist, this method is laudable, but it involves far more work and dedication. Only pesticides considered safe for the environment are used, such as Dipel (Thuricide), Biotrol, or pyrethrin — all products containing natural insect repellants. Pyrethrin, for example, is found in the foliage of chrysanthemums, giving them their distinctive odor. Pyrethrin sometimes is used as a commercial insecticide.

Organic gardeners feed the soil exclusively with organic substances rather than chemical fertilizers. Compost made from grass clippings, coffee grounds, potato peelings, leaves, small twigs, wood ashes, egg shells, and almost anything else that's organic is combined to provide the needed nutrition for the soil. The problem with this method is the time involved; vegetables need nutrients right away for growth, and unless a compost pile has been planned well in advance, growth will be retarded due to insufficient feeding. Cow or sheep manure provides faster feeding, but horse manure is slow in releasing its nutrients and should be used mainly as a soil builder.

Many conflicting statements have been made regarding the relative merits of organic versus chemical fertilizing of gardens. But any living plant will utilize whatever is available, breaking it down naturally just as the human body uses its metabolism to extract the various elements needed for growth and sustenance.

Another unusual method of gardening is called hydroponics, a newer form of raising vegetables. As the name implies, plants are grown totally in water. Roots never touch soil, but grow in water enriched with chemical nutrients. This method involves a great deal of initial expense and effort, such as building the necessary frames, containers, wire mesh, and aeration equipment. For the home gardener, it is much easier and just as effective to grow vegetables in the traditional manner.

A variation of hydroponics is "aggregate culture." A container is filled with some type of mixed aggregate, such as sand, wood shavings, sawdust, pebbles, and similar items, then filled with water and liquid fertilizer. Again, this is for the esoteric-minded hobbyist rather than the practical gardener who has the land, sufficient space, and time to grow a vegetable garden.

HERBS

Herbs have been grown since biblical times. Not only are the leaves used, but stems and roots often make flavorful additions to food, too. Some seeds and flowers go into perfumes and dyes. Fresh parsley is a favorite herb grown in the vegetable garden for garnishes and for flavoring. Nothing beats fresh mint in iced tea as a flavoring.

Some herbs like a semi-sunny spot, but most should be protected from the hot Florida summer sun. Many do well in flower beds and as hanging baskets and border plants.

Herbs are similar to vegetables in that they require well-draining soil, one that has been improved with organic matter such as peat moss, builder's sand, perlite, or dehydrated cow manure. To get your herbs off to a good start, fumigate the soil with Vapam before planting. Fertilize with a good liquid plant food, lightly, once a month. Many of Florida's favorite herbs may be purchased in seed packages or as potted seedlings at your local nursery or garden center.

HERB VARIETIES FOR FLORIDA

There are so many herbs in the horticultural world; it would be virtually impossible to explain each one in detail. The following perennial and annual herb varieties are some of the best for our state.

Perennial Herbs
CATNIP
Tea, made from the leaves of the catnip plant, is said to aid digestion. And cats *do* love it.
CHAMOMILE (Roman)
This herb has delightful, fragrant foliage.
CHICORY (Large-rooted Magdeburg)
Also called coffee chicory, this plant's dried roots are used as a substitute for, or in addition to, coffee.

CHIVE

The delicate, onion-flavored foliage of this herb is used for flavoring and garnishing soups, potatoes, salads, etc. The chives' lavender flower heads are lovely in the garden, too.

CHRYSANTHEMUM *(Cinerarilfolium)*

The petals of this herb are the primary sources of pyrethrin, a natural insecticide.

COMFREY (Russian)

Its leaves are high in vitamins and minerals. Russian comfrey is a reputed remedy for sore throats, wounds, and other internal and external maladies.

WATER CRESS (True)

This plant's tangy leaves are often used for garnishes and salads.

DANDELION

Dandelion leaves are frequently used in salads. They also are used to make wine.

FENNEL (Sweet)

Sweet fennel leaves are a common garnish, and are sprinkled into fish sauces for added zest.

HOREHOUND

The grayish leaves of the horehound plant are employed to make candies and cough remedies.

LAVENDER (Munstead strain)

Its dwarf, deep lavender flowers are delightfully fragrant.

LAVENDER (Vera)

This herb has pleasantly scented, lilac flowers, which are often dried to make sachets. It has attractive, gray-green foliage, too.

LOVAGE

Its aromatic seeds are used in cakes.

ONION (Welch bunching)

These are sweet, mild onions. For a tangy treat, add the bulbs, stalks, and leaves to your favorite salad.

OREGANO

This herb has thick, strongly aromatic, green leaves, which often flavor Italian dishes. Oregano yields lavender-pink flowers.

PEPPERMINT

The oil from the peppermint plant is used to flavor candies.

Oregano

Peppermint

ROSEMARY

Rosemary is an evergreen, "sub-shrub" with pale blue flowers. It frequently seasons pork and lamb dishes.

SAGE

This broad-leaf herb grows to 2½ feet in height, and yields blue flowers. It is widely used as a seasoning for poultry, beef, and sausage.

SAVORY (Winter)

This evergreen, which grows to a foot in height, is a good flavoring for beans.

SOAPWORT

Soapwort is an elegant trailing plant, with showy, rose-like flowers in the spring. It is used to make homemade soap.

SPEARMINT

This herb is used to flavor beverages, sauces, and meats.

TANSY

Tansy leaves are used fresh as a dye, and dried as an insect repellent.

TARRAGON (Russian)

This plant is employed as a seasoning for salads, chicken, and fish.

THYME (English)

This is excellent for flavoring lamb and other meat dishes.

Annual Herbs

ANISE

The anise plant has white flowers. It is used to flavor drinks and pastries.

BASIL

This is the "good basil" of French cuisine. With its small, tender, sweet leaves, it is the fragrant friend of the tomato.

Basil

BASIL (Dark opal)

A fine flavoring, dark opal basil has deep purple leaves, and makes an attractive bed or border in the garden.

BASIL (Sweet)

A very fragrant, handsome plant, this basil is a common seasoning.

BORAGE

The borage plant yields blue flowers. The leaves are used as a flavorful cooking additive. In the garden, this herb attracts bees.

CHERVIL (Curled)

Curled chervil often adds zest to eggs, chicken, and vegetables.

CUMIN

Its seeds are used to flavor curry dishes.

DILL

Dill seeds are employed in the pickling process; its leaves often flavor fish or potato dishes.

PEPPER GRASS (also Curled cress)

Its bright green leaves add tang to salads. Pepper grass may be grown indoors on a sponge or blotter.

MARJORAM (Sweet)

This herb yields sweet flowers on purple spikes. Its leaves flavor sauces, meats, and vegetables.

PEPPER (Chili, Serrano)

Also known as the Tobasco pepper, this is the small-but-pungent ingredient found in Mexican hot sauces.

SAVORY (Summer)

Summer savory is an aromatic topping for many foods, including vegetables.

Dill

Marjoram

Bush beans

VEGETABLE VARIETIES FOR FLORIDA

What follows is a selection of popular vegetables that can be grown successfully in Florida, plus a chart listing varieties and planting dates.

Beans (Lima or Butter)

Lima beans need a rich soil and prefer a warmer and more humid climate than snap beans. They are fairly drought-resistant, but they suffer from insect damage.

Beans (Snap)

Grown as bushes, or pole beans, which need support, snap beans also come in wax-podded varieties. Pole beans are considered to have a better taste, and they freeze very well.

Beans need a fertile soil with ample organic matter, good moisture, and lime. Bush beans require 50 to 60 days from planting to harvest. Pole beans take a little longer. Both varieties can be grown in most of Florida if planted in September or early October. Pole beans often are planted in the spring as soon as the danger of frost is past. More than one planting is suggested to extend the harvest season. Beans are a tender crop and suffer from bean leafhoppers, bean leafrollers, Mexican bean beetles, and bean rust.

Beets (Common or Red)

Although beet leaves and stalks make excellent cooking greens, this vegetable is grown for its enlarged tap root, a favorite cooked, cooled, and sliced in salads.

Beets are hardy and need fertile soil. They need very moist soil for good seed germination and are a cool-weather crop. They suffer from nematodes, caterpillars, and occasionally, fungus on the leaves.

Broccoli

Broccoli

A highly nutritious vegetable, broccoli is easy to grow and prepare for cooking. It is a shallow-rooted plant needing a steady supply of moisture and good soil. Broccoli culture is the same as for its relative, the cabbage. Seeds take four to six weeks to grow large enough to transplant, then 60 to 70 days to harvest. Several crops are possible from one plant, though the first harvest is the best. It is the unopened flower buds that are eaten, together with the stems and some of the smaller leaves near the buds. Never allow flowers to develop. Buy the plant in October and, at the same time, plant seeds for a further supply after the first crop is harvested. Broccoli is attacked by caterpillars and other insects and suffers from several diseases.

Brussels Sprouts

Another relative of the cabbage, Brussels sprouts are rather like a tiny cabbage, growing in clusters up a stem. As the heads begin to get crowded, break off the lower leaves to give them more room. Rather sensitive to environmental conditions, Brussels sprouts develop best during cooler weather and do not always yield satisfactorily. They are targets for aphids, caterpillars, plant bugs, and several diseases.

Brussels sprouts

Harvesting Brussels sprouts

Cabbage

High in Vitamin C, very hardy, and easy to grow, cabbage comes recommended for the home gardener. Good soil, abundant moisture, and lots of fertilizer are needed, and cabbage does best during cooler periods. A hardy vegetable, cabbage is best grown in a seedbed. When transplanting, always plant it deeper than it has been growing before. Spray for caterpillars and plant bugs. Cabbage also is prone to several diseases.

Cabbage (Chinese)

For salads or as a cooked vegetable (especially in Chinese dishes), Chinese cabbage is a pleasant change from the ordinary. A very productive, hardy plant, Chinese cabbage prefers moist soil with plenty of organic matter and grows best in the cooler seasons. If planted in dry soil, it will become tough and will bolt (flower) during hot weather. From seed to harvest takes 75 to 85 days. The young seedlings will transplant easily. The only problem, like with most cabbage-type vegetables, is leaf-eating caterpillars.

An abundant cabbage crop

Chinese cabbage is an unusual but tasty garden crop.

Cantaloupe growing in
the garden

Cantaloupe

Cantaloupes (Musk melons)

The smooth honeydew and the netted honeydew are fairly difficult to grow
in Florida. Preferring a warm, dry climate, they do best in the spring before the
humid weather begins, which also can bring on foliage diseases. Tender to cold,
cantaloupes are heavy feeders and need sandy soil, rich in organic matter. Be
sure to plant only those varieties recommended for Florida, and watch for foliage
diseases such as downy mildew and gummy stem blight.

Carrots

Carrots are an excellent source of Vitamin A. They are hardy; require a rich,
deep, well-prepared soil; and should be grown in the cooler time of the year.
Slow-growing, carrot seeds take about 14 days to sprout and 80 to 110 days to
grow to harvest. Thinning out small carrots will allow the remaining plants to
grow larger and longer. Several plantings are recommended for a longer harvest
season. Carrots suffer from some foliage diseases and nematodes.

Cauliflower

Cauliflower

Very similar in culture and problems to the cabbage, the cauliflower is hard to grow and needs a cool season to thrive. To make the head (the curd) white, wait until it has developed to 2 or 3 inches in diameter, then tie the leaves over the head. This will result in the bleached-white color familiar to us all. Cauliflower suffers from several diseases and is attacked by caterpillars and other insects.

Celery

Celery first was used as a medicine. Now it is popular chopped up in salads as well as cooked as a vegetable. Almost a swamp plant, celery germinates in wet soil and grows only in very moist ground that is rich in organic matter. A hungry feeder, it needs several applications of nitrogen fertilizer to thrive, and the soil must be kept very moist throughout the entire growing cycle. A hardy plant, celery should be grown during the cool periods of the year. A slow grower, it takes from 8 to 12 weeks for seeds to develop into plants, and from 100 to 120 *more* days until harvest time. This vegetable suffers from several diseases, and caterpillars eat the tender stalks.

Collards

Collards are cabbages that do not form heads. Their taste is very distinctive and is enjoyed by many people. Collards are hardy and grow best during the winter months, requiring a fertile soil with good moisture. For improved succulence and taste, fertilize liberally. Collards are ready for harvest 50 to 60 days after the plants are set. The tops can be cut off or only the larger leaves, leaving the younger, upper leaves to develop. Collards suffer from several diseases and are plagued by caterpillars and plant bugs.

Corn (Sweet)

Though cold-sensitive, corn is easy to grow and enjoys warm weather; a rich soil with moderate, continuous moisture; and heavy fertilization. It should be planted in a series of two or three parallel rows to ensure pollination. Two or more plantings per season are recommended for continuous harvesting. Although corn freezes well, it is best when cooked straight from the garden.

Caution: Corn earworm usually is present, as well as budworm. An insecticide such as sevin must be sprayed on the cornsilk every other day after it appears, until it turns black. For budworm, place a small pinch of cutworm bait in each bud of the small corn plants. Corn also suffers from fungus and bacterial diseases.

Cucumbers

Cucumbers are used for salads or for pickles. They need soil high in organic matter and moisture. Fast-growing, cucumbers do not transplant easily. Plant the seeds where the vines are to grow. They are sensitive to cold. Never allow a

Corn

Cucumbers

Eggplant

cucumber to mature on the vine; otherwise, the vine will stop producing. To avoid disease problems, plant cucumbers resistant to downy mildew. This plant also suffers from nematodes, viruses, and pickleworms.

Eggplant

Eggplant fruit must be harvested while still immature, or about two-thirds its full size. Good fruit has a glossy purple skin. This vegetable requires rich, moist soil. The plant is sensitive to cold but, if not frozen, will live for several years. Culture is similar to tomatoes, though eggplants require higher temperatures, need to be fed heavily and given plenty of water. They require 80 to 85 days from plants to harvest. Care should be taken in transplanting. A serious problem with eggplant is the continuing battle with red spiders and nematodes, as well as the tomato pinworm.

Endive (or Escarole)

This plant is a warm-weather substitute for lettuce, with frilled, deep-cut leaves. It is more popular than escarole, which is very similar. To eliminate the slightly bitter flavor, the outer leaves should be tied at the top of the plant with string or a rubber band. In two or three weeks, the leaves will be blanched and the bitter flavor removed.

Endive and escarole take 90 to 95 days from seed to harvest. They have few problems, and the culture is identical to lettuce.

Kale

Kale's culture is the same as for cabbage. Kale is one of the better-tasting cooked greens, a hardy pot herb that is a welcome change as a vegetable. It suffers from several diseases and is attacked by caterpillars and plant bugs.

Flowering kale is an ornamental as well as a vegetable.

Kohlrabi is a sturdy vegetable similar to the turnip.

Kale can be grown as a garden plant or as a potted herb.

Kohlrabi

The enlarged stem of kohlrabi is eaten as a vegetable. Similar to the turnip, it has a milder flavor. Kohlrabi is cold-hardy and needs a fertile, moist soil and cold weather. This is a fast-maturing plant, taking only 50 to 55 days from seed to harvest. It should be picked young, when about 1 to 3 inches in diameter, and will need spraying for caterpillars.

Lettuce

Head lettuce is difficult to grow in Florida. Instead try Bibb lettuce, which has more vitamins and a better flavor. Lettuce is hardy and needs rich soil with

Lettuce is a delicious vegetable crop, but it must be protected from insect and disease damage in the garden.

plenty of organic matter. It grows well in sun or partial shade. Since lettuce has short roots, it needs a continuous supply of moisture. Drought and hot weather induce bolting (flowering). Bibb lettuce takes from 50 to 60 days to mature, and prefers cooler weather.

Leaf lettuce requires less care and is more tolerant of heat than other types of lettuce. There are many varieties, with Cos or Romaine the easiest to cultivate. All lettuce suffers from bolting, aphids, foliage diseases, and viruses.

Mustard (Leaf)

Several varieties of mustard are popular as cooking greens, all easy to grow and ready for picking 40 to 45 days from seed. Mustard greens can be grown all year, but do best during the cool season. They suffer from caterpillars, cabbage loopers, and several diseases.

Okra

Okra will grow on most well-drained soils provided there is plenty of moisture. These are hungry plants and should be fertilized generously every two weeks. Okra is a warm-weather crop that matures in about 50 to 55 days from seed. Planting a second crop 50 days after the first will double your harvest. Pick the pods daily while they are immature; otherwise, they will become woody. Okra suffers from stink bugs and is devastated by nematodes.

Onions

Onions can be grown from seeds, plants, and sets, with most home gardeners choosing sets. This hardy vegetable is available in three types: green, multiplier, and bulbing.

Green onions can be planted anytime sets are available, usually from

Green onions

Onions, a culinary
favorite, require water
and plenty of nitrogen
to yield an abundant
crop.

September through March. This simple and easy way to grow green onions will
give you a harvest in about 50 days.

Multipliers usually are sold in bunches. They do not form a bulb and continue to produce more plants throughout the season. At harvest time, simply
remove a group, replant two or three, and use the rest. Multiplier also can be
grown from seed.

Bulbing onions can be bought in trays as young plants or started from seeds or sets. Set these out as soon as they are available, but no later than November. Bulbs will be ready in late spring and early summer. Tropicana Red and Granex varieties produce bulbs shortly after winter and can be grown from seed quite easily.

Onions must have nitrogen available throughout their growing season. Otherwise, fertilize these plants the same as most other crops. Lack of moisture inhibits growth, so keep your onion plants well watered. They have few problems and are one of the easiest vegetables to grow.

Peas (English garden)

Wait until November to plant peas in Florida, because they only thrive in the coolest months. Peas need improved soil and good moisture. They are ready for harvest 50 to 55 days after seed is sown. Dwarf varieties are the simplest to grow. Peas must be picked often before they get a chance to mature and become hard. They can suffer from leaf diseases.

Peas (Southern cow)

Vigorous but sensitive to cold, Southern peas come in many varieties and grow on bushes or vining plants, doing best early in the season. Plant as soon as danger of first frost is over. After they become established, these plants are drought-resistant, like hot weather, and will flourish in almost any soil. They need a low-nitrogen fertilizer, moderately applied. Several plantings will extend your harvest. Treat for cowpea curculio, caterpillars, plant bugs, and nematodes.

Cool-weather plants, garden peas are most commonly grown from seed.

Some pea varieties prefer to be grown above ground-level on a fence or trellis.

Golden bell peppers

Banana (Butterfinger) peppers are a sweet and flavorful crop as well as an attractive plant in the garden.

Peppers (Bell or Sweet)

Soil rich in organic matter and plenty of water and fertilizer are necessary for a good crop of bell peppers. These plants are tender, but if protected, will live for several years. Usually grown as an annual, they will produce usable peppers in about 65 to 80 days from planting. Pick the peppers when they reach their largest size, before they turn red; however, the red peppers also are good to eat. Problems include nematodes, fungus, bacteria, and virus diseases. Thrips can cause young fruit and flowers to drop.

Peppers (Bird)

Bird peppers are easily grown and can be found growing wild in many parts of Florida. They are very hot and used in cooking and making pepper sauce.

Potatoes (Irish or White)

To plant potatoes, take a seed potato and cut at least one eye in a piece of the flesh, and plant it to grow into a fresh bush. The larger the seed piece, the more vigorous the plant will be. Do not plant table potatoes bought at the store — these have been treated with sprout inhibitors. Potatoes should be sown as soon as seed potatoes are available. This vegetable needs good soil and constant moisture. Fertilize the same as for other crops. Potatoes are hardy, but a hard freeze will kill them. When the vines mature and die down, you may harvest your new potatoes. Late blight and other diseases make it necessary to spray weekly. Nematodes and caterpillars also are a problem.

White potatoes

Budding potato plants

Potatoes (Sweet)

Sweet potatoes (sometimes wrongly called "yams") like a light-to-medium soil that is not too high in nitrogen. If you fertilize too heavily, you will wind up with enormous vines and few sweet potatoes. These are tender plants, susceptible to cold, and take from 120 to 140 days to mature.

Plant portions of the vine about 6 to 9 inches long, burying 4 inches of stem into the soil. Sweet potatoes are prone to weevils and caterpillars. A sweet potato placed in water will sprout vines, which then can be cut and planted for growing new sweet potatoes.

Spinach (Summer or New Zealand)

Summer spinach has a better, milder flavor than the regular spinach, and is easy to grow. Once established, it is fairly drought-resistant and grows all summer. Cut 3 inches of foliage from the ends of branches for cooking. Be warned: The large seeds are slow to germinate, and the plants suffer from caterpillars.

Squash (Summer; includes Yellow crookneck, Yellow straightneck, Patty Pan, and Zucchini)

A bush type with small runners, summer squash is easy to grow in any good soil. Sensitive to cold, summer squash are fast growers, taking 45 to 60 days from seed to maturity. Plant in spring after danger of frost has passed. Plant where they are to grow; the seedlings do not transplant well. A late summer planting will give you a fall crop. Summer squash are subject to nematodes, pumpkin bugs, pickleworms, viruses, and downy and powdery mildews.

Zucchini squash

Squash seedling

Yellow crookneck squash

Butternut squash

Pumpkins, related to squash and gourds, grow well in enriched soil but need plenty of water and insect/disease protection.

Squash (Winter running; includes Butternut, Acorn, and Buttercup)

Picked when the skin has hardened and the vegetable is mature, winter squash grows on long, aggressive vines in any good soil. The recommended varieties for Florida take from 90 to 105 days to mature and can be picked and stored in any cool, dry place for future use. They suffer from the same problems as summer squash, except viruses.

Swiss Chard

Swiss chard is a beet grown for its fleshy stems and leaves. One of the best-cooking greens, it will produce for a long time if only the outside leaves are picked as needed. A rich, moist soil is needed for best growth. Swiss chard can be grown all year but does best in cooler weather, with a hardy, quick crop that takes 55 to 60 days from seed to harvest. It has problems with caterpillars.

Tomatoes

Before you plant tomatoes, you should treat the soil with Vapam first, then follow with organic materials, peat moss and manure, as well as hydrated lime or dolomite. All of this is necessary because Florida's predominantly sandy soil lacks nutritive elements. But do not overfeed with nitrogen fertilizer, as this will promote foliage and few fruit. Once the fruit appears, however, nitrogen and other fertilizer elements are needed in generous amounts. Full sun and plenty of water are essential for healthy tomatoes, possibly more than for any other vegetable. Most of the cherry-type tomatoes do well in Florida. But the larger varieties fruit poorly when the night temperatures get above 68 degrees.

Tomatoes can be grown from seed. For the average homeowner who only needs enought fruit for home use, however, it is more convenient to purchase the plant at a nursery. Before planting, mix a cupful of hydrated lime or two cupfuls of dolomite into each 2 cubic feet of planting media. This will prevent ''blossom-end rot,'' which is caused primarily by a lack of calcium in the soil.

Full sun and plenty of water are essential for growing healthy tomatoes.

Too much nitrogen and uneven watering also can cause blossom-end rot. Using an all-purpose fertilizer will provide your tomatoes with the needed nutrients for healthy plants and good fruit. Once the plants start growing, be sure to stake the branches. This way, they take up less room and are easier to spray for insect and disease control. Also this keeps the fruit off the ground and prevents soil rot.

One of the worst pests for tomatoes is the leaf miner. One species is a small maggot, the immature stage of a fly, that makes a winding tunnel in the tomato leaves, causing them to die. Leaf miners do not attack the fruit itself, but the southern armyworm and hornworm attack and eat everything, often overnight. Diazinon, sevin, Dipel or Thuricide will control armyworms, but hornworms barely are affected. Because of their enormous size, they can be picked off by hand. A watchful eye should be kept for the hornworms (often 6 to 8 inches long). They can strip a tomato plant in a matter of hours.

When buying tomato plants, ask a nurseryman about the best varieties for your area, as well as the recommended spray for insect pests and diseases. Regular spraying is essential to maintain good, healthy tomato plants throughout a season.

Better Boy tomatoes   Bonus VFN tomatoes

Turnips

Both the roots and tops of turnips may be eaten. The Shogoin foliage turnip does especially well in Florida. It is a hardy, cool-weather vegetable that grows rapidly in rich, moist soil. A preventive spray program for aphids will be necessary, because once aphids get established between the leaves, they cannot be eradicated. Watch for leaf-spot diseases, too. Seed to harvest takes 35 to 50 days.

Watermelons

Watermelons thrive in well-drained soil with good moisture content. These plants are cold-sensitive; seeds should be sown after all danger of frost has passed. Seed to harvest is 85 to 100 days. Do not plant seeds in soil that has already produced watermelons or you may encourage fusarium wilt, a soil-borne disease. A weekly spray program is advisable to control such fungus diseases as gummy stem blight, downy mildew, and anthracnose. Other problems with watermelons include viruses, aphids, rindworms, and nematodes.

Ripe watermelons in the garden

FLORIDA VEGETABLE PLANTING GUIDE

CROP	VARIETIES	SPACING IN INCHES	
		ROWS	PLANTS
Beans, lima	Fordhook 242, Concentrated, Henderson, Jackson Wonder, Dixie Butterpea, Florida Butter (Pole)	26-48	12-15
Beans, pole	Dade, McCaslan, Kentucky Wonder, 191 Blue Lake	40-48	15-18
Beans, snap	Extender, Contender, Harvester Wade, Cherokee (wax)	18-30	2-3
Beets	Early Wonder, Detroit Dark Red	14-24	3-5
Broccoli	Early Green Sprouting, Waltham 29, Atlantic	30-36	16-22
Brussels Sprouts	Prince Marvel, Jadecross, Long Island, Improved	30-36	18-24
Cabbage	Copenhagen Market, Marion Market, Badger Market, Glory of Enkhuizen, Red Acre, Chieftan Spray	24-36	14-24
Cabbage, Chinese	Michihli, Wong Bok	24-36	8-12
Carrots	Imperator, Gold Spike, Chantenay, Nantes	16-24	1-3
Cauliflower	Snowball Strains	24-30	20-24
Celery	Utah 52-70, Florida Pascal	24-36	6-10
Chard, Swiss	Swiss Chard of Geneva, Lucullus, Light-Green Rhubarb Chard	15-18	4-8
Collards	Georgia, Vates	24-30	14-18
Corn, sweet	Silver Queen (white), Gold Cup, Golden Security, Seneca Chief, many others	34-42	12-18
Cantaloupes	Smith's Perfect, Seminole, Edisto 47, Gulfstream	70-80	48-60
Cucumbers	Poinsett, Ashley (slicers), Wisconsin SMR 18, Pixie (picklers)	48-60	15-24
Eggplant	Florida Market	36-42	36-48

H — Hardy, can stand frost and some freezing (32 F) without injury.
SH — Slightly hardy, will not be injured by light frosts.

SEED DEPTH INCHES	PLANTING DATES IN FLORIDA			PLANT HARDINESS	DAYS TO HARVEST
	NORTH	**CENTRAL**	**SOUTH**		
1½-2	Mar-June	Feb-Apr	Sept-Apr	T	65-75
1½-2	Mar-June	Feb-Apr	Jan-Feb	T	60-65
1½-2	Mar-Apr Aug-Sept	Feb Mar Sept	Sept Apr	T	50-60
½-1	Sept-Mar	Oct-Mar	Oct-Feb	H	60-70
½-1	Aug-Feb	Aug-Jan	Sept-Jan	H	60-70
½	Sept Feb	Oct Feb	Oct Feb	H	70-90
½	Sept-Feb	Sept-Jan	Sept-Jan	H	70-90
¼-½	Oct-Jan	Oct-Jan	Oct-Jan	H	75-85
½	Sept-Mar	Oct-May	Oct-Feb	H	70-75
½	Jan-Feb Aug-Oct	Oct-Jan	Oct-Jan	H	55-60
¼-½	Jan-Mar	Aug-Feb	Oct-Jan	H	115-125
½	Feb Oct	Feb Oct	Feb Oct	H	50-70
½	Feb-Mar	Jan-Apr Sept-Nov	Sept-Jan Aug-Nov	H	50-55
½	Mar-Apr	Feb-Mar	Jan-Feb	T	80-85
¾	Mar-Apr	Feb-Apr	Feb-Mar	T	75-90
½-¾	Feb-Apr	Feb-Mar Sept	Jan-Feb	T	50-55
½	Feb-Mar July	Jan-Feb Aug-Sept	Dec-Feb	T	80-85

T — Tender, will be injured by light frost.
+ — Tomato varieties best adapted to staking.

FLORIDA VEGETABLE PLANTING GUIDE

CROP	VARIETIES	SPACING IN INCHES	
		ROWS	PLANTS
Endive-Escarole	Deep Heart Fringed, Full Heart Batavian	18-24	8-12
Kale	Dwarf Blue, Curled Scotch, Vate's	24-36	10-12
Kohlrabi	Early White Vienna	24-30	3-5
Lettuce (Crisp) (Butterhead) (Leaf) (Romaine)	Premier, Great Lakes types, Bibb, Matchless, Sweetheart, Prize Head, Ruby, Salad Bowl, Parris Island Cos, Dark Green Cos	12-18	12-18
Mustard	Southern Giant Curled, Florida Broadleaf	14-24	4-8
Okra	Clemson Spineless, Perkins Long Green	24-40	18-24
Onions (Bulbing) (Green)	Excel, Texas Grano Granex, White Granex, Tropicana Red White Portugal or White types, Shallots (Multipliers)	12-24 12-24 18-24	3-4 1½-2 6-8
Parsley	Moss Curled, Perfection	12-20	8-12
Peas	Little Marvel, Dark Skinned Perfection, Laxton's Progress	24-36	2-3
Peas, southern	Blackeye, Brown Crowder, Bush Conch, Producer, Floricream, Snaps, Zipper Cream	30-36	2-3
Pepper (Sweet) (Hot)	Calif. Wonder, Yolo Wonder, World Beater Hungarian Wax, Anaheim Chili	20-36	2-3
Potatoes	Sebago, Red Pontiac, Kennebec, Red LaSoda	36-42	12-15
Potatoes, sweet	U.S. No. 1, Porto Rico, Georgia Red Goldrush, Nugget, Centennial	48-54	18-24
Radish	Cherry Belle, Comet, Early Scarlet Globe, White Icicle, Sparkler (white tipped)	12-18	1-2
Spinach	Virginia Savoy, Dixie Market, Hybrid 7	14-18	3-5
Spinach, summer	New Zealand	30-36	18-24

H — Hardy, can stand frost and some freezing (32 F) without injury.
SH — Slightly hardy, will not be injured by light frosts.

SEED DEPTH INCHES	PLANTING DATES IN FLORIDA			PLANT HARDINESS	DAYS TO HARVEST
	NORTH	CENTRAL	SOUTH		
¾	Feb-Mar Sept	Jan-Feb Sept	Sept-Jan	H	90-95
½	Sept Feb	Sept Feb	Sept Feb	H	50-75
½	Mar-Apr Oct-Nov	Feb-Mar Oct-Nov	Nov-Feb	H	50-55
¾	Feb-Mar Sept	Jan-Feb Sept	Sept-Jan	H	50-80
½	Jan-Mar Sept-May	Jan-Mar Sept-Nov	Sept-Mar	H	40-45
1-2	Mar-May Aug	Mar-May Aug	Feb-Mar Aug-Sept	T	50-55
¾	Jan-Mar Aug-Nov	Jan-Mar Aug-Nov	Jan-Mar Sept-Nov	H	100-130
¾	Aug-Mar	Aug-Mar	Sept-Mar	H	50-75
¾	Aug-Jan	Aug-Jan	Sept-Dec	H	75-105
¾	Feb-Mar	Dec-Jan	Sept-Jan	H	90-95
1-2	Jan-Feb	Sept-Mar	Sept-Feb	H	50-55
1-2	Mar-May	Mar-May	Feb-Apr	T	70-80
1-2	Feb-Apr	Jan-Mar	Jan-Feb Aug-Oct	T	70-80
4-8	Jan-Feb	Jan	Sept-Jan	SH	80-95
	Mar-June	Feb-June	Feb-June	T	120-140
¾	Oct-Mar	Oct-Mar	Oct-Mar	H	20-25
¾	Oct-Nov	Oct-Nov	Oct-Jan	H	40-45
¾	Mar-Apr	Mar-Apr	Jan-Apr	T	55-65

T — Tender, will be injured by light frost.
+ — Tomato varieties best adapted to staking

FLORIDA VEGETABLE PLANTING GUIDE

CROP	VARIETIES	SPACING IN INCHES	
		ROWS	PLANTS
Squash (Summer)	Early Prolific Straightneck, Early Summer Crookneck, Cocozelle, Zucchini, Patty Pan	42-48	42-48
(Winter)	Alagold, Table Queen, Butternut	90-120	48-72
Strawberry	Florida 90, Tioga, Sequoia	36-40	10-14
Tomatoes (Large fruited)	Manalucie, +Homestead-24, Indian River, Floradel, +Tropired, Big Boy +, Walter	40-60	36-40
(Small fruited)	Large Cherry, Roma (Paste)		
Turnips	Japanese Foliage (Shogoin) Purple Top White Globe	12-20	4-6
Watermelon (Large)	Charleston Gray, Congo, Jubilee, Crimson Sweet	90-120	60-84
(Seedless) (Small)	Tri-X 317 New Hampshire Midget, Sugar Baby		

H — Hardy, can stand frost and some freezing (32 F) without injury.
SH — Slightly hardy, will not be injured by light frosts.

SEED DEPTH INCHES	PLANTING DATES IN FLORIDA			PLANT HARDINESS	DAYS TO HARVEST
	NORTH	CENTRAL	SOUTH		
½	Feb-Mar Aug	Feb-Mar Aug	Jan-Mar Sept-Oct	T	45-60
2	Feb-Mar	Feb-Mar	Jan-Feb	T	95-105
	Sept-Oct	Sept-Oct	Oct-Nov	H	90-110
½	Feb-Apr Aug Feb-Apr Aug	Feb-Mar Sept Feb-Mar Sept	Aug-Mar Aug-Mar	T T	75-85 75-85
½-¾	Jan-Apr Aug-Oct	Jan-Mar Sept-Nov	Oct-Feb	H	40-50
2	Mar-Apr	Jan-Apr	Feb-Mar	T	80-100

T — Tender, will be injured by light frost.
+ — Tomato varieties best adapted to staking.

CHAPTER NINE

Vines and Ground Covers

One of the many joys of Florida living is the large number of vines that can be grown here. Their leafy, green runners climb over walls, fences, trellises, and planters. In residential areas and in the wild, these persistent, ever-spreading plants add eye-catching color to the landscape. Their attractive foliage intermingles with blossoms of almost every color.

Vines add to the beauty of any garden, but they also can serve a very practical purpose: blocking out the fierce summer sun and screening windows, walls, and patios from excessive heat. Vines grow quickly and provide welcome shade with a minimum of care and effort. The majority of vines are flowering plants. But many homeowners enjoy vines that do more than beautify. These include the grapevine, or vines such as cucumbers, melons, and climbing figs, which also produce food for the table.

To select the right vine for your particular needs, you should study the characteristics of each variety, learn its growth habits and requirements, and its resistance to cold. Vines are among the easiest plants to grow, and with their sheer mass and moisture content, they create a distinct cooling effect, both physically and psychologically.

For outdoor plantings, March through October is the best time to start a vine in the ground. For container-held vines, planting can be done any time except the dead of winter. Like most plants, vines do best in good, improved soil consisting of one-third peat; one-third dehydrated cow manure; and one-third natural, existing soil. Since vines eventually will grow together, it is best not to place them too close to each other. Planting them 3 to 4 feet apart is a good rule of thumb.

Daily watering is essential after planting, then cut back to about an inch a week once the plant takes hold and begins to mature. Vines planted in full sun require more water than those growing in shade. Test the soil with your finger if you are unsure about watering; if the soil has dried out, step up your watering. Vines must have moist soil to maintain healthy foliage and satisfactory growth. Letting the soil dry out is the quickest way to kill any plant, especially one that has to endure Florida's scorching sunshine.

Vines and ground covers are beautiful plants that act as insulators against our intense summer sun.

Vines are climbers, so they need support. A fence, trellis or rough wall is necessary for all vines. If you do not want a vine to spread out of control, keep it trimmed. The more often you trim a vine, the bushier it will become. Most vines have tendrils that wrap around any available support. But some, such as climbing roses, have to be tied to a fence or trellis.

LANDSCAPING WITH VINES

Vines are particularly useful for covering unattractive fences. A chain-link fence is practical but not aesthetically appealing. Yet this fence provides perfect support for the passion vine, honeysuckle, confederate jasmine and morning glory. Honeysuckle is particularly ideal for growing on a chain-link fence. It will wind in and out of the mesh, creating a solid base from which other branches emerge. It will cover the fence totally (and usually in one season), providing privacy for the garden and a cool, soothing background for the rest of the landscape.

For shady areas, plants such as Algerian ivy, English ivy, philodendron, fat-shedera, and jasmine can be used successfully. The ivy family is suited for climbing up rough, outside walls of houses, where it not only provides a dense screen against the sun, but also enhances the beauty of the home.

Compared to flowering annuals and perennials and vegetables, vines are almost trouble-free. But, despite their hardiness and fast-growth characteristics, they cannot be planted and forgotten. Still, once they are established, vines require little care and will become an admired and useful part of your landscape.

VINES FOR FLORIDA

Allamanda cathartica
ALLAMANDA

Height: 5-10 ft.   Spread: 5-10 ft.   Areas: N (protected), C (protected), S

   Producing trumpet-shaped, yellow, waxy flowers almost 4 inches across, this vine is a fast-grower, blooms 10 months out of the year and can extend to 20 feet in length. Sensitive to temperatures in the 20s, it is used more extensively in central and south Florida. Shoots should be trimmed, and the plant should be pruned before new growth starts in the spring. Allamanda grows well in sun or light shade. As its botanical name implies, all parts of this plant are cathartic (act as a purge).

Antigonon leptopus
CORAL VINE

Height: 5-15 ft.   Spread: 10-15 ft.   Areas: N (protected), C (protected), S

   A prolific grower, the coral vine is covered with delicate pink flowers most of the year and has tendrils that enable it to climb almost any porous or semi-porous surface, such as a low wall or fence. It has unusually heavy growth and should be trimmed after blooming. Otherwise it can get out of control.

Coral vine

This vine can be planted from seed very easily, and during summer and fall, small self-sown plants can be found underneath the mature foliage. In north Florida, frost can injure this vine, but it will grow back again.

Bauhinia Galpinii
BAUHINIA

Height: 5-8 ft.   Spread: 5-10 ft.   Areas: C, S

Similar to the more-familiar bauhinia trees, this vine has to be trained to a trellis. But it grows quite easily from seed and produces exquisite, dark-red flowers. This plant is injured by frost but grows back. Bauhinia is ideal for central and southern Florida.

Bougainvillea sp.
BOUGAINVILLEA

Height: 10-50 ft.   Spread:10-30 ft.   Areas: C (protected), S

Available in brilliant shades of deep pink, almost-red, orange, and yellow, this vine has been known to climb to the top of 50-ft. trees. Frost will injure bougainvillea, but it grows back again. A truly impressive grower, bougainvillea can be used in hanging baskets and as patio plants or allowed to bush into a tall, very thick shrub that can form a remarkably dense hedge blessed with flowers and dark-green foliage. This plant flourishes in most areas of Florida but needs regular feeding with a fertilizer high in phosphorus and potassium.

Bougainvillea blossoms

Clerodendrum Thomsoniae
BLEEDING HEART

Height: 10-15 ft.　　Spread: 5-10 ft.　　Areas: N, C, S

Sometimes called glory bower, this West African vine grows well in Florida, producing white flowers enclosed in heart-shaped calyces that bloom most of the year. The vines should be supported on a trellis or fence. Bleeding heart survives in all parts of the state, but can be injured in colder areas. Long-lasting cut flowers, clerodendrums are very popular for indoor floral arrangements.

Cydista aequinoctialis
GARLIC VINE

Height: 5-8 ft.　　Spread: 4-8 ft.　　Areas: N, C, S

A South American plant that does well in Florida, garlic vine has beautiful pink flowers, sometimes veined with rose or purple coloration. It can be grown from seed and should be protected from severe cold. Best planting time is in the spring, with flowers from summer through fall.

Fatshedera Lizei
FATSHEDERA

Height: 4-8 ft.　　Spread: 5-10 ft.　　Areas: C, S

This vine is a cross between Japanese aralia and English ivy. This evergreen botanical wonder is a leaning vine-shrub growing to 10 feet, with star-studded, dark-green foliage. It needs support to climb and is subject to damage from low temperatures. Against a wall, in a protected corner, or as an indoor or outdoor accent, the fatshedera is most impressive. Plant in good, rich soil with adequate moisture.

Ficus pumila
CLIMBING FIG

Height: 10-15 ft.　　Spread: 10-15 ft.　　Areas: N (protected), C (protected), S

Tolerating heat as well as semi-shade, the climbing fig has dark, evergreen leaves almost 4 inches long. It is a good climber, sometimes reaching a height of 30 feet. This vine does well against walls but has to be staked. Plant every 2 feet for an eventual mass of very attractive foliage. The foliage is popular and used extensively in public places such as Disneyworld in Orlando.

Gelsemium sempervirens
CAROLINA JESSAMINE, CAROLINA JASMINE

Height: 5-8 ft.　　Spread: 5-10 ft.　　Areas: N, C

Best suited to north and central Florida, this plant grows well in full sun or partial shade. It reaches 5 to 8 feet and offers a delightful scent from its bright-yellow flowers that bloom in early spring. The foliage is bright green but shows iron chlorosis when grown in alkaline soil.

Hedera canariensis
ALGERIAN IVY

Height: 10-40 ft.	Spread: 10-40 ft.	Areas: N, C, S

A vigorous grower reaching 40 feet in length, this plant resembles English ivy but with much larger leaves. It is good for covering tree trunks and walls. Plant 12 to 18 inches apart in sheltered locations where winter temperatures do not drop far below freezing for extended periods.

Hedera Helix
ENGLISH IVY

Height: 10-40 ft.	Spread: 10-40 ft.	Areas: N, C, S

This ivy is evergreen, with dark leathery leaves. English ivy is excellent for covering masonry walls and may grow to 40 feet. Plant the vines 12 to 18 inches apart, as close to a wall as possible. However, do not use this ivy for covering hot, reflective walls that receive the afternoon sunlight. English ivy grows best in rich, improved soil with adequate moisture.

English ivy used as a ground cover *and* as a vine

MR. GREEN THUMB RULE

Vines are especially good for hiding unattractive areas, such as fences, and for minimizing objectionable views. Most vines will cover an area in one season.

Hylocereus undatus
NIGHT-BLOOMING CEREUS

Height: 5-12 ft.   Spread: 20 ft.   Areas: C, S

This flowering, climbing cactus does well in central and south Florida, producing delicate, fragrant, white blossoms all summer. This plant will spread its dark-green, ridged branches up to 20 feet, with aerial roots that cling to walls.

Ipomoea sp.
MORNING GLORY

Height: 5-10 ft.   Spread: 10-15 ft.   Areas: N, C, S

Growing 10 to 15 feet in length, morning glory vines do best in full sun, but also flourish in partial shade. They produce abundant amounts of blue, pink, or white flowers that open in the morning and close later in the day. Plant seeds where they are to grow. Soaking seeds in water several days before planting will hasten germination. Blooming six to eight months of the year, morning glories do very well on fences and trellises and cover any area very quickly. This vine self-seeds prolifically; in fact, once introduced into a garden, it is difficult to eradicate, which makes this plant a favorite with lazy gardeners!

Ipomoea tuberosa
WOOD ROSE

Height: 6-10 ft.   Spread: 10-15 ft.   Areas: C, S

This unusual vine does well in south and lower-central Florida and gets its name from its seed pods that resemble carved wooden roses. It will grow from seed and suffers injury below freezing, but will grow back unless killed to the ground.

Lagenaria sp. (and others)
GOURD

Height: 6-8 ft.   Spread: 5-10 ft.   Areas: N, C, S

The name "gourd" generally refers to cucurbits, plants allied to the pumpkin, cucumber, and melon. Some of the more common gourds are: white-flowering gourd, mate or gourd of Paraguay *(Lagenaria siceraria)*; snake or serpent gourd *(L. siceraria* or *Trichosanthes anguina)*; white or wax gourd *(Benincasa hisfida)*; and dishcloth gourd *(Luffa cylindrica)*. Usually exhibiting hard,

Gourds are grown more as ornaments than as foodstuffs.

durable shells, gourds are grown more as ornaments than as foodstuffs. Cultivation techniques are the same as for pumpkins, melons, and cucumbers. Seeds are commonly sown as soon as the weather is consistently warm. Gourds may be started in pots or windowboxes, too, but won't transplant readily if roots are disturbed. The vines of these cucurbits make attractive screens and covers if given proper support. Gourds are frost-tender.

Lonicera sempervirens
TRUMPET HONEYSUCKLE

Height: 5-10 ft.   Spread: 5-10 ft.   Areas: N, C

A native of Florida, the trumpet honeysuckle grows well in good organic soil, producing red, tubular flowers tinged with yellow on the inside. This plant is grown mainly for its dense foliage. It does well in north and central parts of the state and can be started from seed or cuttings.

Passiflora edulis
PASSION FRUIT VINE

Height: 5-10 ft.   Spread: 10-20 ft.   Areas: N (protected), C (protected), S

A rampant, woody vine, the passion fruit has three-lobed, serrated leaves, and climbs with tendrils. The fruit is slightly oval, with a purple, shell-like rind. The pulp is juicy and aromatic, with many seeds. The juice is particularly tasty, and both juice and seeds can be added to fruit salads for interesting flavor. This vine likes full sun, needs a strong support on which to climb (chain-link fence is recommended), and requires good, moist soil. Seeds take two weeks to three months to germinate, and the vine can be grown from cuttings or air-layering. The plants need heavy mulching. New plants should be started every three years. The passion fruit has poor salt-tolerance and suffers from nematodes, caterpillars, and crown rot.

This vine gets its name from its unusual flowers, purple and white with a configuration resembling a crucifix, or "the passion of Christ." Another variety, *Passiflora edulis favicarpa,* has yellow fruit and is very vigorous and productive.

Senecio confusus
MEXICAN FLAME VINE

Height: 5-15 ft.　　　　Spread: 5-15 ft.　　　　Areas: N (protected), C, S

Salt-tolerant, easily propagated from cuttings, and quick to recover from frost damage, this popular vine produces very large, orange-red, daisy-shaped flowers all year. A fast-grower, it does well in most soils and should be shaped to keep it from growing out of control.

Solandra guttata
GOLDEN CHALICE

Height: 5-10 ft.　　　　Spread: 5-10 ft.　　　　Areas: C, S

Grown from seed and soft wood cuttings, the golden chalice does well in fertilized soil with adequate moisture. This vine needs a trellis to climb and has exquisite tubular, golden flowers almost 10 inches long, which open white and slowly darken to their ultimate rich, golden yellow. At night, the blossoms give off a light, pleasant fragrance.

Tecomaria capensis
CAPE HONEYSUCKLE

Height: 5-20 ft.　　　　Spread: 10-30 ft.　　　　Areas: N, C, S

This South African vine is beautiful, shrubby, and blooms most of the year with brilliant, orange-red flowers. A very aggressive vine, it can be propagated easily from soft wood cuttings.

Cape honeysuckle

Trachelospermum jasminoides
CONFEDERATE JASMINE, STAR JASMINE

Height: 10-20 ft.   Spread: 10-20 ft.   Areas: C, S

This vine is a profuse bloomer in early summer. The vines should be planted 24 to 36 inches apart, since they grow rapidly. This vine works either as a ground cover or as an aesthetic addition to fences, trellises, and patio walls. Its foliage is dark green; the brilliant white flowers, resembling pinwheels, have a strong, delightful fragrance. Planted around an entranceway, this vine can fill the house with its perfume. Susceptible to damage from lower temperatures, it does best in central and south Florida. It can be started from tip cuttings or air-layering.

Vitis sp.
GRAPE

Height: 5-15 ft.   Spread: 5-20 ft.   Areas: N, C, S

A grapevine not only enhances the beauty of any garden, but also provides luscious fruit for the table. Used most frequently on arbors and fences, a grapevine will wrap its tendrils around posts, wires, or wooden supports. Several varieties do well in Florida, but you should check with your nurseryman on the best grapevines for your area.

One of the best and easiest to grow is the *Muscadine* grape. It offers tough-skinned, purple, round berries of excellent flavor. Muscadines should be planted in full sun and in soil with good drainage. Bare-root stock is planted while dormant, from November 15 through April. Grapes bought in containers can be planted at any time. These vines must be pruned each winter during their dormant stage. Suckers should be cut off, and tendrils should not be permitted to wrap around and girdle the vine. Muscadines are vigorous, hungry plants and should be well-fertilized once a month after planting. Use ¼ pound of general-purpose or citrus fertilizer, scattered 12 inches from the base of the vine. The second year, use 1 pound of fertilizer for each plant, applied in March, May, and just after harvest. For the third year, and every year thereafter, use 2½ pounds per plant. Vines should not be fertilized after September 15. Keep the area around the base of each plant free of weeds, but be careful to cultivate lightly. Grape roots grow near the surface.

Muscadines are easier to grow than bunch grapes. Muscadines are native to Florida and other southeastern sections of the U.S. Many varieties are resistant to Pierce's disease, a devastating fungus, which renders the growing of European or northern bunch grapes impossible in Florida. However, muscadines must be protected against fungus problems and pests. Spray with a good fungicide such as Manzate D, Diathane M-22, or neutral copper every two weeks from the time the flowers appear until the fruit begins to ripen. This will prevent fruit rot and leaf spots. Spraying is very important during the rainy season, and it should be continued every two weeks until the wet season ends. Spraying with a regular insecticide, such as malathion or sevin, also is advised, except when the vines are in bloom. Spraying then would kill pollinating insects.

Three varieties of bunch grapes, however, can do well in all parts of the state except the southeast coastal regions. *Norris, Lake Emerald,* and *Stover* are resistant to Pierce's disease.

Norris is the largest of these varieties, with deep-purple grapes and skins that are easy to separate from the pulp. A high-yielding, vigorous vine, Norris does well from cuttings, but being self-sterile, it must be planted close to one of the other two varieties to fruit satisfactorily. Susceptible to anthracnose — which causes deformed leaves and lesions — these grapes must be sprayed five or six times with a fungicide, from the time bud growth begins until fruit reaches full size. Be sure to spray when they are in full bloom. Like most grapes, Norris has poor salt-tolerance. But it adapts well to most soils.

Grapevines suffer from several other diseases that must be controlled to ensure good, healthy vines and a fruitful harvest. The most common problem, downy mildew, causes gray patches to appear in spots that eventually turn brown. Black rot shows up as dark brown lesions on leaves, usually round in shape. If untreated, this disease causes the grapes to rot. Leafhoppers, aphids, and the grape leaf folder are three insects that attack grapevines.

All of these problems can be controlled with a fungicide such as Zineb or Dithane M-45. Spray when the first green shoots are about 3 inches long, then every two weeks thereafter, four or five times. Adding malathion and sevin to the spray will take care of many insect infestations.

Grapevines grow on a wooden arbor—one of their most frequent uses.

Wisteria sinensis
CHINESE WISTERIA

| Height: 5-10 ft. | Spread: 5-8 ft. | Areas: N, C |

Wisteria is a very vigorous vine growing to 10 feet or more in length. Over fences and patios, wisteria does best in full or partial sun and can be trained as a small flowering tree. The blossoms are blue-white, pea-shaped flowers hanging in clusters like grapes, and appear in the spring. The foliage is dark green but yellows badly from iron deficiency in alkaline soil. Wisteria can be pruned after flowering. It is an exquisitely showy vine in spring, with plenty of foliage through summer and fall. It loses its leaves during the winter.

Wisteria in bloom

Wisteria trained to a wooden arbor

Ground covers are low-maintenance landscape elements that are particularly suited to patio borders and hard-to-mow areas. Too, there are varieties available for full-sun areas and for those in deep shade, where grass won't grow.

GROUND COVERS

Vines and ground covers are similar horticulturally, but are a bit different in terms of use. While vines are often used for "vertical" gardening, meaning they climb and decorate walls, fences, and trellises, ground covers are horizontal growers, providing an outdoor "carpet" that can hide a multitude of landscape sins when used properly. (Some varieties, such as English ivy, may be used as ground covers *and* vines.)

Most landscapes have areas that are suitable for ground covers. Many people have shady outdoor areas where grass simply won't grow, such as under large shade trees. Here, a planting of English ivy, liriope, or creeping fig would be ideal. Other people have small patches in their landscapes where grass just isn't practical. If it's a sunny area, a good choice would be Blue Rug juniper, wedelia, or kalanchoe.

Too, many people use ground covers in rock gardens. While small cacti are popular here, a succulent type of ground cover, such as sedum, will work well, too.

Ground covers can be energy savers in the garden as well. Paved surfaces reflect sunlight, allowing it to bounce off and pass through windows, heating up the house and raising the electric bill. Ground covers, meanwhile, absorb the sunlight, shade the ground, and prevent that reflected light from heating a home.

PLANTING GROUND COVERS

If you decide to use a ground cover in your landscape, I'd suggest using graph paper to sketch your landscape, indicating where you want to place the ground cover. This will help you get a feel for what the new landscape material will look like in your garden, and will help you decide just how many plants you'll need to fill the areas.

If the ground-cover area used to be a lawn area, it's a good idea to spray the expanse with Round-Up, Kleen-Up, or Kills All (a glyphosate chemical). The glyphosate is taken in through the chlorophyll of the plants, moves to the root zones, and kills the offending grass or weed from the base up.

This shady area is perfect for English ivy ground cover.

Ground covers can act as energy savers, absorbing reflected light that bounces off nearby paved surfaces.

After you've cleaned out the weeds, rototill or hand spade the soil to a depth of 6 inches to 1 foot. (You may have to dig to a shallower depth under a large shade tree.) Next, add peat moss and cow manure at a rate of 25 pounds per 100 square feet of growing space. Then rake the planting area smooth.

Now you're ready to plant. You may want to use a yardstick or string to mark the planting area so your ground-cover rows are neat and evenly spaced. Remove the ground-cover plants from their containers, which may be six-count cell packs, 4- or 6-inch pots, or gallon-size containers. Gently pull apart the root system of each plant, and plant them at the same depth at which they grew in their containers. Water the plants thoroughly, making sure that no air pockets remain beneath the plantings.

To keep your ground cover healthy, I recommend using a good, liquid plant food on a monthly basis during the growing season; always follow package directions. Too, like many people, you may want to apply a pre-emergent herbicide (Balan, Eptam, or Treflan) to the growing area to discourage a rapid return of weeds. A mulch can be helpful around the area, especially if the ground cover is not a spreading type, such as a juniper.

If you do plant a spreading type of ground cover, you may need to prune the growth to keep it where you want it to be. A simple clipping of any new growth should keep the ground cover under control and looking beautiful.

Ajuga in bloom

Ajuga

GROUND COVERS FOR FLORIDA

Ajuga repens
BUGLE-WEED

Height: ½-1 ft.   Spread: 1-3 ft.   Areas: N, C, S

In Florida, bugle-weed grows well year-round; it yields a beautiful, blue flower through much of the year. This plant is strong, cold-hardy, and can be grown in either full sun or partial shade. Bugle-weed, however, does have rather poor salt-tolerance. Occasionally, it may have a problem with aphids on the new growth, but this can easily be controlled.

Alternanthera amoena
JOSEPH'S COAT

Height: 5-10 in.   Spread: 12-24 in.   Areas: C, S

Also called Coat of Many Colors, Joseph's Coat has a multicolored leaf, tinged with pink, red, and green. It is tender, so it should be planted in a protected area. Used in central and south Florida, it will grow in full sun and also does well in partial shade. It is not salt-tolerant, and does occasionally have problems with caterpillars.

Asparagus sprengeri
ASPARAGUS FERN

| Height: 12-24 in. | Spread: 2-4 ft. | Areas: N, C, S |

It is called a fern, but it is really a member of the lily family. The asparagus fern will do well in full sun to partial shade. It is slightly salt-tolerant, and is strong and cold-hardy throughout the state. Homeowners often mistake the white, round, storage part of the root for snake eggs, until they note that the "eggs" are attached to the roots.

Dichondra repens
DICHONDRA

| Height: 4-8 in. | Spread: 3-9 in. | Areas: N, C, S |

Although this plant resembles a common weed, the dollar weed, it *is* a ground cover. Dichondra has been used successfully in southern California. In Florida, we seem to have problems with a fungal disease that may kill large areas of this ground cover. If you like the looks of this plant, give it a try, although you may find other ground covers that will flourish more. Dichondra may be grown from seed.

Hedera Helix
ENGLISH IVY

| Height: 10-40 ft. | Spread: 10-40 ft. | Areas: N, C, S |

This plant is one of the best climbing vines and ground covers for shady areas. Even in the deep shade of oak trees, English ivy and Algerian ivy (*Hedera canariensis,* a close relative), are outstanding choices. They have moderate salt-tolerance, and can be planted in almost any type of soil. Both ivy types occasionally have problems with scale and spider mites but, for a shady landscape spot, these are excellent selections.

A cooling "island" of English ivy amid a sea of pavement

Blue Rug juniper

Blue Rug juniper

Juniperus conferta
SHORE JUNIPER

Height: 1-2 ft.	Spread: 2-4 ft.	Areas: N, C, S

There are a number of junipers that can be used as ground covers. One of the best is the shore juniper. It is flat-growing with blue-green needles. It normally grows to about 1 or 2 feet in height, and to about 2 to 4 feet in width. Like most junipers, the shore juniper does best in a well-drained soil. It is one of the best salt-tolerant plants available, and will grow in full sun to partial shade. This juniper may have problems with juniper blight and spider mites.

Kalanchoe longiflora
KALANCHOE

Height: 1-3 ft.	Spread: 1-3 ft.	Areas: N (protected), C, S

This flat-growing member of the kalanchoe family is great for a seaside planting. Sometimes called "the leaf of life," this kalanchoe is used as a ground cover, and in rock gardens, planter boxes, and many other areas where a bright yellow or reddish flower is desired. Being a succulent, it has good drought-tolerance. It will grow in full sun to partial shade, though it flowers best in full sun. Kalanchoes are cold-sensitive.

Lantana montevidensis
WEEPING LANTANA

Height: 1-3 ft.	Spread: 3-5 ft.	Areas: N (protected), C (protected), S

Weeping lantana, which is somewhat vine-like, bears rosy-lilac or yellow flowers; it blooms best in full sun. The plant has excellent salt-tolerance and will survive in our Florida sand, but does best in an improved, organic soil. The leaves and stems are aromatic when crushed.

MR. GREEN THUMB RULE

Ground covers are tough plants once established, but as with all new plantings, make sure to water them on a daily basis for the first two weeks. Fertilize monthly with a good, liquid plant food.

Liriope muscari
LIRIOPE

Height: 12-18 in.　　　Spread: 10-24 in.　　　Areas: N, C, S

Grass-like in appearance, liriope leaves may reach 18 inches in length, and ¾ of an inch in width. It bears attractive, lilac-colored, spiked flowers. Liriope performs best in partial shade. Commonly called lily turf, this plant is a bulb that can be propagated by the division of its thick, clumpy growth. Liriope should be planted in an enriched, organic, moist soil. It is cold-hardy in our state. Liriope has occasional problems with scale insects and with tip burn, which may force you to trim leaf ends.

Ophiopogon japonicus
MONDO GRASS

Height: 6-8 in.　　　Spread: 6-10 in.　　　Areas: N, C, S

Sometimes called dwarf liriope or monkey grass, mondo grass is used as a ground cover in full sun and in partial shade, such as underneath a canopy of large trees. This plant looks like a little tuft of grass. It is strong, cold-hardy, and has good salt-tolerance. Mondo grass is sometimes used as an edging material along walkways or driveways.

Newly planted mondo (monkey) grass

Peperomia obtusifolia
PEPEROMIA

Height: 6-18 in.   Spread: 1-3 ft.   Areas: S

Peperomias are often thought of as houseplants, since they are used in containers and planters. Still, peperomias are excellent outdoor plants in southern Florida as long as they are shaded and protected from the cold. They have good salt-tolerance. Because of their large, dark-green, oval leaves, peperomias make an attractive addition to the landscape.

Pilea microphylla
ARTILLERY PLANT

Height: ½-1 ft.   Spread: 1-3 ft.   Areas: N, C, S

Artillery plants are enjoying new-found respect as landscape materials. As a young man, I was paid by a nursery to pull these plants out from underneath potting benches where they had become "weedy" growths. A few years later, I was surprised to see them being sold as ground cover. Versatile plants, they do well in full sun to dense shade. Artillery plants have fair salt-tolerance, but are injured at 32 degrees.

Ruellia strepens
RUELLIA

Height: ½-1 ft.   Spread: 1-3 ft.   Areas: C, S

This prostrate grower does well in full sun. If you are looking for a ground cover that flowers and maintains a green appearance, ruellia is a good choice. Still, it is not very salt-tolerant, and gets injured at about 32 degrees. For this reason, ruellia is used mostly in the protected areas of central and southern Florida.

Setcreasea purpurea
PURPLE QUEEN

Height: 6-12 in.   Spread: 6-18 in.   Areas: N (protected), C (protected), S

This plant is often called the giant, purple, wandering Jew. The large purple leaves will reach 8 to 10 inches long. Purple queen makes a good ground cover, since its succulent stems tend to run all over the area where it is planted. This plant has little pink flowers. Purple queen will grow in a number of our sandy soils. It has occasional problems with caterpillars. Purple queen freezes at 30 degrees, but does come back.

Vinca rosea
CREEPING PERIWINKLE

Height: 12-18 in.   Spread: 1-5 ft.   Areas: N (protected), C (protected), S

Often called "the poor man's rose," creeping periwinkle will thrive in full sun or partial shade. It is very salt-tolerant and will grow in just about any of our

Florida soils. The periwinkle is injured at about 32 degrees, but will often come back and reseed itself quite naturally. If you like pink- and white-flowering varieties, you should consider using this easy-to-grow plant.

Wedelia trilobata
WEDELIA

Height: 1-3 ft.   Spread: 10-15 ft.   Areas: N (protected), C (protected), S

If you like a beautiful, yellow daisy-like flower, you'll love the wedelia. This plant blooms during most of the year. It will do well in almost any sandy soil, is easily started from cuttings, and does well in full sun to partial shade. Wedelia is so salt-tolerant that I have seen it growing over a sea wall *into* the salt water. It does get injured at about 30 degrees, but bounces right back. If it gets too large, put your mower on its highest setting, and trim it once a year.

Zebrina pendula
WANDERING JEW

Height: 12-18 in.   Spread: 1-6 ft.   Areas: N (protected), C (protected), S

The wandering Jew is a prolific grower; you can easily plant it in an area that you wish to cover in a short period of time. It will grow in full sun, but does best in partial shade. Wandering Jew has fair salt-tolerance, and should be planted in an area protected from cold. It is injured at about 32 degrees, but normally comes back.

GROUND COVERS AND VINES FOR FLORIDA

COMMON NAME	SCIENTIFIC NAME	FLOWER COLOR	SUN OR SHADE	HEIGHT
Ajuga (Bugle Weed)	Ajuga repens	Bluish Purple	Sun to Partial Shade	6"-12"
Allamanda	Allamanda cathartica	Golden Yellow	Full Sun to Partial Shade	5'-10'
Artillery Plant	Pilea microphylla	Insignificant	Sun to Partial Shade	6"-12"
Black-Eyed Susan	Thunbergia alata	White, Yellow	Sun to Partial Shade	5'-10'
Bleeding Heart	Clerodendrum Thomsoniae	Crimson, White	Sun to Partial Shade	10'-15'
Bougainvillea	Bougainvillea sp.	Purple, Red, Orange, Gold, White	Sun to Partial Shade	10'-50'
Cereus, Night-Blooming	Hylocereus undatus	White	Sun	5'-12'
Coral Vine	Antigonon leptopus	Pink	Sun	5'-15'
Dichondra	Dichondra repens	————	Sun to Partial Shade	4"-8"
Fern, Asparagus	Asparagus sprengeri	————	Sun or Shade	12"-24"
Fig, Climbing	Ficus pumila	Insignificant	Sun or Shade	10'-15'
Flame Vine	Pyrostegia venusta	Orange	Sun to Partial Shade	10'-15'
Flame Vine, Mexican	Senecio confusus	Orange-Red	Sun to Partial Shade	5'-15'
Garlic Vine	Cydista aequinoctialis	Pink	Sun to Partial Shade	5'-8'
Grape	Vitus sp.	Insignificant	Sun to Partial Shade	5'-15'
Grass, Mondo	Ophiopogon japonicus	Blue	Sun or Shade	6"-8"
Honeysuckle, Cape	Tecomaria capensis	Reddish Orange	Sun to Partial Shade	5'-20'
Honeysuckle, Trumpet	Lonicera sempervirens	Red, Yellow	Sun to Partial Shade	5'-10'
Ivy, Algerian or English	Hedera	Insignificant	Sun or Shade	10'-40'
Jasmine	Jasminum sp.	White	Sun to Partial Shade	4'-8'
Jasmine, Confederate	Trachelospermum jasminoides	White	Sun to Partial Shade	10'-20'

*Tops die to ground with first freeze in northern Florida. Plants grow back following spring.
**Will be killed with first freeze in northern Florida. Needs winter protection in central and southern Florida.

SPREAD	GROUND COVER OR VINE	PERENNIAL OR ANNUAL	DECIDUOUS OR EVERGREEN	PLANTING SEASON	BLOOMING SEASON	AREA
1'-3'	GC	P*	E	Feb-Oct	Summer, Fall	N,C,S
5'-10'	V	P**	E	March-Sept	Nearly Year-round	N,C,S
1'-3'	GC	P**	E	Feb-Oct	————	N,C,S
3'-8'	V	A	E	March-Sept	Summer, Fall	N,C,S
5'-10'	V	P**	E	March-Oct	Spring, Summer	N,C,S
10'-30'	V	P**	E	March-Oct	Spring, Fall, Winter	C,S
5'-8'	V	P*	E	Year-round	Summer	C,S
10'-15'	V	P*	D	March-Sept	Summer, Early Fall	N,C,S
3'-9'	GC	P*	E	Year-round	————	N,C,S
2'-4'	GC	P*	E	Year-round	————	N,C,S
10'-15'	V	P	E	Year-round	————	N,C,S
10'-15'	V	P**	E	March-Oct	Nearly Year-round	N,C,S
5'-15'	V	P**	E	Feb-Oct	Summer, Fall	N,C,S
4'-8'	V	P**	E	March-Sept	Summer	N,C,S
5'-20'	V	P	D	March-Oct	————	N,C,S
6"-10"	GC	P*	E	Year-round	Summer	N,C,S
10'-30'	V	P**	E	Feb-Oct	Nearly Year-round	N,C,S
5'-10'	V	P	E	March-Oct	Nearly Year-round	N,C
10'-40'	GC, V	P	E	Year-round	————	N,C,S
5'-10'	V	P	E	March-Oct	Year-round	N,C,S
10'-20'	V	P	E	Year-round	Spring, Summer	C,S

GROUND COVERS AND VINES FOR FLORIDA

COMMON NAME	SCIENTIFIC NAME	FLOWER COLOR	SUN OR SHADE	HEIGHT
Jasmine, Madagascar	Stephanotis floribunda	White	Sun to Partial Shade	5'-10'
Jessamine, Carolina	Gelsemium sempervirens	Yellow	Sun (for best flowering)	5'-8'
Joseph's Coat	Alternanthera amoena	White	Sun to Partial Shade	5"-10"
Juniper, Shore	Juniperus conferta	————————	Sun to Partial Shade	1'-2'
Kalanchoe	Kalanchoe longiflora	Red, Yellow, Pink Orange	Sun	1'-3'
Lantana	Lantana montevidensis	Yellow, Purple, White	Sun to Partial Shade	1'-3'
Liriope	Liriope muscari	White, Blue	Sun or Shade	12"-18"
Morning Glory	Ipomoea sp.	Bluish Purple	Sun to Partial Shade	5'-10'
Peperomia	Peperomia obtusifolia	Insignificant	Sun or Shade	6"-18"
Periwinkle, Creeping	Vinca rosea	Pink, White	Sun to Partial Shade	12"-18"
Purple Queen	Setcreasea purpurea	Insignificant	Sun or Shade	6"-12"
Queen's Wreath	Petrea volubilis	Bluish Purple	Sun to Partial Shade	5'-8'
Rose, Wood	Ipomoea tuberosa	Yellow	Sun to Partial Shade	6'-10'
Ruellia	Ruellia strepens	Pale Blue, Violet	Sun	6"-12"
Trumpet Creeper	Campsis sp.	Red, Orange, Yellow	Sun to Partial Shade	10'-15'
Trumpet, Herald's	Beaumontia grandiflora	White (large)	Sun	10'-12'
Trumpet, Painted	Clytostoma callistegioides	Lavender	Sun to Partial Shade	3'-5'
Wandering Jew	Zebrina pendula	Insignificant	Sun or Shade	12"-18"
Wedelia	Wedelia trilobata	Yellow	Sun or Shade	1'-3'
Wisteria, Chinese	Wisteria sinensis	Bluish Purple, White	Sun to Partial Shade	5'-10'

*Tops die to ground with first freeze in northern Florida. Plants grow back following spring.
**Will be killed with first freeze in northern Florida. Needs winter protection in central and southern Florida.

SPREAD	GROUND COVER OR VINE	PERENNIAL OR ANNUAL	DECIDUOUS OR EVERGREEN	PLANTING SEASON	BLOOMING SEASON	AREA
5'-8'	V	P**	E	March-Oct	Summer	N,C,S
5'-10'	V	P	E	March-Oct	Spring	N,C
1'-2'	GC	P**	E	Feb-Oct	Summer	C,S
2'-4'	GC	P	E	Year-round	————	N,C,S
1'-3'	GC	P*	E	Feb-Oct	Year-round	N,C,S
3'-5'	GC	P*	E	Year-round	Spring, Summer, Fall	N,C,S
10"-24"	GC	P	E	Year-round	Summer	N,C,S
5'-20'	V	P**	E	Feb-Oct	Summer	N,C,S
1'-3'	GC	P**	E	Feb-Oct	————	S
1'-5'	GC	A (but may reseed)	E	March-Oct	Spring, Summer, Fall	N,C,S
6"-18"	GC	P**	E	Feb-Oct	————	N,C,S
5'-10'	V	P**	E	March-Oct	Spring, Summer	N,C,S
10'-15'	V	P	semi-E	March-Oct	Fall	C,S
1'-3'	GC	P**	E	Feb-Oct	Summer	C,S
10'-15'	V	P	D	March-Oct	Summer, Fall	N,C,S
10'-15'	V	P**	E	May-Sept	Summer	N,C,S
3'-5'	V	P	E	March-Sept	Early Summer	N,C,S
1'-6'	GC	P**	E	Feb-Oct	————	N,C,S
10'-15'	GC	P**	E	Feb-Oct	Spring, Summer, Fall	N,C,S
10'-30'	V	P	D	Year-round	Spring	N,C

CHAPTER TEN

Florida Lawns

Having a healthy, green lawn around your home is like having a nice frame around a work of art. It adds beauty to your home. Selecting the right grass for your lawn is important. Factors such as the pH of your soil and determining the amount of money, time, and care you want to put into your lawn should be taken into consideration. I often make the analogy, when teaching, that it's better to have an old, reliable Chevy that's properly maintained than to have a Cadillac you can't afford to keep up. The suitability and maintenance demands of your lawn can be just as exacting as with the upkeep on your car.

LAWN GRASSES

Most newcomers to Florida face the problem of selecting the right lawn. The fescues and blue grasses of the North are not adaptable to Florida. Many homeowners have tried to grow them, but without success. In Rome, do as the Romans do; in Florida, grow the grass or lawn that is best adapted for Florida. The following discussion will provide some basic guidelines for establishment and care of your Florida lawn.

A lawn pays a special dividend in Florida. Compared with concrete, it can reduce garden temperatures from 3 to 6 degrees, an appealing aspect during hot, humid summers. Above all, lawns provide the background against which the colors and textures of your other plants are displayed to their optimum aesthetic potential.

The type of lawn that should be grown depends in large measure on the size of your property, the amount you wish to spend, and the time you can devote to its upkeep. Those who have semi-rural property on several acres possibly can get by with fertilizing and mowing the grasses already in the soil. This will provide an orderly expanse of green that looks neat and attractive. But for the majority of homeowners with homes on normal-sized city lots, a lawn should be planned and started from scratch. This means total preparation of the soil, careful selection of the type of grass, and proper upkeep of the lawn to maintain its appearance and keep it free of insects and disease.

Florida lawn grasses are a vital part of any landscape. They help to create a green, living environment, but need regular care, a regular feeding program, and frequent watering.

A lawn should serve the particular needs of the property owner. Few people have the time or inclination to care for a "putting green" lawn. Those are best left to professional landscapers. The bent grasses needed for this type of lawn are difficult to raise and are prone to disease. In addition, they require constant and frequent mowing, often three or four times a week. Golf-course greens usually are mowed daily, which is beyond the capabilities of the average household.

No single species of grass can meet the demands of every lawn situation. Only tough, coarse grass will survive in a high-traffic area. Grass with fine leaves makes a beautiful display but requires more care, attention to fertilizers, and control of pests and fungi.

MR. GREEN THUMB RULE

Select the right lawn grass for your area. Bitter Blue St. Augustine does better in shade. Bahia is the most drought-tolerant. Bermuda is the finest looking, but also the highest in maintenance. Select by learning about your lawn areas and knowing what is the best choice for you.

St. Augustine *(Stenotaphrum secundatum)*

The grasses most widely used in Florida lawns are the St. Augustine varieties. These are easy to maintain and take shade well. In fact, St. Augustine is the most shade-tolerant grass grown in our state, and it is excellent for coastal areas because of its high salt-tolerance.

St. Augustine grass has much to commend it: rich, blue-green color; adaptability to shade or sun (depending on the variety); and rapid, healthy growth. Even though this grass is coarser than other varieties, it tolerates almost any type of soil, from sand to muck-type soil. St. Augustine needs deep watering, but it has fair drought-resistance.

Its major weaknesses are its lack of resistance to brown-patch disease and chinch bugs, but both these problems are relatively easy to handle with the proper sprays. St. Augustine also can develop thatch problems due to overfeeding and mowing the lawn too low.

The most common types of St. Augustine used in Florida are hybrids of an older, seldom-used variety that gives today's improved grasses their hardiness.

Seville St. Augustine, often sold in plug-form, creates an attractive, low-growing lawn.

St. Augustine varieties are the most popular grasses for Florida lawns.

Bitter Blue has dark, blue-green leaves that do well in shade. An improved variety, *Floratine,* has closer nodes at the beginning of each leaf blade.

Floratam is another good variety, developed by the University of Florida and Texas A&M. It is an extremely vigorous grass with larger inner nodes, and is resistant to SAD (St. Augustine decline) virus and chinch bugs. Floratam is not as shade-resistant as the other varieties and should not be planted in shady areas.

Another variety is *Seville,* which makes a beautiful, low carpet-like lawn. Seville often is sold in plug form rather than flats.

Unlike other grasses, St. Augustine does not grow from seed but from plugs or sod. It is usually sold in flats a yard square, which can be placed edge-to-edge to fill in the desired lawn area or cut into smaller squares and arranged in a checkerboard pattern to grow together to form the lawn. Once established, St. Augustine puts out vigorous growth in the form of long runners which can be cut off and replanted to fill in other areas.

Do not make the mistake of mowing St. Augustine grass too low. Set your mower at 3 inches for most types, including Floratam. Dwarf types such as Seville must be kept at 2 inches. These heights are better for the health and growth of the grass, as well as for giving a lush, rich look to your lawn. While it is an aggressive, vigorous grower, St. Augustine does not tolerate heavy-traffic areas.

Bermuda *(Cynodondactylon)*

Although St. Augustine is considered an elegant grass, the true aristocrat is Bermuda, a fine-bladed grass with a rich appearance, often used on golf-course greens and fairways. A Bermuda lawn can be most spectacular but requires frequent mowing and a lot of care, plus frequent fertilizing, to maintain its deep, rich, green color.

Planted from seed (common varieties) or sod (improved varieties), Bermuda is a vigorous grower that can overrun flower beds or other unwanted areas unless these are edged with some type of impenetrable border such as metal strips, wood, or brick. In some parts of the world, Bermuda grass is known as "devil grass" because of its tenacious growth habits. Once introduced into a garden, it

Tifway Bermuda   Bermuda grass

Bermuda can be beautiful, but it needs frequent mowing.

is almost impossible to eradicate. This characteristic makes it a most desirable lawn grass, but it has to be kept under control. Bermuda can be cut very low, preferably with a reel-type mower. The best varieties for Florida are *Tifway* and *Ormond*.

Zoysia *(Zoysia)*

Very similar in appearance to Bermuda is zoysia grass, which has been advertised extensively in recent years by mail-order nurseries. An attractive grass, zoysia is very slow-growing, taking as long as two years to cover a desired area. In Florida, it suffers very badly from nematode problems. Despite its ultimate good appearance, zoysia is expensive and cannot compete with existing grasses. It requires heavy feeding. Zoysia adds up to higher initial cost, costly upkeep, and debatable results in the long run. In Florida, *Emerald* zoysia and *Mayer* zoysia are preferred varieties. Many grasses are better buys, but if you do decide to plant zoysia, buy your plugs locally, not through the mail. Zoysia can be started from sprigs, plugs, or sod.

Bahia, seeded out

Bahia, ready to plant

Bahia *(Paspalum notatum)*

The most drought-tolerant grass available is bahia, with two recommended varieties: *Argentine* and *Pensacola*. The Argentine, which is the more popular, is a flatter-growing grass without the long seed stalks typical of Pensacola. Both varieties can be started from seed or sod. Argentine is a very attractive lawn if mowed frequently; Pensacola will put out tall seed heads two or three days after mowing, giving the lawn an untidy appearance.

Plant 5 to 10 pounds of bahia seed per thousand square feet of ground, tilling the seed in lightly. Scarified seeds, which are prepared for easier germination, will sprout faster and make a more successful lawn planting. Bahia grass is tough and looks better if cut with a rotary mower, though the blade will have to be very sharp. Bahia grass can dull a mower blade faster than most other grasses.

Manhattan rye

Centipede *(Eremochloa ophiuroides)*

In northern Florida, centipede grass is recommended. Its lack of salt tolerance makes it unsuitable for the coastal areas. Centipede looks like a dwarf St. Augustine. It needs ample moisture, though it can tolerate short dry spells. In high-alkaline soils, it tends to look yellow, or iron-deficient, and it will brown out after a harsh winter. Plant centipede grass in full sun, either from seed, at the rate of 4 ounces per thousand square feet, or from sprigs. I haven't seen any named varieties of this type; it is simply labeled "centipede" grass.

Rye Grass *(Lolium multiflorum)*

For winter color in any lawn, rye is a good, temporary grass. Plant from seed (5 pounds per thousand square feet) from October through November for a lush, rich, green spread until May, when it dies off. Rye grass must be fertilized in December and January and replanted every year. It is sold as "winter" or "Italian" rye.

PLANNING AND PREPARING YOUR LAWN

Installing a lawn means more than merely filling the open spaces between trees, shrubs, and flower beds. You have to determine how much of each open area gets full sun or partial sun and which is fully shaded all day. These factors are crucial to your choice of the type of grass to plant. Soil analysis also will help you choose a variety that will do well. For example, in south Florida, St. Augustine does best in a high pH soil while bahia grass tends to turn yellow. The following chart can help you determine the best grass for your area of the state, and the conditions existing in your garden.

WEED CONTROL

Weeds are like a red flag that signals you have a turf problem. If the pH of the soil is unbalanced, weeds are more likely to invade your property. Check your pH and make sure you have the proper balance for your type of grass. The presence of spurge weed may indicate a nematode problem. Dead spots and brown patches may indicate that feeder roots have been damaged by mole crickets or fungus diseases. New lawns that have been thrown on top of old lawns without adequate sterilization often succumb to nematodes.

Watering should also be checked. Too much water can encourage dollar weeds; too little water and the grass will weaken, allowing beggar weed or creeping Charlie to take over. Lawns that are overly compacted are also more susceptible to weed infestation. Again, a healthy lawn is the best defense against weeds; but if you have a problem, here are some tips for getting rid of these uninvited guests.

Grassy Weeds

Grassy weeds are the most difficult to control. It is hard to kill a grassy weed because of the possibility of damaging the lawn. One control for grassy type weeds, however, is glyphosate, sold under the name of Round-Up or Kleen-Up. This material is non-selective, meaning that it kills any green plant it comes in contact with. It is translocated from the green leaf to the root system where it kills the plant.

One of the most obnoxious grassy weeds is the sand bur. Not only does it stick you, but it is hard to remove from the skin. One way to pick up the sand-bur seed is with a broom covered with an old piece of burlap. Sweep the broom over the lawn, allowing the burlap to catch and pick up the burs. When all the burs are removed from the lawn, simply throw away the burlap.

A member of the reed family, sedge is also difficult to control. Resembling the sand bur, sedge has a triangular stem and a soft seed. The best way to combat sedge is by spot-treating affected areas with Round-Up or Kleen-Up.

Crabgrass is another troublesome weed; to eradicate it, you may have to dig it out by hand, but you can probably kill this weed with a local application of glyphosate.

Glyphosate (sold as Round-Up or Kleen-Up) may be used to kill grassy weeds along a fence, eliminating the need for back-breaking work.

Clover

Dollar weed thrives in
wet areas, but can be
deterred by chemicals.

Broadleaf Weeds

Clover is often very attractive with its tiny white flowers, but it is, nevertheless, a weed. Treat it with 2, 4-D in bahia lawns, and with Atrazine in St. Augustine lawns.

Creeping beggar weed is sometimes called "stick tight." Its tiny, jointed seed pods will stick to almost anything they touch. This woody vine weaves its way through your lawn. Repeated applications of 2, 4-D or Atrazine should control beggar weed.

The shamrock or yellow wood sorrel is a variety of the oxalis weed. Although it is often sold in nurseries, it can be considered a weed; after all, the definition of a weed is "a plant that's out of place." Having shamrocks growing throughout your yard probably won't bring you good luck, and it can harm your grass. Repeated applications of Atrazine in St. Augustine; and 2, 4-D with dicamba in bahia will control this weed.

Dollar weed is sometimes called pennywort. A round-leaved type, dollar weed grows in wet areas, and can be partially controlled by reducing the amount of water your lawn receives. For control, spray St. Augustine with Atrazine; and bahia with 2, 4-D.

Chickweed tends to be a problem during the winter. This vining weed is a succulent and prefers moist soil. Again, spraying St. Augustine with Atrazine; and bahia with 2, 4-D; will control this weed.

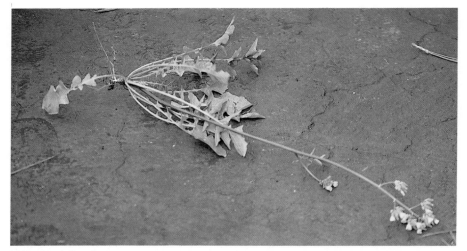

False dandelion

Match weed tends to
creep into lawn grasses.

Another common broadleaf weed is false dandelion. Although it looks much like the northern dandelion, false dandelion is a member of a different family. To control this weed in bahia grass, use 2, 4-D or Trimec; in St. Augustine, use Atrazine; in Bermuda, use DSMA or MSMA weed killers.

Match weed is a broadleaf that looks like a kitchen match, with a purplish flower on a 3-inch-long stalk. Match weed can be controlled in bahia with 2, 4-D or Trimec. Use Atrazine to control this weed in a St. Augustine lawn.

TYPES OF WEED KILLERS FOR FLORIDA LAWNS

Selective weed killers are designed to kill the weed and not injure the lawn. Of these types, the most common are 2, 4-D and dicamba, which are considered hormone weed killers. They are often sold as Trimec, Weedone, Weed-Be-Gone or just 2, 4-D. 2, 4-D can be very damaging to tomato plants, poinsettias, and papayas. Spraying should be done on a day with little or no wind. Most weed

For best results, use weed-killer sprays as soon as the offending weeds are spotted, preferably when they are young, tender, and actively growing.

killers are more effective when the weeds are young, tender, and actively growing. It is better to use a light application more than once than to spray heavily and risk burning the surrounding grass. Atrazine is a good pre- and post-emergent herbicide to use on St. Augustine. Use caution when applying, and, as with any herbicide, use according to label directions. Atrazine is sometimes sold under the trade name Purge. It is different from most other herbicides since it does give you some pre-emergent weed control, which stops the germination of weed seeds. Some of the other common brand names for pre-emergents are Balan, Dacthal, and Balfin.

Non-selective herbicides, such as glyphosate, will kill any plant they come into contact with. This chemical is absorbed through green foliage. Cacodylic acid is also absorbed through the foliage. It differs from glyphosate in that it burns the foliage and does not have the long-lasting or deep effectiveness of glyphosate.

HOW TO PREPARE A PROPER LAWN

Step 1: Determine the pH of the soil, which will be an important factor in the selection of your lawn grass and whether you will need to add chemicals.

Step 2: Evaluate the amount of light your lawn will receive. If you have dense shade, your choice may be St. Augustine. For a bright, sunny area where watering may be less frequent, bahia is a possible choice. A lawn need not consist of only one variety. For example, St. Augustine may well fill any large, shady areas, but you still can plant Bermuda in portions of the lawn that receive full sun. As a general rule, plant the grass best suited to the soil and sun/shade ratio in the various areas of your property. Remember, no grass will grow in dense shade.

Step 3: Next, rototill the soil to a depth of 6 or 8 inches. Add Florida, Canadian, or Michigan peat. Till this in to a depth of 6 inches. The peat should be 2 to 3 inches thick over the surface area. Also till in a 10-10-10 or 20-10-10 fertilizer, one that is high in phosphorus, to promote good growth.

Step 4: Roll or rake the soil smooth, going as close to the final grade as possible. If this intended lawn area adjoins your home, slope the soil gently away from the house to ensure good drainage. This need not be a perceptible incline, which might spoil the aesthetics of your lawn. But the grade should be enough to allow water to drain off and not lay stagnant after a heavy rain. Poorly drained lawns soon develop diseases and root rot.

Step 5: Decide which process you want to use to install your lawn, such as seeding, sodding (the easiest way), sprigging, or plugging.

Seeding

Seeding is the way most people from the North are accustomed to starting their lawns. It can be done here, but not as quickly or with the same success. Our sandy soils dry out rapidly. Seeds must be kept moist, if any success is expected. A sprinkler system is almost a necessity when seeding.

Sodding

Sodding is the easiest way to an instant lawn, but it is also the most expensive. Sod should be laid on the final grade, on an evenly raked surface. One piece of sod should butt up against the next piece. Rolling is desirable for an even turf. You will need frequent waterings until the root base is established.

Sprigging

Sprigging is a time-consuming method for starting a lawn. The sprigs must be kept moist, like seeds, or they will die. A sprig is one strand of grass that has nodes, leaves, and roots. Commercially, some sod farms have large tractors called sprig spreaders. The workers use this equipment to chop up sprigs, spread

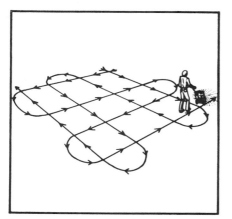

Sow seed and spread fertilizer by applying half of it in a north-south direction and the other half in an east-west direction: in other words, lengthwise and then crosswise over the entire area.

For best coverage, install checkerboard sod plugs across the area.

MR. GREEN THUMB RULE

Never use a sprayer for weed killer and then reuse it for insecticides or fungicides. Mark the weed-killer sprayer for WEED KILLER ONLY! Even thorough washing may not get rid of these potent chemicals, so don't risk contamination. Each chemical has its own special purpose; use them all accordingly.

---

them over the sod field, and roll it level. Then they apply water on a daily basis and produce sod. Many people do not cover their sprigs with enough soil; consequently, they don't often get the quality lawns the commercial growers produce. For the average homeowner, plugging or sodding is generally a more efficient method.

Plugging

Plugging is another relatively easy way to start your lawn. Plugs are normally sold in 2- to 4-inch squares, which are planted 12 to 18 inches apart. Often a checkerboard pattern is used.

WATER: THE KEY TO A GOOD LAWN

After you've installed your grass, watering is crucial. Some people water their lawns only during drought periods, and some won't water for some time after it has rained, mistakenly thinking that the rain offered sufficient moisture. Lawns use an abundance of water, especially during the warm, humid season. As discussed in Chapter 1, water is one of the most important factors in growing plants of any kind. Lawn grasses are constantly giving off moisture; it is part of their respiration process. That moisture has to be replaced, which means your lawn will need either frequent rain or frequent deep watering. Watering is, of course, the most reliable means. The average lawn grass will be up to 85 percent water. This high percentage should help us realize how important water is to a healthy lawn.

Whatever watering system you use, check to make sure you are getting adequate coverage. Sprinkler systems are designed to overlap, thus curbing brown spots, but even the best sometimes miss a few patches. Check out your system and find ways to compensate. A healthy lawn will demand a reliable deep-watering system.

Your lawn will get some additional moisture from rain, normal condensation, and even morning dew; but you can't really rely on these. Nor can you rely on occasional short waterings. It is better to water once or twice a week with ½ to 1 inch per application than to sprinkle lightly every day. This develops a stronger and deeper root system opposed to a shallow one. After watering for 15 minutes,

---

MR. GREEN THUMB RULE

Check the watering system! Use either rain gauges or a simple tuna can to measure how much your system is putting out. Normally, your lawn requires 1 to 2 inches of water per week.

Open cans, such as tuna cans, may be used as rain gauges to check the amount of water actually reaching the lawn. As a rule-of-thumb, each watering should deliver from ½ inch to 1 inch of water to the lawn.

I check the level of water in a tuna can sitting on my lawn. By multiplying the amount by 4, I have a good idea how many inches per hour my sprinkler system is putting out.

By and large, the best time to water is in the early morning when the temperature is moderate and the water can do the most good. However, if this time is a problem, afternoon or midday waterings are better than no watering at all.

A lawn *must* be fertilized; if it isn't, the neglect is clear.

LAWN CARE AND FEEDING

Your grass also will need feeding — not merely to promote health but also to help it choke out weeds that inevitably invade any lawn. Healthy grass will fight for its own space in the ground, and this battle should be reinforced with fertilizer to enable the grass to hold its own. Many horticulturists believe in fertilizing only once or twice a year. But more frequent, lighter fertilizer applications seem to be the secret to continuing the good growth of turf.

Two very efficient methods will distribute granular fertilizer over a lawn. The first method is the drop spreader. It must be pushed back and forth across the lawn in parallel paths until the entire turf is covered. Set the spreader according to the recommendations on the bag of fertilizer. This will ensure that the proper amount of fertilizer is dispensed. The second mechanical means is the rotary spreader, which broadcasts fertilizer granules over a wider area than the drop spreader and provides a better chance for proper coverage.

A method of fertilizing that has become quite popular in recent years involves adding a liquid fertilizer dispenser to the hose line leading to your sprinkler. This is very reliable and provides an easy way to water and fertilize lightly at the same time.

All lawns need NPK — nitrogen, phosphorus, and potassium — but other minor elements, such as iron, also are advisable for optimum turf growth. Check the label on your fertilizer to make sure you are feeding your lawn all the elements needed for best results.

MOWERS AND MOWING

Many gardeners spend considerable money, time, and effort installing a lawn, then attack it with a mower that does little more than lacerate the grass. Then they wonder why the turf deteriorates after a few weeks with rough brown tips on the leaves.

Every lawn deserves care and consideration when it is being mowed, just as attention should be given to the type of mower being used and its condition.

Fertilizer must be applied in smooth, even strokes to avoid a "zebra" effect.

Mowers come in two types: rotary and reel. The rotary mower is the more widely used because of its versatility. The rotating blade can cut not only grass, but also small shrubs and vines. It can be used to level wild ground before tilling, as the blade is, in actuality, a lethal weapon that slices off almost anything in its path. Despite warnings, many people lose fingers and toes that have been foolishly placed beneath the protective housing. Rotary mowers will also hurl debris, stones, and small twigs at frightening speed from the chute, a potential danger that has caused serious injury to people and pets. When mowing with a rotary mower, always check the surface of the lawn for foreign objects and remove them before you get started.

Rotary mowers often have an attachable bag fastened to the chute, which catches the grass clippings. Still, letting the cut grass sink back into the sod after being clipped is good for the soil. It provides natural nourishment to supplement applied fertilizers.

The reel mower was popular years ago before the rotary mower was invented. Still used in some small-space situations, the reel mower has one basic advantage over the rotary type; the reel mower does a better job of cutting tender-leaved grasses, such as Bermuda and zoysia. A reel mower's mechanism actually *cuts* the grass in the same way scissors cut, rather than *slicing* the grass, which is what a rotary mower does. A manual reel-type mower does require a little more muscle because, in addition to pushing the mower across the lawn, you are producing the power to turn the wheels, which, in turn, rotate the blades.

For small lawns, some people prefer an electric mower, which is a rotary type, powered by electricity rather than a gasoline motor. Electric mowers are somewhat quieter and give off no fumes. But they do require a very long extension cord, and that demands careful planning of your mowing pattern to avoid running over the cord.

The height at which you should set your mower depends upon the type of grass you have. St. Augustine should be kept at 3 inches and the dwarf variety at 2 inches. Bermuda and zoysia look best when cut to 2 inches, as do most other lawn grasses.

After you have planted a lawn, allow it to grow fairly high before mowing, then mow once at a setting of about 5 or 6 inches. Then make another pass to cut it down to the final, desired height. Place your mower on level concrete to make the height adjustment, measuring from the blade to the ground for accuracy. Never try to mow very high grass down to 2 inches as this may result in damage to the grass. Mowing grass is like having a haircut at the barber: gradual shortening will achieve the desired results better than a heavy-handed attack!

Lawnmower Maintenance

The blades on a rotary mower should be kept sharp. Next to nematodes and insect infestations, a dull blade is probably the most common killer of lawns. Mowing is meant to cut grass evenly and smoothly, not beat it to death. Professional gardeners sharpen their mower blades daily. But once a month during the mowing season should be sufficient for the average homeowner. Otherwise, sharpen every two or three months, depending on the amount of mowing being done.

Sharpening a mower blade is relatively simple, with a file or a grinder. Be sure to take off equal amounts of metal on both sides of the blade to maintain proper balance. As a safety precaution, always disconnect the spark plug before working on a mower. An accidental start or a sudden release of compression can throw the blade into motion, causing serious injury. For foolproof safety, the spark plug can be removed totally to ensure the motor does not start.

Standard maintenance on a mower includes checking and changing the oil, the spark plug and, if needed, the air filter. Generally, a full crankcase of oil will last a season, but like your automobile, your mower will operate at peak performance only if the oil is clean. Replacing a worn spark plug will eliminate difficult starts and conserve gasoline. The air filter seldom needs replacing, but it does require regular cleaning. Squeezing a warm solution of detergent through the filter will remove most dirt. Before replacing, dry the filter between layers of paper towels, then spray with WD-40 or a similar thin lubricant, which will improve the filter's capability to trap dust particles.

Before storing the mower for the winter, be sure to drain the gasoline from the fuel tank. If left standing for long periods, gasoline tends to separate, producing a gummy residue that will clog the fuel line. After every use, hose the underside of the mower to remove finely packed grass clippings from the housing, as well as any impacted soil. Allow the motor to cool before this washing, otherwise the cold water from the hose may crack the engine block. Occasional oiling of the wheels and crankshaft also will help maintain your mower in peak condition for years of good service.

SOD CUTTING AND THATCHING

To remove old sod, you can rent a sod cutter. Set the depth at 2 inches and move the machine in parallel lines in order to scoop out the soil evenly. A sod cutter is a neat, time-saving alternative to digging up the old sod by hand.

Thatching is not the undesirable condition some gardeners believe, because this layering of lawn clippings can create a natural foundation over which new growth can flourish. Thatch also allows a cultivated lawn to grow over and replace an older lawn or other grasses, as often happens with St. Augustine and Bermuda. And thatch is a vital element for providing a solid base for a lawn, for walking or for mowing. Without a solid thatch base, it is difficult to run a mower across a lawn.

However, thatch sometimes can become too thick and compact, providing a breeding ground for insects and disease. When this occurs, you need to loosen the thatch and remove some of it to allow air and moisture to circulate down to the soil.

You can rent a verti-cutter, which should be set ½ inch into the soil, allowing the teeth to reach down into the thatch and pull it out without damaging the lawn itself. A power rake is another method of dethatching bahia lawns. It slices through the layers of rhizomes and stolons, allowing air and water to flow through. However, a power rake is liable to remove almost one-third of your grass, and using one is, quite truthfully, a major job for the average gardener. Many homeowners hire a professional landscape company to handle dethatching.

COMMON LAWN PROBLEMS IN FLORIDA

Contrary to popular belief, a general-purpose insecticide is *not* the total answer to the varied problems that can affect lawns in Florida. Certainly it will help, just as malathion and diazinon will take care of the majority of insect pests that affect flowers and vegetables. But proper diagnosis of any condition is the key to the cure.

A wise gardener gives his lawn a regular checkup and takes note of anything that appears out of order, such as dry-looking areas, brown patches, poor growth, and unhealthy turf. You must take into consideration the type of grass in which any unwanted condition is present. Is your Bermuda fading away while the St. Augustine is flourishing? Has the bahia lost its fresh, sparkling-green appearance? Is the zoysia simply not spreading?

Note *where* the problem exists — in sun or in shade? Is the unusual patch circular? Does it perhaps follow a clearly defined line through the turf?

Often, an odd-looking section denotes a simple lack of water. Perhaps your sprinkler-system heads are clogged and not dispensing water properly. You may have spilled some gasoline on the grass when refilling your mower. Gasoline and oil will affect grass very quickly, causing a growth setback and poor appearance. Too, a handful of granular fertilizer, carelessly dropped, will burn out a patch of grass.

Check for insects by parting the grass and examining the soil. Look for raised tunnels or trails, or a yellow, mottled look that usually follows an attack by juice-sucking insects. A distinctive patch of dead grass 2 to 3 feet in diameter can indicate a fungus infection.

Your lawn will tell you when it's being attacked by insects or diseases; diagnosis and a quick response to the problem are the keys to a cure.

Once you have found the problem, you can go about diagnosing the cause. Do not allow any unusual condition to persist, thinking that it will go away. Uncontrolled insects or disease can wipe out an entire lawn in a single season. For this reason, a regular program of insect and disease control is a valuable insurance policy against loss of your total investment in your lawn.

If you are uncertain as to the cause and what to do, consult your nurseryman. He can recognize and prescribe suitable treatment.

The following are the problems that most often afflict lawns in Florida:

Lawn Insects

Sod webworms: No lawn is safe from these predators. Watch for large moths at dusk, usually ½ to ¾ of an inch long, fluttering about the grass, then disappearing into the turf. The moths lay tiny eggs, evidenced by fine webbing over the turf. The webbing is best seen in the early morning when the dew is still present. Unchecked, these eggs hatch into tiny worms that chew the grass steadily, destroying the turf. During the day, the worms stay curled up under the thatch. Quick and easy control of sod webworms is possible by spraying with Dipel, Thuricide, diazinon, Dursban, or sevin.

White grubworms: Like sod webworms, white grubworms attack all grasses, eating away at the root system, sometimes so severely (especially with St. Augustine) that the turf ends up looking like a loose carpet on the ground. To check for white grubworms, cut a 1-foot square of sod a few inches deep, lift it up, and check the root system. If present, the grubs will stand out starkly against the soil, curled up in thick, white little balls, about 1 to 1½ inches long and ½ inch wide. Dangerous as they can become, white grubworms can be controlled by thoroughly drenching the soil with diazinon, Dursban, or Spectracide. Apply the granular insecticide, followed by a deep watering. Control is most effective when applied about six weeks after the main emergence of June beetles, which appear after the grubs have pupated. Regular annual application will help keep your lawn free of these pests, which are most evident in spring and fall.

Armyworms: Laying from 50 to 100 eggs at a time, the armyworm moth is another plague that attacks all types of grasses. Upon hatching, the worms start eating the grass, crawling across the lawn somewhat like an army — hence the

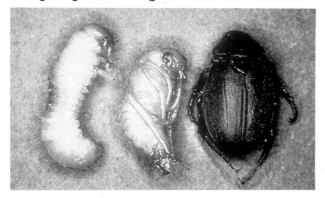

If left unchecked, grubs will destroy root systems in short order.

Mole crickets

Chinch-bug damage in a once-healthy lawn

name. Armyworms are very heavy feeders and, if not checked, can completely destroy a lawn. For good control, spray with diazinon, Dursban, sevin, Dipel, or Thuricide.

Mole crickets: A major cause of damage to bahia and Bermuda lawns, the mole cricket is easily detectable by its tunnel trails on the soil surface: raised mounds about ½-inch high, spreading in all directions. A soft sponginess, along with 5-inch-wide holes, are other indications of mole crickets. This annoying pest can be controlled by spraying with Dursban, diazinon, or Baygon. Oftonal, once used only by professional exterminators, is now available for homeowners and provides a longer residual effect than other products. Oftonal and Mocap are used by certified pest-control operators. Both these insecticides have an offensive odor. Special masks, boots, and gloves usually are worn by the professionals when they apply these toxic insecticides.

One preventive measure that can be taken safely by any gardener is to sprinkle mole-cricket bait throughout the lawn in May through late August. Use mole-cricket bait *after* you have watered the lawn thoroughly. Watering (or an unexpected rain shower) will diminish the bait's effectiveness.

Chinch bugs: Chinch bugs are the primary problem with St. Augustine grass. These tiny, heat-loving insects attack the leaves and stems, sucking the life fluids from the grass, which then turns yellowish brown and looks as though it has been burned. Chinch bugs can be detected in the sunniest parts of the lawn and along sidewalks and patios. Spray with diazinon, Spectricide, Dursban, Ethion, or Baygon.

Lawn Diseases

Helminthosporium sp. — **Leaf Spot:** Ultimately fatal, leaf spot begins as brown, purple, or yellow areas with a dark border and a black spore center. Blades of grass turn yellow and die. A serious problem with Bermuda grass, leaf spot also can attack zoysia and St. Augustine lawns. This disease attacks throughout the year and is best controlled with Daconil, Tersan, or Fore.

Piricularia grisea — **Gray Leaf Spot:** Gray leaf spot causes brown and gray lesions on stems and leaves, with a dark-brown margin around the infected areas. It usually affects rye and St. Augustine grasses in the hot, humid, summer months. Spray with Thiram, Fore, or Daconil for control of this fungus.

Rhizoctonia solani — **Brown Patch:** This is a cool-weather fungal disease that affects St. Augustine, rye, zoysia, centipede, Bermuda, and bahia grasses. It is more common when the temperature is above 70 degrees with high humidity. Grass turns brown quickly and leaves pull loose from runners easily. This fungus is not fatal but can damage a lawn and weaken the turf. Spray with any good fungicide labeled for brown patch, including Fore, Daconil, Tersan, benomyl, maneb, or Terrachlor.

Sclerotinia homoeocarpa — **Dollar Spot:** An easy fungus to identify, dollar spot starts by turning the grass a pale yellow in areas 2 to 3 inches in diameter, spreading to form larger diseased areas. Often seen in fall and spring when fog and dew are present, dollar spot is a major problem with Bermuda and zoysia and occasionally bahia, but can sometimes attack St. Augustine and centipede lawns, as well. Two applications of Daconil, plus complete fertilization, usually will take care of this problem.

Three more fungal diseases that attack Florida lawns include:

1. *Pythium,* associated with newly planted grass and prevalent in poorly drained areas. Control with Subdue.
2. *Fairy ring,* a circle of mushrooms inside which the grass will die. In severe cases, soil fumigation may be necessary, but usually, hand-picking the mushrooms, fertilizing, and increasing the watering will eliminate this problem. *Caution:* Do not attempt to eat any mushrooms picked from a fairy ring. They are poisonous.
3. *Slime mold,* an unattractive black mold, sometimes gray or yellow. It is harmless and can be washed off with a hose. Proper mowing usually takes care of this minor problem.

When spraying for fungal diseases, it is best to spray an entire area rather than to try spot treatments. When examining your turf for possible fungal disease, use a magnifying glass. Most of the fungal organisms are too small to be seen with the naked eye.

Mold on grass

COMPARISONS OF FLORIDA TURF GRASSES

GRASS	TEXTURE	SOIL pH ADAPTABILITY	SHADE TOLERANCE*	SALT TOLERANCE
ST. AUGUSTINES Varieties:				
Floratam	Coarse	Wide range	Poor	Excellent
Florantine	Coarse	Wide range	Good	Excellent
Bitter Blue	Coarse	Wide Range	Good	Excellent
Floralawn	Coarse	Wide Range	Moderate	Excellent
Seville	Coarse	Wide Range	Good	Excellent
Raleigh	Coarse	Wide Range	Good	Excellent
BERMUDAS Varieties:				
Common	Fine	Wide range	Poor	Good
Ormond	Fine	Wide range	Poor	Good
Tiflawn	Fine	Wide range	Poor	Good
Tifway 419	Fine	Wide range	Poor	Good
ZOYSIAS Varieties:				
Japonica	Intermediate to Fine	Wide range	Good	Good
Meyer-Z-52	Intermediate to Fine	Wide range	Good	Good
Matrella	Intermediate to Fine	Wide range	Good	Good
Emerald	Intermediate to Fine	Wide range	Good	Good
CENTIPEDE Type:				
Common	Intermediate	Acid soils	Good	Poor
BAHIAS Varieties:				
Pensacola	Intermediate to Coarse	Acid soils	Poor	Poor
Argentine	Intermediate	Acid soils	Poor	Poor
RYE Type:				
Common	Fine	Wide range	Fair	Fair

*All the grasses shown in the chart tolerate at least partial sun.

DROUGHT TOLERANCE	MOWING FREQUENCY	FERTILIZER REQUIREMENTS	PEST PROBLEMS	PROPAGATION
Moderate	Every 5-10 days	Moderate to High	Low	
Moderate	Every 5-10 days	Moderate to High	Moderate	Sod, Plugs, Sprigs
Moderate	Every 5-10 days	Moderate to High	Moderate	Sod, Plugs, Sprigs
Good	Every 5-10 days	Moderate to High	Moderate	Sod, Plugs, Sprigs
Good	Every 5-10 days	Moderate to High	Moderate	Sod, Plugs, Sprigs
Good	Every 5-10 days	Moderate to High	Moderate	Sod, Plugs, Sprigs
Fair	Every 3-7 days	High	High	Sod, Plugs, Sprigs
Fair	Every 3-7 days	High	High	Sod, Plugs, Sprigs
Fair	Every 3-5 days	High	High	Sod, Plugs, Sprigs
Fair	Every 3-5 days	High	High	Sod, Plugs, Sprigs
Fair	Every 10-14 days	Moderate to High	High	Sod, Plugs, Sprigs, Seed
Fair	Every 10-14 days	Moderate to High	High	Sod, Plugs
Fair	Every 10-14 days	Moderate to High	High	Sod, Plugs
Fair	Every 10-14 days	Moderate to High	High	Sod, Plugs
Fair to Good	Every 10-14 days	Low	Moderate	Sod, Plugs, Sprigs, Seed
Good	Every 7-10 days	Very Low	High	Seed, Sod
Excellent	Every 7-10 days	Low	High	Seed, Sod
Fair	Every 5-10 days	Moderate	Low	Seed

CHAPTER ELEVEN

Houseplants

For centuries, man has brought plants indoors to brighten his home and add year-round color. But there are *no* true houseplants. Anything grown indoors has its origins in nature. For this reason, the indoor gardener should try to duplicate as closely as possible the conditions under which plants grow in their outdoor environment. Water, light, and soil are as important in the home as they are in the garden, because all plants rely on these elements for nourishment, growth, and healthy foliage and flowers.

Many people are misled by the lush appearance of houseplants in stores and florist shops, not realizing that the healthy condition comes from an ideal greenhouse environment, proper feeding, and the right amount of light. These folks buy a plant, take it home and then wonder why it droops, yellows, and dies after a few weeks. They blame the store when *they* are to blame for not taking proper care of the plant. You must discover the specific needs of every plant grown indoors. Some need more sun than others. Many can survive with a cup of water once a week; others need daily watering. Each houseplant has individual requirements. You cannot expect any plant to flourish when it is dumped in a corner and neglected. Take care of your plants as you would any member of your household. Check them daily, testing the soil with your finger to make sure there is sufficient moisture, and position them so they receive enough direct or filtered sunlight.

The more common types of indoor plants, such as ivy, can be bought at supermarkets and dime stores. But for more esoteric varieties, go to a reputable garden shop where you can get advice and instructions on establishing the proper conditions for continued growth and healthy appearance.

Knowledge is power — and learning all you can about the plants in your home will give you the capacity to keep your indoor garden in the best possible shape.

Indoor plants are not immune to disease and insect problems. A rich, sterile potting soil is the only guarantee of avoiding such hazards from the outset. Never use soil from your garden for indoor plantings, because you run the risk of bringing in fungal diseases and insects. If you notice a plant showing symptoms of wilting or poor growth, it may be infected and will need treatment just like outdoor plants.

Take care of your foliage and flowering houseplants as you would any member of your family.

One of the biggest mistakes made by indoor gardeners is overwatering. Many plants should be allowed to dry out between waterings; others need light, daily watering. Knowing what a particular plant needs will enable you to gauge the amount and frequency of water.

SOIL FOR INDOOR PLANTS

Good, commercial soil mixes are available at garden shops. Most are sterilized and adaptable for indoor gardening needs. Soil is the basic material in which almost every plant grows, but certain additives are useful for adapting soil to certain plants or for particular purposes. These include:

Vermiculite: A very light, mica-like mineral that has been expanded by extremely high heat. Its porosity allows it to hold water like a sponge, and it also improves the drainage of heavy soils. A sterile medium, it can be used to start seeds or root cuttings.

Perlite: A white, sterile medium that has been produced from the heat explosion of volcanic rock. Its rough edges will hold water, though not as long as vermiculite. Perlite is recommended as a good addition to a soil mix for plants that prefer to be kept on the dry side. Perlite is a good rooting medium for succulent stems that tend to rot if given too much moisture.

Sand: Finely ground particles of stone, mostly quartz. Coast sand will improve the drainage of any soil and is a necessary component of a soil mix for growing cactus. Sand also is one of the best mediums for rooting clippings.

Leaf Mold: Partially decayed leaves, usually oak leaves. Leaf mold improves the quality and fertility of any soil and is one of the best sources of organic material.

Humus: Decayed vegetation that increases the soil's water absorption. Humus also improves the quality and fertility of soil.

From left: Pothos, Dracaena marginata, syngonium, Red Princess philodendron.

Peat Moss: The decomposing remains of plants. Sphagnum moss is by far the best type of peat, since it resists further decomposition. Peat has good water-retention properties and helps lighten soil texture.

FERTILIZING INDOOR PLANTS

No aspect of gardening is more misunderstood than fertilizing. Most people presume that a sick-looking plant needs feeding. Actually, lack of plant food seldom is the cause. More often that not, problems with indoor plants stem from inadequate light, improper watering, or an insect or disease infestation.

Many good houseplant fertilizers are on the market. Two of them — Peters and Nutri-Sol — are excellent for indoor *and* outdoor plants.

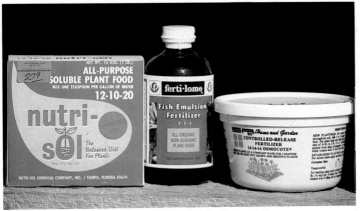

Fertilizers are available in many types and concentrations.

Plants that actively grow during spring and summer will benefit from a monthly feeding. Fertilization should be discontinued or lessened during winter, when many plants slow down and even become dormant.

It can be confusing to examine the great variety of plant foods available: powders, liquids, and tablets; fast-release and slow-release compounds; organic and inorganic nutrients; monthly fertilizers; others to be given with each watering. The best method is to follow the directions for each particular plant, and feed accordingly rather than to fertilize everything you have. The only exception to this would be to add a little Nutri-Sol every time you water, thereby ensuring your plants not only get moisture but also a little "shot in the arm" as well. However, major feeding should be done only at the recommended intervals for each plant.

Choice of fertilizer is important, however, with acid-loving plants such as azaleas, gardenias, camellias, and all citrus plants. Select an acid-type fertilizer from your garden shop for these plants.

HOUSEPLANT PROBLEMS

Warm temperatures and low humidity are the general rule in a house, and these conditions are ideal for many pests that plague indoor plants. Without the presence of their natural enemies, insect pests can multiply rapidly and destroy a plant quickly. For the indoor gardener, therefore, pest control is a continuing process.

Before adding a new plant to your indoor garden, it should be isolated for a two-week period — put in quarantine. Check the undersides of the leaves thoroughly for any signs of insects. The younger leaves at the growing tips of plants are especially vulnerable to attack. If you find no trace of insect infestation, place your new plant with the rest of your indoor garden, but maintain a watchful eye. Prevention is the best possible method of pest control, because once insects or diseases appear, it is often a losing battle to try to cure the condition.

For example: A chemical spray is effective in controlling the adult fungus gnat, but there are six other stages in the gnat's life cycle which may not be affected at all. It would take more than a month of proper spraying to eradicate this pest completely, using an insecticide that kills only the adult. Consult a garden shop for the proper compounds to handle *all* stages of insects as they develop among your plants.

Common Insect Problems

Fungus Gnat: Generally considered harmless, the fungus gnat is a familiar indoor plant pest. With black bodies and grayish-brown abdomens, the adult gnats are smaller than fruit flies, for which they are sometimes mistaken. The female lays from 100 to 300 eggs in the soil. At the usual household temperature of 72 degrees, the eggs hatch in only four days. The emerging maggot feeds on the root hairs of young seedlings. The larvae are seen easily when the plant is watered. They look like white "bugs" floating on the surface. A severe fungus-gnat infestation will cause a plant to droop and look unhealthy with yellowing leaves. The plant also will get root rot because of the damaged root hairs. Fungus gnat is a sure sign of overwatering. Use only sterile soil, and if you notice a fungus-gnat infestation, spray weekly to control the adults. Use a soil insecticide to destroy the larvae.

Whitefly: These are some of the most difficult of all indoor pests. Brushing the leaves of an infected plant will send these small insects scattering. Whiteflies lay their eggs on the undersides of leaves. The larvae feed on plant sap, causing leaves to turn yellow. If unchecked, whiteflies eventually will kill a plant. Control of whiteflies is not easy, but it can be done by scraping the eggs from the underside of leaves with your finger and thumb and washing the leaves with a mild solution of warm water and household detergent, followed by spraying every four days. Undersides of leaves should be checked often for evidence of eggs, larvae, or adult whitefly.

Red Spider Mite: Although red spider mites are hard to see with the naked eye, the damage caused by them is very obvious. Yellow or brown speckles on new foliage indicate an infestation. So do fine webs on the leaves, especially on the undersides. An infested plant slowly will stop growing and die. Treat in the same manner as for whiteflies, described above. If a plant is severely infected, it is often wiser to discard the plant, to keep the red spider mites from infecting other indoor plants.

Mealybug: This insect resembles a small cluster of cotton. Attacking all parts of a plant, mealybugs usually are found in leaf axils. Mealybugs suck sap, eventually killing the plant. They are especially fond of cacti and succulents. To kill individual bugs, take a swab of cotton or a Q-tip, dip it into rubbing alcohol, and touch the mealybug. Next, spray with an outdoor insecticide — a fine, enveloping spray from about 18 inches away from the plant — and follow up the next day with a total washing of the plant. Use warm water and a mild household detergent. Quarantine the plant for several weeks after treatment to ensure the problem does not recur.

Scale: Scale insects are the most annoying of all household plant pests, because they often go unnoticed until the infestation has become severe. Overall yellowing or yellowing in circular spots can be clues to these insects, which appear as brown blisters or white scales. Spraying is ineffective; the insects have hard shells. Washing with warm water plus detergent can help, but in many cases, it may be necessary to destroy plants infected with scale. Regularly washing your plants with warm water and detergent can serve as a preventive measure against scale, as well as many other plant problems.

MR. GREEN THUMB RULE

Drooping or yellow leaves may be caused by overwatering, chilling of the plant, root decay (which may be caused by insects or diseases in the soil), or by poor soil drainage.

Aphid: Although aphids are the most common insect problem, they are the easiest to handle. Adult aphids are green and large enough to be seen easily and removed by hand. Aphids reproduce rapidly and can disfigure a plant if allowed to breed unchecked. Any indoor plant spray will destroy aphids effectively.

Plant Diseases

Fortunately, few diseases cause major problems for houseplants. Using a systemic fungicide usually takes care of most fungi. But many problems such as rhizoctonia, pythium, and phythophthora (which cause root and stem rot) usually are the result of improper watering, and cause "damping off" in seedlings.

LIGHTING CONDITIONS FOR INDOOR PLANTS

There is a difference between an indoor plant *surviving* and *thriving,* a factor that can be traced directly to the amount of light it receives. Plants that demand a sunny location should be placed where they get the maximum amount of light entering the room, preferably near a window with southern or western exposure. For plants needing filtered light, an east window is preferred, though light filtering through sheer drapes against a south window is acceptable. If a plant is described as low-light tolerant, it will continue to grow in any room where there is a natural light source, including a northern-exposure window.

If natural light is limited in a room, you might want to install supplemental electric lights such as "grow-lamps." These valuable light sources come in round

Plants—such as this Ficus benjamina—should be turned in a circular fashion every few days when placed near a window; this action promotes attractive, upright growth.

or tubular forms and provide the ultraviolet light essential for good plant growth and health. While these lamps do give out a light that is harsh on the eyes and aesthetically unappealing, they can be turned on during periods when a room is not being used. Many indoor gardeners switch on their grow-lamps after their families have gone to bed, giving plants six to eight hours of artificial sunshine while everyone else is asleep.

If plants are placed near a window, you may need to turn their pots every few days to maintain straight, upright growth. Plants bend naturally towards their light source. This is why many indoor plants bend towards a window, causing disfigured stems and an unbalanced look.

The most desirable light levels will vary from one plant to the next. But all plants *must* have light to complete the process of photosynthesis, which enables them to take in sufficient nutrients for growth. Matching the right plant to the light level is very important. Hardy, light-loving plants will favor an east window. Plants thriving in partial shade will do well by a north window. Check with your garden shop for information on the light needs of any plant you decide to purchase.

TYPES OF INDOOR PLANTS

Hanging Baskets

Hanging baskets provide interesting focal points in any room decor. Plants suspended in the air always seem to hold a greater appeal than those merely placed on a shelf or on a coffee table. For plants with long, trailing vines, a hanging basket is the only practical way to provide near-natural growth conditions.

Many people place hanging baskets in stairwells, but no plant will survive in an area without windows, unless it receives 14 to 16 hours of artificial light daily.

As a general rule, one 2-inch, pot-size plant can be used for every 2 inches of basket diameter. Three plants of this size could fill a 6-inch-diameter basket, with four plants to an 8-inch basket, and so on. Hanging wire baskets are very popular but should only be used outdoors, where dripping does not constitute a problem. Indoor baskets should be plastic with attached saucers to catch excess draining water. Do not use ceramic baskets. They lack drain holes in the bottom.

Hanging baskets are very attractive, and ideal for displaying asparagus fern, English baby tears, ivy, and pothos, as well as the very popular airplane plants and piggyback plants.

Begonias are among the best and most colorful plants for indoor hanging baskets.

Here are five easy steps for making a moss-lined hanging basket:

1. Pack moistened, long-fibered sphagnum moss tightly against the sides of the basket.
2. Mix equal parts of loam, vermiculite, and peat moss, and fill the basket to within 1-inch of the top.
3. Pot your plants in the basket — as many as the basket will hold.
4. If the basket is wire, hang it in a suitable spot from a tree, making sure that enough light filters through to it. If the basket is plastic, hang it in any desired spot indoors where it will get enough light from a nearby window or grow light suspended above it.
5. Check the moisture content daily. Indoor baskets may need only weekly watering, but outdoors, you may need to water twice a day during the heat of summer.

Ferns and Foliage Plants

From the elegant stateliness of the Australian tree fern to the dainty maidenhair, ferns are unrivaled in variation and versatility. They do not flower, but the delicacy of their foliage is more than sufficiently attractive.

With good soil and regular misting, the bird's nest fern will thrive indoors and out.

Most ferns are not difficult to grow, but the low humidity in most houses in winter can create a problem. In winter, ferns require daily misting with distilled water. A dry atmosphere also may encourage mealybugs and scale, which has to be treated manually because many ferns are too sensitive to stand chemical sprays.

Apart from true ferns, there are popular fern-like plants, such as the asparagus fern, the peacock fern, and the "air-fern," which is really not a plant at all, but the dyed skeletal remains of a moss animal living in the sea.

Like ferns, foliage plants are grown for their attractive leaves. Although these plants bloom, their indoor flowering is rare or insignificant. These various species are used as indoor trees, in dish gardens and terrariums, and are especially attractive when combined with other indoor plants to form a lush, miniature jungle.

Cacti and Succulents

Cacti and other succulents are a most intriguing group of plants. In addition to their unique appearance, they can produce some of the showiest and most unusual flowers. This group can withstand extreme climatic conditions and, as a result, are ideal for indoor use. If their basic needs are met, these plants can grow indefinitely.

Contrary to popular belief, cacti do not grow in sand. Their native soils usually are quite rich in organic matter, and these plants fail to produce lush vegetation only because of lack of water. A cactus soil should contain 25 percent decayed leaf mold and humus, 25 percent loam, and 50 percent coarse sand.

Cacti not only need organic matter, but they also need water. Outdoors, you must water them twice a week; brought indoors, a cactus needs water only every two weeks. Make sure your soil mixture is light and airy. A heavy soil that remains too moist can cause a succulent to rot. Most insects do not constitute a problem for cacti, except mealybugs, which should be treated by touching them with a cotton swab dipped in rubbing alcohol. Do not use malathion or any other strong insecticide. These will damage cacti.

Cacti are perfect plants for indoor use.

Cacti and other succulents can be propagated from cuttings. Slice off a stem with a sharp knife, allow it to dry for several days, then place it in sand to root.

While lacking the lush foliage of other plants, cacti are interesting variations for an indoor garden and are not to be overlooked when planning your selection of plants.

Flowering and Colorful Foliage Plants

Chrysanthemums, lilies, azaleas, and poinsettias often are thought of as indoor plants as well as outdoor plants. But any potted specimen of these plants did not get that way in a house — rather, in a *greenhouse!* They give a house a welcome splash of holiday color, but these flowering plants do not survive well indoors. When their blossoms fade, move the plants outdoors and sink them into your flower bed for further growth.

True indoor flowering or foliage plants include a fairly wide variety, from crotons with their variegated leaves, to orchids with their breathtaking blooms. African violets, of course, are an old standby that have the unique advantage of being able to bloom under artificial light. A tip to remember: Plants with variegated foliage require more light than all-green plants.

HOUSEPLANTS FOR FLORIDA

The following selections are some of the more popular indoor plants for our state.

Aglaonema sp.
CHINESE EVERGREEN, SILVER KING, SILVER QUEEN, SPOTTED EVERGREEN

Height: 2-3 ft.　　　　Spread: 2-3 ft.

The Chinese evergreen has bold, lance-shaped leaves that are often a foot or more in length. Some varieties have all-green leaves; others display creamy white patterns. Although this plant will grow well in low-light and high-light indoor situations, it doesn't like full sun. (If you decide to give it a little fresh air outdoors, provide some shade.) Like many houseplants, the Chinese evergreen prefers temperatures between 70 and 85 degrees, and must be protected from freezing temperatures. When watering this variety, keep it moist but not saturated.

These plants are used as decorative, indoor specimens for desktops, dish gardens, even shopping malls.

Aphelandra squarrosa 'Dania'
ZEBRA PLANT

Height: 1-1½ ft.   Spread: 1 ft.

With dark-green, white-veined leaves that resemble a zebra's hide, this is a most attractive plant, especially when it produces its bright yellow blossoms with showy, golden yellow bracts. It prefers filtered light and moist, rich soil. Ideally suited to high humidity, the zebra plant flourishes in a terrarium, which is the only way to cultivate this plant to its maximum potential. If allowed to dry out, the leaves will drop. Lasting only a few months, the zebra plant is, nevertheless, worth having for its exceptional beauty. It should be pruned after watering to prevent the plant from getting leggy.

Aralia sp.
ARALIA

Height: 5-8 ft.   Spread: 5 ft.

A large plant, the aralia grows as tall as 20 feet outdoors, but normally grows to 5 to 8 feet indoors. This plant branches freely and has bright green leaves, some with white borders.

Aralia

Asparagus fern

Asparagus Sprengeri
ASPARAGUS FERN

Height: 2 ft.   Spread: 3-4 ft.

Not a true fern, this plant is a member of the lily family. The plumosus variety has very delicate leaves and reaches a height of 4 feet. For a hanging basket, use the Sprengeri variety. It likes rich soil and filtered sun. Low-light conditions will cause the needle-like leaves to drop.

Aspidistra elatior
CAST-IRON PLANT

Height: 2-3 ft.   Spread: 2-3 ft.

Brown thumbers, rejoice; this may be the plant for you! This native of China can survive under a great range of conditions. It will grow in low light and high light, although it should be kept out of full sun. It will survive even in a window with a northern exposure. The cast-iron plant will tolerate temperatures between 32 to 90 degrees. Fertilize this plant every two months in a high-light area, and every three months in a low-light area.

Begonia sp.
BEGONIA

Height: 1-3 ft.   Spread: 1-4 ft.

Begonias offer dark, flat green leaves and a variety of shapes and flower colors. They need bright light to maintain their rich leaf color. Some of the thousands of varieties, such as the Rex begonia, have marbled red and greenish white leaves. With its colorful blossoms and lush appearance, the begonia is truly a rewarding houseplant.

Brassaia actinophylla
SCHEFFLERA

Height: 6-7 ft.   Spread: 3-4 ft.

The schefflera is sometimes called the umbrella plant. This attractive and very popular specimen grows leaves that are more than 12 inches in length, with a total plant height of 6 or 7 feet. These plants need moderately high light levels and should be watered only after the soil dries out. They are sensitive to temperatures below 40 degrees. *Caution:* Overwatering will cause the leaves to drop, one of the most common complaints about this plant. It is also subject to spider mites.

Bromeliaceae
BROMELIAD

Height: 2-3 ft.   Spread: 2 ft.

Grown epiphytically (in air) or terrestrially (in soil), these spiny plants reach 2 or 3 feet in height, with beautiful, multicolored, spiked flowers or bracts that are similar to the poinsettia's. The pineapple is a bromeliad; so is Spanish moss. The most common variety grown in Florida is the Billbergia. Another member of this family is the Aechmeas, which grows to 3 feet, with spiny leaves and colorful bracts that bloom during most of the winter and spring. Most bromeliads respond well to liquid fertilizer and to water that is placed inside the "cups" of the plant leaves.

Bromeliad

A healthy, indoor-grown schefflera

Chamaedorea sp.
VARIOUS INDOOR PALMS

Height: 2-10 ft.   Spread: 3-6 ft.

There are a large number of palms that can and *should* be used indoors. They vary in height from 2 to 10 feet. Most palms require high-to-medium light levels for best growth; the seifrizii grows best in high light. An exception is the *Chamaedorea elegans,* which prefers low light. If overwatered, palms are subject to root rot; therefore, do not saturate the soil around them. Fertilize palms in medium-to-high light areas once every two months with a good, liquid plant food; in low-light areas, use the liquid fertilizer every three months. Protect palms from temperatures below freezing.

Chlorophytum commosum 'Variegatum'
SPIDER PLANT

Height: 1-1½ ft.   Spread: 2-3 ft.

Ideal for hanging baskets, spider plants (also called airplane plants) send out long, flowering racemes that form new plants that can be cut off and rooted. Foliage is slender and graceful, in shades of green or green and white. The tips of spider plants sometimes turn brown; don't panic, as this condition is not an indication of disease. Simply snip off the brown tips with a pair of scissors. The spider plant prefers filtered sun and rich organic soil, and does better if allowed to dry out between waterings.

This cascading spider plant (on stand) prefers filtered sun and rich, organic soil.

A tall Chamaedorea palm, accented by a small peace lily

Cissus rhombifolia
GRAPE IVY

Height: 1 ft.   Spread: 2-3 ft.

With a mass of tendrils and attractive, shiny green leaves, this plant is excellent for a hanging basket. Grape ivy is actually a member of the grape family. This plant likes filtered light and moist, rich soil. Spider mites can be a problem, but frequent, overhead sprayings with water usually will control this pest. New plants may be started from stem-tip cuttings.

Codiaeum variegatum
CROTON

Height: 2-5 ft.   Spread: 2-3 ft.

Used outdoors in central and southern Florida, crotons have variegated leaves in red, yellow, green, and brown. Like all multicolored foliage plants, the croton needs plenty of light or the colorations will fade. *Caution:* Croton leaves are toxic.

Crassula argentea
JADE PLANT

Height: 2-5 ft.   Spread: 2-4 ft.

With fleshy leaves and waxy stems, the jade plant is one of the more common succulents. It does best in full sun, where it will display a reddish margin on its leaves. The soil may be allowed to dry out slightly between waterings without endangering this plant. When grown in partial shade or limited indoor light, the jade plant's leaves are pure green.

Crotons adapt well to the indoor environment but need plenty of sunshine to retain their rich colorations.

Cryptanthus bivittalus
EARTH STAR

Height: 4-12 inches   Spread: 12-18 in.

The botanical name means "hidden flowers." Earth stars — which grow from a few inches to a foot in height — have colorfully marked leaves of green, white, red, and pink. They do best in high-to-medium light levels. The leaves will lose some color if light levels are too low. Allow the surface of the soil to dry slightly between waterings. Fertilize lightly every 2 to 3 months with a good, liquid plant food. Earth stars are used as table plants and in terrariums.

Dieffenbachia picta
DIEFFENBACHIA or DUMB CANE

Height: 3-6 ft.   Spread: 2-4 ft.

A very popular indoor plant, the dieffenbachia has wide, green leaves with white-patterned centers. They grow well in rich soil kept on the dry side; water only occasionally. As this plant gets older, it loses its lower leaves. To rejuvenate the plant, it should be cut off at the base. New shoots will arise from the main root. The top, shorn portion of the dieffenbachia may be rooted; too, portions of

Dieffenbachia is a particular indoor favorite, partly because it thrives with little attention.

the bare stem may be dried out and placed sideways in moist sphagnum moss (or a similar propagation material) to root, producing new plants. *Caution:* The name "dumb cane" stems from the fact that all parts of this plant are toxic. If chewed, the tongue of the "eater" will swell so badly that speech becomes impossible.

Dizygotheca elegantissima
FALSE ARALIA

Height: 3-6 ft.   Spread: 3-5 ft.

False aralias (as well as the Balfour and Ming varieties) will grow well in high, interior light levels. If aralias don't receive enough light, they may become spindly and die. It's best to let surface soil dry slightly between waterings. Aralias grow best at temperatures between 65 and 85 degrees, and should be protected from temperatures below 45 degrees.

Dracaena fragrans 'Massangeana'
CORN-PLANT DRACAENA

Height: 3-6 ft.   Spread: 2-4 ft.

This plant's leaf pattern resembles edible corn, hence the common name, corn-plant dracaena. On certain varieties, the long, strap-like leaves will display yellow stripes. I recommend planting dracaenas in a good potting soil, such as Hall's. If overwatered, these specimens may develop root rot. Protect them from temperatures in the low 40s and below. Fertilize dracaenas every two months with a good, liquid plant food.

Dracaena massangeana

Dracaenas do very well indoors, particularly if planted in a quality potting soil.

Ficus lyrata
FIDDLELEAF FIG

Height: 3–8 ft.   Spread: 3–6 ft.

The fiddleleaf fig got its name because each of its leaves resembles a fiddle. Its leaves may be 12 to 18 inches long, and are dark green and glossy. These figs grow best in high light but will tolerate lower light levels for a surprisingly long period of time. The soil surrounding these plants should be kept moist but not saturated. They should be protected from temperatures below the mid 40s. Fertilize fiddleleaf figs every 3 to 4 months with a good, liquid plant food, such as Nutri-Sol.

Fittonia Verschaffeltii argyroneura
FITTONIA

Height: 1 ft.   Spread: 1–3 ft.

Sometimes called the silver-nerve plant, this attractive variety has white-veined leaves. The red-nerve plant has red veins on its leaves. Fittonia requires high light levels and must be protected from temperatures below 40 degrees.

Gynura sarmentosa
PURPLE PASSION

Height: 1 ft.   Spread: 2–3 ft.

A striking specimen for use in a hanging basket, this plant needs constantly moist soil. It is sometimes called the velvet plant because of the soft texture of its green-and-purple leaves.

Fittonia

Hedera Helix
ENGLISH IVY

Height: ½-1 ft.   Spread: 2-3 ft.

Preferring temperatures below 70 degrees, and suffering from red spider mites, English ivy is difficult to grow indoors but well-worth the effort because of its lustrous, variegated leaves. English ivy likes rich soil and low light conditions. Saturate the soil when watering, then allow it to dry out before watering again.

Hoya carnosa
HINDU-ROPE PLANT

Height: 1-3 ft.   Spread: 2-3 ft.

The Hindu-rope plant is sometimes called the wax plant because of its unusual, waxy, twisted stems. This plant needs moist soil for best growth.

Maranta leuconeura Kerchoviana
PRAYER PLANT

Height: 12-18 in.   Spread: 18-24 in.

A splotchy, maroon pattern runs along the middle of each velvety leaf. This plant folds its leaves at night — hence the name. Because of the pattern on the leaves, it is sometimes called "rabbit tracks." It likes moist soil, but prefers to be slightly drier from December through February.

Monstera deliciosa
SPLIT-LEAF PHILODENDRON

Height: 2-5 ft.   Spread: 3-5 ft.

The split-leaf philodendron is one of the most popular indoor plants in existence. Extremely easy to grow, it will tolerate low light, but needs bright conditions for maximum growth. It prefers rich, organic, moist soil. Aerial roots will hang from the stems of this plant. Do not cut off these roots, but direct them

Used indoors or out, philodendrons are lush, beautiful plants.

down into the potting soil. New plants may be rooted from stem sections imbedded in damp sphagnum moss. *Caution:* Allow plenty of room for this plant. It may start out relatively small (12 to 18 inches tall), but, in a very short time, it can climb to impressive heights.

A smaller variety, the heart-leaf philodendron *(Philodendron oxycardium)*, has the same characteristics as its larger relative, and makes an excellent basket or floor plant, which will climb when staked to a wooden support.

Nephrolepis exaltata 'Bostoniensis'
BOSTON FERN

Height: 1-3 ft.   Spread: 2-4 ft.

The Boston fern requires high light levels. The most common of the many ferns available, it may be used to create a very impressive, leafy hanging basket. The Boston fern needs protection from temperatures below 50 degrees. It does best in rich, moist soil. A similar — and very popular — variety is the Fluffy Ruffle fern.

Peperomia sp.
PEPEROMIA

Height: 4-18 in.   Spread: 1-2 ft.

Peperomias have heart-shaped or rounded leaves and vary from a few inches to 18 inches in height. This plant (from the same general family as the table pepper) prefers high light levels but not full sun.

Peperomias make pretty, cascading hanging baskets; give them plenty of light, but not full sun.

Pilea Cadierei
ALUMINUM PLANT

Height: 8-24 in.   Spread: 8-24 in.

This attractive plant grows from 8 to 24 inches high, with silver, waffled leaves. It tolerates medium-to-high light levels.

Plectranthus australis
SWEDISH IVY

Height: 1½-2 ft.   Spread: 2-3 ft.

This member of the mint family is a native of Australia, although its common name stems from its popularity as a houseplant in Sweden. It has beautiful, round, bright-green waxy leaves. Available in a variegated form, Swedish ivy grows best in high-to-medium light levels. Soil should be kept moist, with a short dry-out period between waterings. Swedish ivy is often used as a hanging-basket plant or as a table plant. Protect it from temperatures below 50 degrees.

Sansevieria trifasciata 'Laurentii'
SANSEVIERIA

Height: ½-3 ft.   Spread: 1-3 ft.

Also called the snake plant or mother-in-law's tongue, this tender perennial has stiff, erect leaves that are about 2 feet long and marked with white and green or yellow and green. Overwatering is harmful, but this plant can tolerate more neglect than any other houseplant.

Sansevieria will tolerate more neglect than any other houseplant.

Pothos

Scindapsus aureus
GOLDEN POTHOS

Height: 1-2 ft.   Spread: 2-4 ft.

Particularly suited to indoor culture, pothos ivy can grow halfway around a room if allowed to trail. Sometimes called a variegated philodendron because of its leaf patterns, this plant should be grown in rich, moist soil and provided ample, filtered light. Allow the soil around pothos to become almost dry before watering again. New ivy plants may be grown from stem-tip cuttings.

Senecio mikanioides
GERMAN IVY

Height: 1-2 ft.   Spread: 2-4 ft.

A slow grower, German ivy prefers cool temperatures and strong, filtered light. Plant this ivy in rich, moist soil; water sparingly. Soggy soil can be the downfall of German ivy.

Spathiphyllum sp.
PEACE LILY

Height: 2-3 ft.   Spread: 1-2 ft.

Tolerating low light levels, this unusual plant grows dark green leaves that may reach 30 inches in length. The peace lily produces a striking white shield and a flower cluster from a central stalk.

Tolmiea Menziesii
PIGGYBACK PLANT

Height: 10–15 in.   Spread: 10–18 in.

A long-stemmed favorite, this plant is interesting in the way in which new plantlets ride "piggyback" on mature leaves. These "babies" can be rooted by cutting them off and planting them in moist vermiculite. The piggyback plant has rich, green leaves with a crinkled, frilly appearance. It prefers rich, moist soil and filtered light.

The peace lily's leaves may reach 30 inches in length.

Peace lily

CHAPTER TWELVE

Insects and Diseases

Florida has one of the most appealing climates in the world. In fact, the sub-tropical weather of southern Florida has brought people from far away to live and enjoy the balmy ambience, especially in the coastal regions. Florida is blessed with lots of sunshine, tropical rain showers, and multiple growing seasons. It's a virtual paradise for the gardener.

Still, no paradise is perfect. The absence of a long, cold spell in southern Florida means that the pests never really become completely inactive through the year, although they do less damage in January and February.

Though insects and diseases are certainly plentiful in all parts of Florida, because of the difference in temperature ranges, the bugs and blights are less abundant in kind and number the further north you travel in our large state. Florida is so vast, in fact, that northern Florida is actually a temperate region. Here, temperatures dip below freezing regularly from January through March, bringing critter activity to a halt during these months.

Because insects and diseases are a "given" in Florida, the successful gardener regularly inspects his or her plants (vegetables, ornamentals, shrubs, and shade trees) on a regular basis, keeping a keen watch for signs and symptoms of insect infestation or disease infection. Unless recognized and treated early, these bugs and blights can decimate a garden very quickly.

Chewed leaves, nips in flower buds, squiggly lines on leaves, and black sooty mold are all positive indications that your garden has been invaded. Other problems, such as fungi, viruses, and nematodes, need closer inspection to determine their presence.

You cannot grow flowers or vegetables, or have a healthy lawn or beautiful shrubs and trees, without taking some steps to control the insects and diseases that are present in Florida. There are various ways in which to accomplish this: with careful preventive practices, and with physical, cultural, and chemical controls. You may find that the best way to combat garden insects and diseases is to implement a combination of the following controls.

PREVENTIVE MEASURES

Preventive practices mean starting out your garden on the right foot. You can safeguard against some bugs and blights by fumigating the soil prior to

Chewed leaves are a clear indication that your garden has been invaded by some type of pest.

planting, by planting insect- and disease-resistant varieties, by eliminating trash sites (pests love 'em), by minimizing foliage watering, and by promoting irrigation of the soil alone.

PHYSICAL CONTROLS

Controlling insects and diseases with physical controls requires extra time and effort on the part of the gardener, but these measures can pay off. Physical controls include the picking or pruning and then the removal and destruction of pest- or disease-ridden plant parts or the beasties themselves.

For these procedures, helpful tools include a pair of long tongs and a pair of heavy duty gloves.

MR. GREEN THUMB RULE

To combat your plants' pests and diseases, proper identification is important. Inspect your plants on a weekly basis. Look for chewed leaves, mangled flowers, and burned edges to determine which insect or critter is causing the problem.

CULTURAL PRACTICES

Cultural controls can be effective against insects and diseases, too. Such measures involve planting the proper plant in the proper place at the proper time. Using the correct amount of fertilizer is also a cultural control; some diseases, especially those that attack lawns, are aggravated by too much fertilizer, especially if it's high in nitrogen. Why? High concentrations of nitrogen encourage a lot of growth, which results in an abundance of succulent tissues; many fungi go nuts when they have access to nice, moist, plant tissues. If you're a bit stingier with high-nitrogen fertilizers, you'll actually be doing your lawn a favor!

CHEMICAL CONTROLS

Chemical control of insects and diseases is often an important part of maintaining a beautiful, healthy garden or landscape. Because crawling pests and insidious plant diseases are diverse in their habits and effects, it is crucial to diagnose the particular problem and then use the correct control. (Later in this chapter, I'll discuss specific insects and diseases, and what chemicals may be used against them.)

Most of the remedies are highly sophisticated chemical compounds that cure certain problems. Unwisely applied, they can kill plants as well as become dangerous for humans, animals, and birds. Be *sure* to read label directions on any product you use, and do *not* exceed recommended amounts.

TYPES OF APPLICATORS

After you've decided what chemical control you need to use, you'll need to decide how to apply it. There are many convenient instruments for applying insecticides and herbicides (and fertilizers, for that matter) in the lawn and garden. The following covers the most readily available types.

Hose-end sprayers are inexpensive and easy to handle. They allow you to mix prescribed amounts of material with the flow of water, and spray either a fine mist on plants and lawns, or a stream of water on trees and hard-to-reach foliage.

Hand-held compression sprayers are versatile and convenient for almost any garden use. They can be heavy when full, but they do spray either mist or stream uniformly, and are handy for getting to hard-to-reach spots. They employ a pump device, have an adjustable nozzle, and vary in price according to the material from which they are constructed.

Dusters spray powder material such as sevin or sulfur evenly and without the weight or transport problems of other applicators. Dusters are inexpensive and most are adjustable for fine or heavy dusting. One caution: Use these applicators only on windless days.

Trombone sprayers act on a compression system, drawing material from a pail or other container. Their greatest advantage is the ability to spray long distances and into high tree foliage.

Hose-end sprayer

Hand-held compression sprayer

Duster

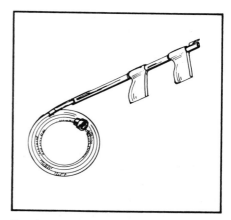

Trombone sprayer

Atomizer

Bait

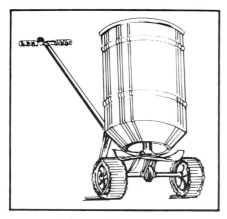

Hand-propelled spreader

Power compression sprayer

Atomizers are best when used on houseplants and small, delicate plants. The principle here is the same as the hand-held compression sprayer.

Bait is normally applied in dry form directly from a box or can. It is used to combat insects such as cutworms, slugs, and snails. Bait, an inexpensive choice, is usually used for small, specific infestations.

Hand-propelled spreaders are used in applying certain granular products, both insecticides and fertilizers; either a drop spreader or a rotary type is effective. If you want to use a hose-adaptor spreader for liquid fertilizer or insecticide, buy the type with calibrated dial settings. These units are more accurate and help guard against overapplication, which is particularly crucial when spraying products like malathion, a highly effective insecticide that kills the majority of garden pests. Malathion must be properly applied because it will kill flowers, shrubs, and trees, *too,* if the mixture is too strong.

Power compression sprayers are usually used by professionals rather than home gardeners. These instruments work faster and have more power to reach, say, the top of a 50- or 60-foot tree. The main disadvantage of power compression sprayers is their cost. These units cost between $1,000 and $20,000 *each.*

SAFETY PRECAUTIONS

The chemicals we gardeners apply in a routine fashion are potentially dangerous if caution and restraint are not used. Chemical insecticides and fertilizers are formulated to be used in certain prescribed dilutions. To ignore the directions may endanger not only your plants, but also people, animals, and birds. For example, never spray on a windy day, because the liquid chemicals can burn skin and eyes. Inhaling sprays (such as malathion) can cause grave internal damage, too. After use, insecticides and herbicides should be stored in a safe place in their original containers, out of reach of children and animals.

If you do get chemicals on your skin while spraying, wash with warm, soapy water as soon as possible. Wearing rubber gloves, goggles, and a respirator are good preventive measures against exposure to the chemicals. Long-sleeved shirts and trousers also are recommended to prevent any spray from touching the body and possibly causing an adverse reaction.

All pesticides are *poison* — they have to be to do their intended job — and great care must be taken in handling, mixing, applying, and storing.

KNOW YOUR ENEMY

Once a week you should examine all of your plants for signs of insect damage or disease. Look at the flowers, leaves, stems, and, if necessary, the roots as well. Keep an eye out for evidence of pests or plagues. Turn over leaves, because many problems start on the undersides of these plant parts. Pull away mulch from the plant bases to check for insects. Most bugs are nocturnal, so they will hide during the day from the hot Florida sunshine.

A cupping or curling of a leaf can indicate a fungus, virus, or stray weed killer. To determine the exact cause, you should be familiar with the variety, culture, and characteristics of a plant before making a diagnosis and starting treatment. Small annual seedlings may be healthy and dark green one day, and wilted the next, a sure sign of a fungal disease known as "damping off." Other diseases cause wilt, canker, leaf spot, root rot, and stem problems.

Do not mistake deficiency diseases for fungal problems. For example: Frizzle top on queen palms may look like a disease, but it is caused by insufficient watering. Newly planted flowers and shrubs that are inadequately watered may

Inspect your plants regularly for insects and diseases; unchecked problems may result in disheartening damage, such as the chewed leaves of this once-thriving squash plant.

> **MR. GREEN THUMB RULE**
>
> Many fungal diseases are manifested by a brown circle in the leaf, followed by little black dots, which are the spores of the disease. It may take more than one application of a fungicide to bring this problem to a halt.

exhibit symptoms that look suspiciously like an infection; actually, these symptoms may be caused by a combination of transplant shock and lack of water.

To be truly successful in your garden, you must properly identify and treat any problems that may arise there. If you can't seem to make a correct diagnosis on your own, take a representative cutting of the infestation or infection to your nurseryman; he'll be able to help you identify the problem and suggest ways to treat it.

FLORIDA'S COMMON INSECTS

The following is a listing of some of the more common insects and plant diseases encountered in Florida. Studying the descriptions will help you to identify and control the particular problem in your garden.

Ants

There are many varieties of ants, ranging in color from red to brown and black. The most dangerous ants are fire ants, which build large, porous mounds above the ground. A fire ant's bite is painful and results in pustular, itching bumps on the skin. Amdro bait is most effective against this quick-tempered ant. Dursban or diazinon will control most other types.

A fire-ant mound

Some ants are actually friends of the gardener, because they prey on other insects. The carpenter ant is one such beneficial bug; it grows to ⅜ of an inch in length, with a black abdomen and red thorax and head. This ant often will build tunnels in dead trees and logs; more importantly, it eats other bugs.

Beneficial aspects aside, the presence of ants in the garden may indicate that a scale or aphid population is on the rise. This is because ants feed on the sucking insects' honeydew, and, in return, protect the sap suckers from parasites and predators.

Aphids

Aphids are 1/6 of an inch long and vary in color depending on the foliage they feed on. They may be green, blue, white, red, yellow, or black. Aphids insert their stylets (needle-like mouth parts) into plant tissues and feed on the juices, resulting in deformed, tightly curled new leaves or stippled, chlorotic leaves. Aphids are particularly prone to attack ornamentals in the garden. Spraying with diazinon, sevin, or malathion will control these pests. Also very effective is the systemic insecticide known as Orthene.

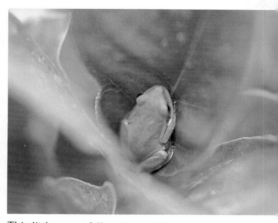

This little green fellow is actually a garden "good guy"; like the ladybug, he, too, preys upon pesky insects.

Aphids, which are sucking insects, will attack most garden plants but can be controlled with regular spraying.

There are some beneficial residents of the garden. The ladybug is one of the "good guys," as it preys upon the damaging aphids.

Chinch bugs are the biggest threat to St. Augustine lawns; here, they've turned a green lawn into a brown, brittle mess.

Although orange-red in its youth, the chinch bug turns brown or black at maturity.

Chinch Bugs

The chinch bug can do serious damage to St. Augustine grass by sucking the sap from the stems and blades of grass. The chinch bug ranges from 1/16 to 1/5 of an inch in length and is orange-red in color, changing to brown or black when mature. One or more applications of diazinon, dursban, or other chinch-bug spray (Baygon, Oftanol) usually controls this pest.

Lace Bugs

Only ¼ to ⅓ of an inch long, lace bugs are light-colored and appear to have lacy wings. Their favorite foliage is found on pyracanthas, azaleas, oaks, avocados, sycamores, and elms. They feed on the leaves and deposit a silvery residue that ultimately turns brown. Affected plants may lose their vigor prematurely; look for chlorotic stippling on affected leaves that results from the lace bugs' sucking habits. Two applications of malathion, diazinon, Cygon, or Orthene usually will control these pests.

Stink Bugs

Stink bugs are green-to-brown insects that are almost an inch long. Stink bugs get their name from the offensive odor present after they are crushed. These pests attack citrus fruit trees, blackberries, tomatoes, and many other vegetables and ornamentals. Spray with malathion, diazinon, or dursban for good control.

Mole Crickets

A particular problem in bahia, Bermuda, and similar Florida lawns, the mole crickets tunnel and feed on the roots of the grass as well as attack vegetables and young seedlings. From 1 to 1½ inches in length, mole crickets are able to move easily through sandy soil due to their powerful front legs that act somewhat like bulldozers beneath the ground. In winter they hibernate 3 to 5 feet down, emerging in summer to mate, at which time they are often seen in great quantities near street lights and other brightly lit areas.

From late June through mid-August, mole cricket bait (dursban or Baygon) can be effective, spread evenly over moistened ground. Another way to control mole crickets is to apply Oftanol in early June.

Cutworms

These large caterpillars, which are about 2 inches long and ¼ of an inch wide, literally cut off plants at ground level. Cutworms feed at night and are particulary fond of tomatoes, peppers, and practically all vegetables and annuals. Spraying with diazinon or sevin will help control these pests. Sprinkling cutworm bait on the ground before planting also is effective. A non-chemical means of protecting plants is to cut the bottoms from paper cups and encircle the base of each plant with the cylinders, which keeps the cutworm away from the stem. Similarly, a toothpick placed next to the plant stem may discourage the worm from encircling and killing the plant.

Fleas

I'm including these pests because they do infest lawns, although they don't damage the landscape per se. Fleas attack warm-blooded animals rather than plants. Any dog or cat owner will need no introduction to fleas, which lay their eggs in animal fur. These eggs then are carried into the house, where they fall on carpets and get into furniture. The eggs develop into tiny wormlike larvae that then pupate into adult fleas. Very tenacious, fleas have been known to live for 18 months without a host animal to feed on.

Initially, any animals should be treated with sevin or any pet spray fatal to fleas. Indoor areas should be sprayed with Precor to stop development of the flea larvae. All outside areas should be sprayed with diazinon or malathion. If your property is badly infested, you will have to repeat this program every 10 days until you're rid of the problem.

Tomato Hornworms

A menacing-looking monster, the tomato hornworm is harmless to humans but devastating to tomatoes and poinsettias. Growing to 4 inches or more in length, with a horn-like projection on its tail, this ravenous eater can strip a tomato bush in a matter of hours, eating only the leaves and leaving the stems. Spraying with sevin or *Bacillus thuringiensis* (Dipel, Thuricide, or Biotrol) will control the hornworm. Because of its size, however, many people prefer to keep a watchful eye out and pick each worm off the plant by hand. This is often the best way to control hornworms once they have gained a foothold in the garden.

Cabbage Loopers

Broccoli, cauliflower, Brussels sprouts, and kale are very susceptible to attack from this insect. The cabbage looper is a large caterpillar from 1 to 3 inches in length. It gets its name from the way it pulls itself forward like an inchworm, "looping" its body as it moves. Loopers normally appear in spring and early fall and are dark green to lime green in color. They are best controlled by spraying with insecticides such as Dipel or Thuricide, which are called biological insecticides; or traditional insecticides, such as diazinon or sevin.

Mealybugs

Mealybugs are ¼ of an inch in length, with a waxy covering on their bodies. These insects are a common problem on crotons, citrus trees, mangoes, ivy, and many other indoor and outdoor ornamentals. They are easily controlled by spraying with malathion, diazinon, Cygon, or Orthene.

Spider Mites and Eriophyid Mites

Mites are not true insects; they're related to spiders and ticks. Still, mites are serious garden pests. They are difficult to see without the aid of a magnifying glass. A stippled, yellowish white dot pattern with a brownish cast on the leaves is evidence of spider mites. They suck the juice from plants. Some gardeners plant marigolds to keep away spider mites, only to find these flowers covered with a shiny, silky web — evidence that the mites have destroyed the plant. Spider mites are a major problem in summer, especially in areas that do not get good air flow, such as porches or entranceways. The pests are very prolific and hatch a new generation every five days.

Spider-mite damage on junipers

Spider mites, resistant to natural pyrethrins found in plants such as marigolds, can spread webs quickly and destroy healthy plants.

MR. GREEN THUMB RULE

Malathion and diazinon will control the majority of insect infestations; using Vapam on the soil prior to planting will minimize disease in the garden. Keep these three chemical aids to good gardening on hand at all times, to maintain the healthiest growing conditions for your plants.

Eriophyid mites are often called gall mites, rust mites, or bud mites. They commonly cause abnormal plant growths.

Regular spraying with a miticide is essential when combating mites. Kelthane, diazinon, and malathion are some recommended controls.

Nematodes

These microscopic eel worms or roundworms, also called thread worms, are a major problem in Florida. They exist in the soil in every area of the state. Nematode damage is identified by a lack of feeder roots, blackening of root systems, or thickening of the roots with the galls or raised knots caused by these pests.

Nematode control in lawns is best handled by a certified pest control operator, as there is no easy way to exterminate nematodes other than by sterilizing the soil, preferably before planting a lawn. With nematodes, prevention is easier, cheaper, and better than a cure.

Should you choose to sterilize your entire lawn area yourself, you will have to wait two to three weeks before replanting, and be sure to keep the sterilant (Vapam) at least 2 to 3 feet away from the root zone of existing trees or shrubs.

For a small fee, you can obtain a nematode soil-testing kit from your local county extension service. To request a kit, call your local county agent; his or her office will be listed in the phone book under "Government Offices — County/Cooperative Extension Services/Agricultural Agents Office."

If you'd prefer to let a professional test your soil for nematodes, send a pint of moistened soil, dug from 2 to 6 inches below the surface, to the nematology department at the University of Florida in Gainesville.

Scales

There are several types of scale insects, almost all of which can be controlled by spraying with an oil emulsion or a systemic such as Cygon or Orthene. Malathion is also commonly used. It is important to do two sprayings, the second about 10 to 14 days after the first application.

A few of the most common scales are wax, red, hemispherical, cottony cushion, snow, and tea.

Scale

Tea scale on a camellia plant

Cottony cushion scale grows ⅛ to ¼ of an inch long. It is brownish red in color, with a small, cottony white mass about ½ inch long. This scale is found on many ornamentals, as well as on pittosporum and citrus.

Hemispherical scale is ⅛ of an inch wide and about 1/10 of an inch high, ranging from light to dark brown in color. It often is found on ixoras, gardenias, roses, and cycads.

Florida red scale is 1/10 to 1/12 of an inch in diameter, dark red to black in color, with the center slightly raised. It attacks many Florida plants, including citrus and hibiscus.

Snow scale (female) is 1/12 of an inch long, dark brown, and difficult to see. The male scale is 1/24 of an inch long and snow white, giving the appearance of confectioners' sugar sprinkled on twigs and branches. Snow scale is a serious problem on citrus, hibiscus, and many ornamentals.

Tea scale can devastate camellias, often infesting the lower sides of the leaves so heavily that they look as if they are painted white. The white-colored scales are immature male scales. Female scales are 1/20 of an inch across and brown. Only the males can fly.

Wax scales are creamy white scales ⅛ to ¼ of an inch in size. They look like small drops of wax. Very common on podocarpus, they also attack hibiscus, camellias, and mangoes.

Slugs

Slugs look like snails without shells, and leave a slimy, silvery trail of dried mucous behind them. From 1 to 3 inches long, slugs feed at night, attacking tender foliage on most plants, then hide during the day. (If you think your garden may contain slugs, inspect it at night with a flashlight; that's the best time to catch them at work.)

Although they are mollusks — not insects — slugs are, nevertheless, a serious garden pest and should be treated with slug-and-snail bait containing Mesurol or Methaldehyde. For the organic gardener who prefers not to use chemical insecticides, a flat saucer can be sunk into the soil and filled with beer, which will attract slugs in great numbers. The beer does not kill the slugs but enables them to be swept up and disposed of early in the morning.

Slugs love to shade themselves under boards, brush, and burlap sacks. Keep this and all other debris out of the garden to deter slugs.

Thrips

Florida is plagued by many varieties of thrips, which are small, flying insects. Adults range in color from reddish brown to dark brown and black. When the leaves or blossoms of an infected plant are disturbed, the thrips will take rapid flight, though they tend to stay close to or on the plant most of the time. Numerous ornamentals, shade trees, and fruit trees are affected by these pests, including amaryllises, chrysanthemums, grapes, ficuses, and avocado trees.

The larvae and adults feed on foliage and fruit. Damage is marked by distorted leaves; injured fruit; dark blotches on leaves; and leaf drop, which can denude trees. Recommended controls include malathion, lindane, meta-systox-R, and dimethoate; apply the control twice, the second treatment about 7 to 10 days after the first application.

Fall Webworms

From spring through fall, these many hairy, creamy white worms spin large silk webs over ornamentals, shrubs, and trees, destroying the foliage. The webs can be removed by hand, but the insects are destroyed by sprayings of sevin or diazinon. There is more than one generation of webworms produced each year; therefore, repeated control measures may be necessary to rid your garden of webworms.

Whiteflies

Whiteflies are true bugs, not flies. Their sap-sucking feeding habit leads to black sooty mold on ornamentals. Adults and nymphs feed on plant juices of citrus, gardenias, and many ornamentals. For fruit trees, malathion or diazinon are strongly recommended. For ornamentals, use a systemic insecticide such as Cygon or Orthene.

Whitefly damage on a citrus plant

FLORIDA'S COMMON PLANT DISEASES

Fire Blight

Plants damaged by this disease appear badly burned, with leaves turning brown and hanging on the limbs for months. Pyracanthas are the main victims, as well as pears, loquats, and camellias. Loquats can be treated for this disease by spraying with streptomycin at 5- to 7-day intervals, a method that also is effective with other plants. Fire blight can be controlled manually by trimming 6 to 9 inches below the infected wood with clippers that have been sterilized in physan (a hospital sterilizer) or in a 10-percent chlorine solution. This is very important to avoid spreading the blight. Be conservative when fertilizing a fire-blighted plant. Overfertilization aggravates the problem.

Damping Off

A number of fungi attack small plants before they emerge from the soil, or shortly thereafter. Stems have the appearance of being pinched. Sterilizing the garden soil with Vapam or drenching young plants with Captan, Dithane M-45, and other approved fungicides will control damping off.

Crown Gall

Crown gall starts out as round knots or blisters on shrubs and trees. On larger plants with light infections, the diseased spot can be trimmed away by cutting out the entire affected area. On small plants, it is best to remove and destroy the infected plant. The only preventive measure is to buy gall-free plants. There is no cure.

Powdery Mildew (Numerous Fungi)

Spraying with Karathane, Acti-dione, Benomyl, or other approved fungicides will control powdery mildew, a white powdery or mealy fungal growth found on the top and bottom leaf surfaces of many plants, especially crape myrtles, roses, cucumbers, watermelons, and zinnias. Sulfur is another remedy, though care should be taken because sulfur can burn some plants.

Powdery mildew

Sooty Mold

Not really harmful to plants, sooty mold is an indication that aphids, whiteflies, or scales are attacking your garden. This fungal growth does, however, cut down on the plant's ability to produce food, and grows on the secretion (honeydew) left by feeding insects. Getting rid of the insects will help cure the mold problem. The mold can be washed off plants with a mild, soapy solution or a strong stream of water.

Mottling, Ring Spot

Mottling and ring spot are caused by viruses. Viruses must invade other living cells to survive, since they have no cellular structure of their own. Only an electron microscope is able to single out the presence of a virus, which can cause mottling, curling, and twisting of leaves; as well as a mosaic pattern. Infected trees should be destroyed. As a preventive measure, always buy healthy plants and trees with certified bud wood.

Brown Patch

During warm, humid weather, this disease appears as a small, brown, circular area in the lawn. In the early morning hours, you may see grayish purple rings around the patches. If the infection spreads, large areas of turf can be destroyed. Spray with Daconil, Fore, or Benomyl.

Mushroom Root Rot

Ornamentals and trees that die suddenly may be victims of this disease. It can be identified by peeling back the bark near the base for the telltale, "chicken pox-like" white film that is the mycelium of this fungus. In the fall, this disease can be detected by its clusters of fleshy, tan-to-brown toadstool mushrooms. After destroying the infected plant, be sure to sterilize the soil with Vapam before replanting (with a different variety) in the same area.

Black Spot

Black, circular spots on leaves, often surrounded by a yellow halo, are signs of this disease. If not treated, black spot can cause persistent defoliation and can

Brown patch damage

Black spot on roses

weaken the plant. Water remaining on the leaves for several hours will aggravate this disease and cause it to spread. Susceptible plants, such as roses, should not be watered just before nightfall, but rather in the early morning when the sun has a chance to dry the leaves and lessen the chances of black spot. Raking up black-spotted leaves will minimize the chance of further infection in your garden.

A persistent disease, black spot needs spraying every two weeks to keep it under control, especially during rainy periods. Daconil, Fore, Benlate, and Funginex are recommended to cure black spot and keep it from reappearing.

Leaf Spot

Spraying with Benlate, Dithane M-45, or zineb, can control leaf spots, which are caused by fungi and bacteria. After small spots appear on leaves, larger brown areas may show up. The dead spots will fall off, leaving large holes in the leaves. This type of damage often is wrongly attributed to caterpillars. As with most fungal infections, sanitation is important. Rake up fallen leaves for disposal. This will help prevent the spread of the infection to other plants.

Lethal Yellowing

Lethal yellowing is caused by a primitive microorganism called emycoplasma. It is thought to be transmitted by leafhoppers. In coconut palms affected with this disease, the coconuts drop and the fronds yellow, blacken, and die. Tetracycline injections every three months give temporary relief, but replacement of an infected plant is the best solution. In southern Florida, Jamaican coconut palms are susceptible to lethal yellowing and usually are replaced with resistant varieties such as the Malayan dwarf palm.

INDEX